THE FAITH

THE FAITH

A Popular Guide Based on
The Catechism of the Catholic Church

John A. Hardon, S.J.

CHARIS

Servant Publications
Ann Arbor, Michigan

Imprimi potest: Very Reverend Joseph Daoust, S.J. Provincial, Detroit Province, August 8, 1994.

Imprimatur: Bishop Alvaro Corrado, S.J., October 4, 1994

The Nihil obstat and the imprimatur are declarations that this work is considered to be free from doctrinal or moral error. It is not implied that those who have granted the same agree with the contents, opinion, or statements expressed.

References to *The Catechism of the Catholic Church* have been translated by the author from the French edition of this work (*Catéchisme de l'Eglise Catholique*) with gratitude to the publishers Mame-Librairie Editrice Vaticane, © 1992, Paris.

All Scripture references have been translated from the Latin vulgate by the author, unless otherwise noted.

Charis Books is an imprint of Servant Publications especially designed to serve Roman Catholics.

Published by Servant Publications
P.O. Box 8617
Ann Arbor, Michigan 48107

Cover design by Gerald Gawronski, The Look

03   04   12   11   10

Printed in the United States of America
ISBN 0-89283-875-2

Library of Congress Cataloging-in-Publication Data

Hardon, John A.
    The faith : a popular guide based on the Catechism of the Catholic Church / John A. Hardon. S.J.
        p.   cm.
    Includes index.
    ISBN 0-89283-875-2
    1. Catholic Church. Catechismus Ecclesiae Catholicae.   2. Catholic Church—Catechisms.   3. Catholic Church—Doctrines.   I. Catholic Church. Catechismus Ecclesiae Catholicae.   II. Title.
BX1959.5.H37   1995
239'.2—dc20

94-41457
CIP

Contents

ACKNOWLEDGMENTS

THE AUTHOR OWES SPECIAL THANKS to many people whose generous assistance has made possible the publication of this book.

To Heidi Hess and her associates at Servant Publications, for their patient cooperation in editing the manuscript.

To my Jesuit Provincial, V. Rev. Joseph Daoust, S.J., for the *Imprimi potest.*

To His Eminence James Cardinal Hickey, for his encouraging Foreword.

To Bishop Alvaro Corrado, S.J., for his *Imprimatur.*

To Mrs. Carol Egan, for long hours of word processing the manuscript and assembling the Index.

To His Eminence Jose Cardinal Sanchez, for his strong moral support.

To Mr. and Mrs. John (Dolores) O'Connell, for their indispensable help as coordinators in the publication of this manual for *The Catechism of the Catholic Church.*

FOREWORD

THE PUBLICATION OF *The Catechism of the Catholic Church* is one of the most significant events in the life of the Church in this century and beyond. The new *Catechism* is an authoritative, reliable and complete summary of what the Catholic Church believes and teaches.

In preparing a question-and-answer compendium of the *Catechism*, Fr. John Hardon, S.J., has done the English-speaking Catholics a great service. This compendium renders the content of the new *Catechism* accessible to many readers and serves as an invitation to them to read the complete text. Fr. Hardon helps the reader to see the principal points of doctrine, moral teaching and spirituality conveyed so beautifully in the *Catechism*.

I believe that Fr. Hardon's latest book will be especially useful in helping both parents and teachers to train young people in the faith. Our young people need to know clear, concise and accurate ways of expressing what the Church believes and teaches. It is important for them to commit these doctrinal statements to memory, for these serve as building blocks for the development of a strong life of faith and active membership in the Church, the Body of Christ.

With that pastoral need in mind, I am happy to commend Fr. Hardon's new book. I hope and pray that it will be well received.

James Cardinal Hickey
Archbishop of Washington

General Introduction

Understanding *The Catechism of the Catholic Church*

The twentieth century is the most critical in the history of Christianity. The decades since 1900 are more than so many years that might just as well apply to any other period of history. They mark the beginning of a new age in human civilization and, correspondingly, of the Christian religion.

What does this have to do with our subject, "Understanding *The Catechism of the Catholic Church*"? Everything. Unless we realize the providential period through which the Church is now passing, we shall look upon *The Catechism of the Catholic Church* as just another book, or just another piece of religious literature.

This catechism is of historic importance. Depending on how seriously we take it, the future of the Catholic Church will be shaped accordingly. We may legitimately look forward to the twenty-first century as the most glorious since the coming of Christ. But we must capitalize on the gift He is giving us in *The Catechism of the Catholic Church*.

UNDERSTANDING THE FAITH TAUGHT BY *THE CATECHISM*

The Catechism of the Catholic Church (hereafter *The Catechism*) is not a mere collection of doctrines. It provides the groundwork for understanding what we Catholics believe. On this level, *The Catechism* is unique.

The Holy Spirit guiding the Church knows that the modern world is the most academically sophisticated in history. In America alone, over five million students go to college every year. We are trained to the hilt in every humanistic subject under the sun. But most Catholics are undereducated in their faith. The result is predictable. By the time they finish even their secondary education, they find themselves in conflict in their own minds. They are trained in science, history, and world literature. At the same time, their minds have been, to say the least, undertrained in the religion they profess. What happens? They abandon their Catholic faith as a remnant of childhood.

The Catechism provides the beginning of what should be considered the single greatest Catholic need in the world today, namely, to understand what we believe.

Recall the sower parable of Our Lord as narrated by St. Matthew. The sower in the parable sows all good seed, but on four different kinds of ground. Only the last soil produces any yield. It is especially the first fruitless soil that applies to these reflections here.

In the words of Christ, as the sower sowed the seed, "some seeds fell on the edge of the path; and the birds came and ate them up."

When the disciples asked Jesus to explain the parable, He told them, "When anyone hears the words of the kingdom without understanding, the Evil One comes and carries off what was sown in his heart. This is the man who received the seed on the edge of the path" (Matthew 13:10, 18-19).

That's it! It is both that simple and that serious. The seed of God's revealed truth has been sown in our hearts at Baptism. But that was only the beginning. We must do everything in our power to grasp the meaning of what we believe. Otherwise, the devil will come along and steal the faith from our hearts.

There has never been a substitute for understanding our Christian religion. There is no substitute today. But now this understanding is absolutely imperative. The world in which we live is too determined to take from our hearts what we believe.

That is why *The Catechism* is such a providential godsend. It not only provides the believing Catholic with information about what to believe; it also gives us an explanation of the *meaning* of what we believe.

Of course, *The Catechism* is only a start. But it promises to be a powerful initiative for waking up a sleeping Catholic world to the duty we have to know:

- what we are to believe on the revealed word of God;
- what the faith we profess is all about;
- that Christianity is the most credible religion in the world and, within Christianity, that the Catholic Church has the fullness of the truth;
- that, as a result, we Catholics have a grave responsibility for educating a world that is starving for knowledge of Christ and His truth.

UNDERSTANDING WHY *THE CATECHISM* IS SO IMPORTANT

It is one thing to know theoretically what Catholics are to believe. It is something else to know where to find the true faith expressed in straightforward and unambiguous language.

The confusion among Catholics on even the most fundamental doctrines of faith and morals is widespread.

There is no ambiguity in *The Catechism*. People may not want to accept what *The Catechism* teaches. That is their problem.

Someone somewhere in the Church founded by Christ must be in a position to tell the faithful, "This is true, and that is false," or, "This is morally good, and that is morally bad." Otherwise, the very existence of Christianity is in danger and the survival of the Catholic Church in any given country or locality is in jeopardy.

That is why *The Catechism* has not been released one month too soon. It is *the* hope of restoring unity in a widely dismembered Christianity.

UNDERSTANDING HOW TO USE *THE CATECHISM*

We still have one important aspect to explain. It is also the most important practical question that needs raising. How is *The Catechism* to be put into apostolic use?

Before going any further, certain things should be made clear.

- *The Catechism* is no mere reference work that we may occasionally consult, like a standard dictionary or encyclopedia.

- *The Catechism* is no mere summary of religious ideas or ideals that provides a readable handbook on how Catholics think.

No, *The Catechism of the Catholic Church* is an indispensable arm of instruction on every level of the teaching apostolate.

We now have a one-volume reservoir of Catholic truth and practice for everyone who wants to bring others to Christ, if they are not yet Christians; to deepen and solidify the faith of those who have been baptized.

The question, however, still remains: How to use *The Catechism* in the apostolate of evangelization and catechesis?

Know *The Catechism*. Our most fundamental duty is to know *The Catechism*. How do you come to know anything? By reading, by discussing, by hearing it explained by competent persons.

Speed reading of *The Catechism* would be self-defeating. If anything, *The*

Catechism should be not only read but prayerfully meditated. I mean it. Set aside some time for reflecting, in God's presence, what *The Catechism* teaches through more than five hundred pages of print.

How much time people waste in useless reading, or worse. Is it too much for Christ to expect us to spend a few hours a week in reading, alone or with others, what promises to be the food that feeds the soul on revealed truth?

Trust *The Catechism.* Already, critics have appeared who discredit *The Catechism* on both sides of the spectrum.

- Some criticize it for being outmoded and out of touch with the times.

- Others criticize it for giving in to Modernism and therefore discredit what the Vicar of Christ is offering the believing faithful for their spiritual sustenance.

Pay no attention to these critics. To distrust *The Catechism* is to play into the hand of the spirit of division, who fears nothing more than security of doctrine among the followers of Christ.

Adapt *The Catechism.* *The Catechism* is not simple reading. But neither is it sophisticated and out of touch with the vocabulary of the people. In any case, *The Catechism* contains all the essentials for Catholic faith, morality, and divine worship.

In using *The Catechism* to teach others, adjust the language to the mentality of those you are teaching. Adapt the ideas, without watering them down. Accommodate what *The Catechism* says to the mental and spiritual level of those with whom you are sharing God's truth.

Live *The Catechism.* This is no pious platitude. Teaching the true faith is unlike any other form of pedagogy.

The purpose of teaching the Catholic faith is to enable those you are teaching to practice the virtues that Christ expects of His followers. Very well. But how do you enable those you teach to practice what they have learned? You don't! Only Christ can give them the grace they need to practice what they believe. So how do they get the grace they need? From Christ, of course. But *through* you, their teachers.

What are we saying? We are saying that God uses holy people as channels of His grace to others. In the measure of our own union with Him, He will communicate to those we teach the light and strength they need to live the Christian faith. God uses humble people to give others the gift of humility. He uses chaste people as conduits of His grace of chastity, patient people to inspire patience, prayerful people to make others prayerful.

In a word, if we live *The Catechism,* we become instruments of divine faith to everyone whose life we touch. This, we may say, is the law of spiritual generation. Sanctity is reproductive; holiness is procreative.

Share *The Catechism.* As we close this introduction on understanding *The Catechism of the Catholic Church,* we should make one thing clear. On the last day, we shall be judged on our practice of charity. How we hope that when Christ appears, He will say to us, "Come, blessed of my Father, and possess the kingdom prepared for you from the foundation of the world. I was hungry, and you gave me to eat; thirsty and you gave me to drink; naked and you clothed me; sick and in prison and you visited me."

How does this affect our apostolic use of *The Catechism of the Catholic Church?* Profoundly! This masterpiece of sacred wisdom provides us with all the resources we need to meet the spiritual needs of our times. But we must be convinced that we have at hand, in the words of our Holy Father, the means of saving the soul of our society.

PREPARATORY NOTE

This compendium of *The Catechism of the Catholic Church* is just that: a compendium. It concentrates all the essentials of the catechism in question-and-answer form.

The source of the compendium is the original French, *Catéchisme de l'Église Catholique,* issued by Pope John Paul II October 11, 1992, on two memorable anniversaries:

- the quincentennial of Christopher Columbus' bringing the Catholic faith to the New World, October 11, 1492;

- the thirtieth anniversary of the opening of the Second Vatican Council, October 11, 1962.

Why the publication of this compendium? In order to provide a reliable digest of all the main areas covered by *The Catechism of the Catholic Church.* Another reason is to offer, in clear and simple language, a reference source for what the larger catechism treats at greater length and in more detail.

My prayer is that those who use the compendium will find it a valuable means of "getting to the heart" of the Church's faith in Jesus Christ, our Way, our Truth, and our Life.

John A. Hardon, S.J.

Editor's Note: The numbers that appear in parentheses in the right margins of this work serve as cross-reference guides to *The Catechism of the Catholic Church.*

PROLOGUE

1. *Why did God create us?*

God created us to know and love Him with our whole heart, and thus come to share in His own divine happiness for all eternity. (1)

2. *How do we come to know and love God?*

We come to know and love God by freely responding to the call of His divine Son, Jesus Christ, through the Apostles whom He sent to preach the Gospel to all nations. (1-2)

3. *Are we to hand on the Gospel to others?*

Yes, we have the duty to hand on the treasure of the Gospel that we have received from the Apostles and their faithful successors over the centuries. (3)

4. *How do we pass on the Gospel?*

We do so by professing our faith, living it with other believers, and celebrating it through the sacraments and prayer. (4)

5. *What is catechesis?*

Catechesis is the Church's effort to make disciples by enabling people to believe in Jesus Christ and thus build up His Mystical Body, which is the Church He founded. (5)

6. *How is catechesis a form of education?*

Catechesis is education in Christian doctrine of children, young people, and adults. Catechetical instruction is given in an organized way for training believers in the fullness of the Christian life. (5-6)

7. What are the outstanding periods in catechetical history?

They are periods when the Church had special need for self-renewal and reformation. Such were the age of the Fathers of the Church like Sts. Cyril of Jerusalem, John Chrysostom, Ambrose, and Augustine. Such, too, was the sixteenth century, when the Roman catechism was published after the Council of Trent. Such is the period after the Second Vatican Council, which council Pope John Paul II called the great catechism of modern times. (7-10)

8. What is the purpose of The Catechism of the Catholic Church?

Its purpose is to provide an organic synthesis of the essential and fundamental Catholic doctrines of faith and morals. These doctrines are presented in the light of the Second Vatican Council and the whole of the Church's Tradition. Their main sources are Sacred Scripture, the Fathers of the Church, the liturgy, and the Magisterium, or teaching authority of the Church. (11-12)

9. What is the basic structure of The Catechism?

Its basic structure is inspired by the great catechisms of Catholic Tradition. The four pillars of its foundation are the profession of baptismal faith, or the Creed; the Sacraments of faith; the life of faith, or the Commandments; and the prayer of faith, the Lord's Prayer. (13)

10. What is the special emphasis of The Catechism?

Its special emphasis is on explaining Catholic doctrine to deepen our understanding of what we believe and thus to provide for deeper roots in our Christian life and a more effective witness of our faith to others. (23)

11. How is The Catechism to be adapted to different people?

The Catechism is to be adapted especially to the religious maturity and the mental level of those who are being taught. All the while, however, the fullness of the faith is to be communicated. (24)

12. What is the basic principle for teaching The Catechism?

The basic principle for teaching The Catechism is divinely revealed love. Everything we believe and everything we hope for is founded on the fact that God is infinite love who became incarnate out of love for us. We are to spend our lives here on earth giving ourselves in selfless love to God in return. (25)

PART ONE

THE PROFESSION OF FAITH

SECTION I:
"I BELIEVE" — "WE BELIEVE"

Before we look at our Catholic faith to see what the Church's creeds tell us we must believe, we should first ask ourselves, "What does it mean to believe?" (26)

CHAPTER ONE
THE HUMAN CAPACITY FOR GOD

I. The Desire for God

13. *What is the deepest desire of every human being?*

Our deepest desire is to know and love God. Our minds want to know the truth, and our wills want to be happy. Both desires can be satisfied only by knowing and loving God. (27)

14. *Is man a religious being?*

Yes, in the depths of their hearts all human persons want to know and respond to God. This knowledge and love of God is what makes a person religious. (28)

15. *Does everyone always act on these religious instincts?*

No, selfishness and sin, scandal, and suffering can estrange people from God. (29)

16. *Does God abandon those who ignore Him?*

No, on the contrary, God continues to call all human beings to know and love their Creator. He knows that we shall find true happiness only in Him, by Whom and for Whom we were made. (30)

II. Ways of Coming to Know God

17. *What is the natural way of coming to know God?*

We can know God naturally by the use of our native reason, reflecting on the world of nature created by God. (31)

18. *What does this mean?*

It means that the beauty and power, wisdom, and goodness in the world are a proof of the beauty, power, wisdom, and goodness of God. He made the world and keeps it in constant existence as a reflection of His own divinity. (32)

19. *Do we have to be open to seeing God in His creation?*

Yes, our sincere desire for the truth, for virtue, for true freedom, and for happiness is a precondition for recognizing God in the world that He made.

(33)

20. *To what does the history of humanity testify?*

It testifies to the universal search for God. Unlike the world, He is the being who must exist, who alone is without beginning and without end. (34)

21. *How can we enter into real intimacy with God?*

We can do so only by the help of His grace. Building on our knowledge of God by reason, we can come to freely accept His supernatural revelation of Himself by faith. (35)

III. The Knowledge of God According to the Church

22. *Can we know God by reason alone?*

Yes, we can. In fact, we must know Him by reason. Otherwise we would lack the necessary foundation for a credible faith in His revealed Word. (36)

23. *Do we need divine revelation even to know the naturally knowable truths of religion?*

Yes, we need supernatural revelation because our minds are darkened by passion, the imagination, and sin. We call this the moral necessity for everyone to know religious and moral truths easily, firmly, and without error.

(37-38)

IV. How Can We Speak about God?

24. *Can we dialogue with persons who have no religion or whose religion is different from ours?*

Yes, because our knowledge of God is reasonable. (39)

25. *Is our language about God limited?*

Yes, it is limited by our human capacity for thinking and knowing. (40)

26. *Are all creatures a reflection of God?*

Yes, so much so that the more we know about the perfections of creatures, the more we can know about the attributes of their Creator. (41)

27. *Why must we purify our language about God?*

We must do so because our natural tendency is to speak about the infinite God in the finite and changeable terms of His creatures. (42)

28. *How can we describe our knowledge of God?*

We can never penetrate the inner Being of God. We can only know that He is not like His creatures and know how they are related to Him. (43)

CHAPTER TWO
GOD'S INITIATIVE

Beyond what we can naturally know about God, He has freely revealed Himself in the person and mission of Jesus Christ.

ARTICLE 1: REVELATION

I. God's Plan Revealed

29. *Why has God revealed Himself?*

He has revealed Himself and the mystery of His will in order to draw us nearer to Himself and enable us to know and love Him as the adopted children of His grace. (51-52)

30. *What was God's plan of revelation?*

It was a gradual disclosing of Himself over the centuries until He finally revealed Himself in the person and mission of Jesus Christ. (53)

II. The Stages of Revelation

31. *How did God reveal Himself at the beginning of the human race?*

He revealed Himself to our first parents, and did not withdraw His self-manifestation even after they sinned. (54-55)

32. *What was God's covenant with Noah?*

After the flood, God made a covenant with Noah by which the stability of the course of nature against catastrophe was assured. Also, the basic precepts of the law were revealed. (56)

33. *What is paganism?*

Paganism is the constant threat to pervert God's plan for the human race. It is a combination of idolatry and polytheism that continued after the flood and the covenant with Noah. It has been active to this day. (57)

34. *How long did the covenant with Noah continue?*

It paved the way for the covenant with Abraham and remained active until the coming of Christ. (58)

35. *Why did God choose Abraham?*

God chose Abram, a Chaldean, to leave his own people and become Abraham, "the father of a multitude of nations." He is also the father of all believers. His descendants were the stewards of the promise made to the patriarchs and prophets of the Old Testament. When Christ came, the Gentiles who believed in Jesus were grafted onto the Chosen People. (59-60)

36. *Are any Old Testament figures honored as saints by the Church?*

Yes, personages like Adam and Eve, Abraham and David, Esther and Judith, Deborah and Hannah are venerated as saints and invoked by the Christian faithful. (61)

37. *Who are the people of Israel?*

They are the descendants of Abraham, whom God chose as His very own. Through Moses, He gave them the Law to know and worship the one true God and await the Messiah who would save His people from their sins. (62)

38. *How did God form His people, Israel?*

He formed them into a priestly nation that would become the channel of revealed truth to the whole world. This truth was kept alive by the prophets sent by God, and by the holy women of Israel, the greatest of whom was the Blessed Virgin Mary. (63-64)

III. Jesus the Christ: Mediator and Fullness of All Revelation

39. *How is Christ the final Revelation?*

As the Son of God who became man, Jesus Christ is the completion of God's revelation. In Jesus, God has revealed everything the world needs to know for its salvation and sanctification. This is called "public revelation." (65)

40. *Will there be any further revelation?*

No, the objective content of God's revelation was completed in Jesus Christ. But we are to grow in our subjective understanding and living of this revelation all through life and, in fact, until the end of the world. (66)

41. *What, then, are private revelations?*

Private revelations are supernatural communications that God gives to certain chosen persons. These revelations must be approved by the Church. Their purpose is to help people grasp and live out the public revelation, which is necessary for the human race. (67)

ARTICLE 2: REVELATION COMMUNICATED

Since God wants everyone to be saved, He wants His revealed truth to be made known to all nations in every generation.

I. The Apostolic Tradition

42. *To whom did Christ entrust the preaching of the Gospel?*

He entrusted the preaching of the Gospel to the Apostles. They were to proclaim the fullness of His saving truth and moral laws to all people. (75)

43. *How did the Apostles fulfill their mission?*

They did so "orally," by what they said, and in written form, by both the Apostles themselves and by others who were associated with the Apostles. (76)

44. *What is Tradition?*

Tradition can be understood in two different ways that are closely related to each other:

- *Sacred Tradition* is the oral and personal communications of divine revelation that began at the dawn of human history and continued through the Apostolic Age. In this sense, it is distinct from Sacred Scripture.

- *Tradition* is the carrying on of divine revelation as found in Sacred Scripture and Sacred Tradition and as preserved, explained, and spread by the bishops as successors of the Apostles. (77-79)

II. Connection between Tradition and Scripture

45. *How are Sacred Scripture and Sacred Tradition related to each other?*

Both have the same divine source. They complement one another, and together they form a single reality with the same goal, which is to make the mystery of Christ present and fruitful to the end of time. (80-82)

46. *What are ecclesial traditions?*

Ecclesial traditions are the various theological, liturgical, and disciplinary expressions of Tradition that have come down over the centuries. Ecclesial traditions are, therefore, changeable and even removable under the Church's authority—as, for example, the eucharistic fast. (83)

III. Interpretation of the Faith Heritage

47. *To whom did the Apostles entrust the heritage of faith?*

The Apostles entrusted the heritage of faith (*depositum fidei*), contained in Sacred Scripture and Tradition, to the whole Church. (84)

48. *Who in the Church has authority to interpret the heritage of faith?*

Only the Magisterium, or teaching authority in the Church, has the divine right to interpret the heritage of faith. The Magisterium is the bishops in communion with the successor of Peter, the Bishop of Rome. (85)

49. *What is the role of the Magisterium?*

The Magisterium is the servant of God's Word. Its role is to listen to this Word, preserve it, and teach it to the faithful. (86)

50. *What are dogmas of faith?*

Dogmas are truths that are either divinely revealed or necessarily connected with revelation and which the Church teaches as irrevocably binding on all the faithful to accept. Some examples of dogmas are the Divinity of Christ, the Real Presence, and the Immaculate Conception. (88)

51. *How are dogmas related to the spiritual life?*

Dogmas provide the faith foundation for the spiritual life. And our fidelity in the spiritual life enlightens our understanding of the dogmas and enables us to put them into generous practice. (89)

52. *How are the dogmas interrelated?*

They are related in a "hierarchy of truths." Some dogmas are more basic than others. But all are expressions of the same deposit of faith. (90)

53. *Do all the faithful share in the right understanding and passing on of revealed truth?*

Yes, by virtue of the Holy Spirit dwelling in the faithful, they are enabled to grasp the meaning of God's revelation and pass it on to others without error. (91-92)

54. *What is the sense of faith?*

Under the guidance of the Holy Spirit, the sense of faith is the instinctive adherence to what God has revealed, a deeper penetration into its meaning, and a more generous response to its responsibilities. (93)

55. *How does the Church grow in understanding the faith?*

The Church grows in her understanding of the faith:
- through prayerful contemplation, study, and research;
- through the experience of living the faith;
- through the preaching of the episcopal successors of the Apostles. (94)

56. *How are Sacred Scripture, Tradition, and the Magisterium to be used?*

They are to be used together, not in competition but by each assisting the others for the salvation of souls. (95)

ARTICLE 3: SACRED SCRIPTURE

57. *How is Christ the unique Word of Sacred Scripture?*

Christ is the unique Word of Sacred Scripture in two ways:
- The Scriptures are the wisdom of God revealed to us in human words and language.
- The Scriptures reveal the Word of God who became Man and therefore human like us in all things except sin.   (101-102)

58. *How are the Bible and the Eucharist related?*

The Church is nourished both on the Word of God revealed in the Bible and on the Word of God who became flesh and physically gives Himself to us in Holy Communion.   (103)

59. *Why is the Bible a source of nourishment?*

The Bible nourishes the faithful because it is literally the Word of God. (104)

60. *How is God the author of Sacred Scripture?*

He is the author of Sacred Scripture because everything in the Bible has been inspired by the Holy Spirit.   (105)

61. *How did God inspire the human authors of the Bible?*

He inspired them by choosing certain people to write, as true authors, all that He wanted them to write and only that.   (106)

62. *Does the Bible teach the truth?*

Yes, the Bible teaches the truth because the Holy Spirit, who is the Truth, is the author of the Bible.   (107)

63. *Why is Christianity not a religion of the book?*

It is not a religion of the book because, while using the Bible, the Church is constantly enlightened by Christ through the Holy Spirit to understand the Scriptures.   (108)

64. *How are we to interpret the Scriptures?*

We must be attentive to both what the human writer wanted to say *and* what the Holy Spirit intended to communicate.   (109)

65. *How can we find what the human author intended to say?*

We must consider the time and culture, the literary forms then current, and the manner of thinking and speaking in vogue when the text was written.

(110)

66. *What are the norms for interpreting the Bible as divinely inspired?*

There are three basic norms:
- Pay attention to the content and unity of the Bible as a whole.
- Read the Bible in the light of the Church's entire Tradition.
- Be attentive to the analogy of faith, which means the coherence of the truths of faith among themselves and in the context of the whole of Revelation. (112-114)

67. *What are the senses of Scripture?*

They are the meanings that the biblical words are meant to convey. (115)

68. *How many senses do the Scriptures express?*

There are two main senses of Scripture, namely the *literal* and the *spiritual*.

1. The *literal* sense is that which the actual words directly convey. This again is twofold.
    - The *precise literal* sense is that which the written words have in their own exact meaning, like the narrative of the Passion.
    - The *literal figurative* sense is the meaning expressed in a metaphor, as when Christ is spoken of as a lamb, or a lion, or a vine.

2. The *spiritual* or *mystical* sense is not in the words themselves but is suggested by the things signified by the words. This can be:
    - *allegorical,* when some account in the Bible refers to a doctrine of the faith. For example, the story of Jonah refers to Christ's burial and resurrection.
    - *moral,* when a biblical event teaches us a lesson for our spiritual life. For example, Abraham's faith teaches us the obligation to believe in Christ.
    - *immortal,* when realities or events have a meaning for eternity. For example, the Church on earth is a sign of our heavenly destiny.

(116-117)

69. *What is the canon of Scripture?*

The canon of Scripture is the catalogue of books that the Church recognizes as divinely inspired. (120)

70. *What are the inspired books of the Bible?*

In biblical order, the following are the books of the Old and New Testaments:

Old Testament

Genesis	Gn	Proverbs	Prv
Exodus	Ex	Ecclesiastes	Eccl
Leviticus	Lv	Song of Songs	Sg
Numbers	Nm	Wisdom	Wis
Deuteronomy	Dt	Ecclesiasticus	Sir
Joshua	Jos	Isaiah	Is
Judges	Jgs	Jeremiah	Jer
Ruth	Ru	Lamentations	Lam
1 Samuel	1 Sm	Baruch	Bar
2 Samuel	2 Sm	Ezekiel	Ez
1 Kings	1 Kgs	Daniel	Dn
2 Kings	2 Kgs	Hosea	Hos
1 Chronicles	1 Chr	Joel	Jl
2 Chronicles	2 Chr	Amos	Am
Ezra	Ezr	Obadiah	Ob
Nehemiah	Neh	Jonah	Jon
Tobit	Tb	Micah	Mi
Judith	Jdt	Nahum	Na
Esther	Est	Habakkuk	Hb
1 Maccabees	1 Mc	Zephaniah	Zep
2 Maccabees	2 Mc	Haggai	Hg
Job	Jb	Zechariah	Zc
Psalms	Ps(s)	Malachi	Mal

New Testament

Matthew	Mt	1 Timothy	1 Tm
Mark	Mk	2 Timothy	2 Tm
Luke	Lk	Titus	Ti
John	Jn	Philemon	Phlm
Acts	Acts	Hebrews	Heb
Romans	Rm	James	Jas
1 Corinthians	1 Cor	1 Peter	1 Pt
2 Corinthians	2 Cor	2 Peter	2 Pt
Galatians	Gal	1 John	1 Jn
Ephesians	Eph	2 John	2 Jn
Philippians	Phil	3 John	3 Jn
Colossians	Col	Jude	Jude
1 Thessalonians	1 Th	Revelation	Rv
2 Thessalonians	2 Th		(120)

71. *How important are the books of the Old Testament?*

They are an essential part of the Bible for several reasons:
- They are all divinely inspired.
- They bear witness to God's redemptive love.
- They prepare us for the final coming of Christ, even as they prepared Israel for His first coming.
- They are an integral part of the liturgy.
- They are integrated into the New Testament.
- They provide us with an indispensable understanding of God's providence. (121-123)

72. *What are the New Testament Scriptures?*

They are the ultimate truth of divine revelation, whose central object is Jesus Christ, the Incarnate Son of God. (124)

73. *How are the Gospels the principal writings of the Bible?*

They are the principal writings of the Bible because they give us the primary witness of the life and teachings of our Savior, the Incarnate Word.
(125)

74. *What are the three stages in the formation of the Gospels?*

They are, in sequence:
- the actual historical events of the life and teaching of Jesus Christ;
- the oral tradition, passed on by the Apostles under the guidance of the Holy Spirit;
- the written Gospels, which give us the honest truth about Jesus. (126)

75. *How are the Gospels unique in the Church's history?*

The Gospels are unique in the veneration they have received over the centuries in the Church's liturgy and in their role in producing saints. (127)

76. *What is the unity of the Old and New Testaments?*

It is a unity based on typology. This means that what God did under the old covenant prefigures what He would do in the fullness of time in the person of His Divine Son, Jesus Christ. (128)

77. *How are the two testaments related?*

As St. Augustine tells us, the New Testament lies hidden in the Old, while the Old Testament is unveiled in the New. Each testament needs the other to give us the fullness of God's revealed Word. (129-130)

78. *What are some biblical directives of the Second Vatican Council?*

The Council tells us:
- "Access to the Sacred Scriptures should be opened wide to the Christian faithful" (*Dei Verbum*, 22).
- "The study of the 'sacred page' should be the very soul of sacred theology" (*Dei Verbum*, 24). (131-132)

79. *Why should the faithful frequently read the Scriptures?*

Because, as St. Jerome says, "Ignorance of the Scriptures is ignorance of Jesus Christ" (*Dei Verbum*, 25). (133)

Chapter Three
Humanity's Response

Faith is our response to God's revelation. He speaks and thus reveals Himself; when we listen, we believe. (142-143)

ARTICLE 1: "I BELIEVE"

80. *What is the obedience of faith?*

It is the free submission to God's Word because its truth is guaranteed by God, who is Truth itself. (144)

81. *How is Abraham the father of all who believe?*

Abraham is the father of all who believe because:
- He was chosen to be the ancestor of all believers on account of his faith.
- He fulfilled the definition of faith in the New Testament, "Faith is the assurance of things hoped for, the conviction of things that are not seen" (Heb 11:1, NAB).
- His faith was a prelude of what our greater faith should be, "believing in Jesus, the Son of God." (145-147)

82. *How is the Virgin Mary our highest pattern of faith?*

Mary is the supreme model of faith because:
- She believed the angel's words that she was to be the mother of the Most High.
- Throughout her life on earth, she believed that all the promises made by God would be fulfilled. (148-149)

83. *What is divine faith?*

Divine faith is a free assent to everything revealed by God. (150)

84. *What is divine faith for Christians?*

For Christians, divine faith is believing in Jesus Christ. It is a commitment to Christ as God-become-man, and acceptance of everything that Jesus taught. (151)

85. *What is divine faith in the Holy Spirit?*

It is a commitment to Christ because we share in His Holy Spirit, who, we believe, is truly God. (152)

86. *What do we believe by divine faith?*

We believe in everything "contained in the Word of God, written or handed down and... proposed for belief by the Church as having been divinely revealed" (*Dei Filius*, 3). (152)

87. *How is faith a gift from God?*

Faith is a gift from God because it "can exist only with the help of God's preceding grace, and the interior help of the Holy Spirit, who moves the heart and turns it to God, opens the eyes of the mind, and gives 'to all joy in assenting to the truth and believing it'" (*Dei Filius*, 3). (153)

88. *How is divine faith a human act?*

Divine faith is a human act because it is fully consistent with our human nature. We naturally trust people and accept their word. How much more should we trust the word of God? (154)

89. *How do we define divine faith?*

Divine faith is an act of the intellect, assenting to the divine truth by command of the will moved by God through grace. (155)

90. *What is the credibility of our faith?*

Our faith is credible because it is perfectly reasonable to believe what God has revealed. To believe anyone, we must know by reason that the person has knowledge of what he or she is saying and is honest in saying it. God is all-knowing, thus He cannot be deceived, and all-truthful, so He cannot deceive. The only question is, how can we be sure that God has spoken? We can be sure He has spoken when He performs miracles that testify to His revelation. That is why Christ worked so many miracles during His public ministry. That is also why He continues working miracles in His Church, to verify the truth of her teaching. (156)

91. *Why is divine faith certain?*

It is certain because it is founded on the word of God, who cannot lie. (157)

92. *Are we to understand our faith?*

Yes, with God's grace and our own effort we are to grow in our understanding of what we believe. Of course, we shall never fully understand or comprehend God's revelation. We have a duty to grow in our grasp of the meaning of what we believe. Otherwise, as Christ warns us in the parable of the sower, we run the risk of losing our faith. (158)

93. *What is freedom of the faith?*

Our faith is a voluntary submission of our intellect to accept what God has revealed. We believe with the mind, but our will must freely command the mind to believe. We must *want* to believe. (160)

94. *Is divine faith necessary for salvation?*

Yes, as the New Testament says, "without faith it is impossible to please God." And the absolute minimum is to "believe that God exists and is a rewarder of those who seek Him" (Heb 11:6). (161)

95. *Must we persevere in the faith?*

Yes, because we can lose the gift of faith. We must, therefore, practice the faith, pray for perseverance, and nourish the faith by hearing and meditating on the Word of God. (162)

96. *How is faith the beginning of eternal life?*

Faith is the beginning of eternal life because by believing in God's revealed Word already on earth, we begin to enjoy a foretaste of the peace of mind and happiness of heart awaiting us in a heavenly eternity. (163)

97.   *What does it mean that we walk by faith, not by sight?*

This means that we must expect our faith to be tested by trials and temptations. Here on earth, we perceive God as in a mirror, dimly, and only in part (1 Cor 13:12).   (164)

98.   *What should we do when our faith is tested?*

We should turn to the great models of faith in the Bible, like Abraham and Our Lady. We should find inspiration in the lives of the saints, whose faith was so tried.   (165)

ARTICLE 2: "WE BELIEVE"

99.   *How is faith a social virtue?*

Faith is a social virtue because every believer has received his faith from other believers. Moreover, we have the duty to share our faith with others. Finally, our faith supports the faith of others, even as their faith sustains us in our believing in the Word of God.   (166)

100. *How should we profess our faith?*

We should profess our faith personally, as individuals, and socially, as co-believers with other Christians. Thus, the Church tells us to say "I believe" and "We believe."   (167)

101. *How does our salvation come through the Church?*

Our salvation comes through the Church because she nourishes and sustains our faith through her teaching, her sacraments, and her treasury of merit as the Mystical Body of Christ.   (168-169)

102. *What is the language of faith?*

The language of faith is the expression of the truths we believe, which are preserved and handed on in set formulas of doctrine.   (170)

103. *How is the Church the pillar and bulwark of faith?*

She is this by faithfully guarding the words of Christ and passing them on from generation to generation, teaching her children to understand and put them into practice in their lives.   (171)

104. *How has the Church preserved the one faith received from the Lord?*

In spite of the variety of nations and languages, the Church has kept the one faith intact by the grace of the Holy Spirit. This unity of faith is both a historical continuity over the centuries and a geographic identity throughout the world. It testifies to the fact that humanity has only one God and one Father. (172-175)

SECTION II:
THE PROFESSION OF THE CHRISTIAN FAITH

INTRODUCTION:
THE CREEDS OF THE FAITH

From apostolic times, the Church expressed and transmitted the faith in brief formulas for all believers. (186)

These formulas are called "professions of faith" because they synthesize what believing Christians profess to believe. They are also called "Creeds," from the Latin word *credo* (I believe). Finally, they are called "symbols of faith," from the Greek word *symbolon* (a collection or summary). (187-188)

105. *When is the believer's first profession of faith made?*

It is made at Baptism. Since Baptism is conferred in the name of the Trinity, the faith is professed in three parts:
- faith in God the Father and the creation of the world;
- faith in God the Son and the redemption of the human race;
- faith in God the Holy Spirit and the sanctification of mankind.

(189-190)

106. *What are the articles of the Creed?*

They are the individual truths of faith, each distinct from the others, like the separate members of our body that are united in one whole. (191)

107. *Are there many creeds?*

Yes, in the two millennia of the Church's history, many professions of faith were formulated. Each creed was meant to serve a special need. Among the more important symbols of faith are:

- the Athanasian Creed, from the late fourth century, attributed to St. Athanasius;
- the creeds of certain councils of the Church, like those of Toledo (400 A.D.) and Trent (1564 A.D.);
- the creeds of the Bishops of Rome, like that of Pope Paul VI (1968 A.D.). (192-193)

108. *What are the two most important creeds?*

They are the Apostles' and the Nicene Creeds. (193-195)

109. *What is the Apostles' Creed?*

This is the creed that professes the faith of the Twelve Apostles. (194)

110. *What is the Nicene Creed?*

Also called the Niceno-Constantinopolitan Creed, it comes from the first two general councils of the Church, Nicea in 325 A.D. and Constantinople in 381 A.D. To this day, it is professed by all the great Churches of the East and West. (195)

111. *On what creed is* The Catechism *based?*

It is based on the Apostles' Creed, which is really the oldest Catholic catechism. However, we shall constantly refer to the Nicene Creed to supplement and make more explicit the teaching of the Apostles' Creed. (196)

112. *Why is the Apostles' Creed called "the treasure of our soul"?*

St. Ambrose used this name to show how the articles of the Apostles' Creed are like the principle of our supernatural life of faith. (197)

CHAPTER ONE:
"I BELIEVE IN GOD THE FATHER ALMIGHTY, CREATOR OF HEAVEN AND EARTH"

We begin our profession of faith with God. He is the origin, or beginning of everything created, and the end or purpose for which everything in the world exists.

We open the Creed with the first Person of the Holy Trinity, and with creation, which is the foundation of everything that God has made.   (198)

ARTICLE 1: "I BELIEVE IN GOD THE FATHER ALMIGHTY, CREATOR OF HEAVEN AND EARTH"

I. "I (We) Believe in One God"

113. *Why does the Apostles' Creed open with the words "I believe in God"?*

The reason is that this is the most fundamental truth of our faith. Everything else we believe depends on this, even as everything else derives from our belief in the existence of God.   (199)

114. *Why does the Nicene Creed begin with "We believe in one God"?*

There are three reasons for this:
   • The plural "we" is used to emphasize the social character of our faith as a believing community.
   • The attribute of God's oneness is affirmed to exclude any kind of polytheism or plurality of gods.
   • Also, the oneness of God is professed to bring out the fact that God is only one in nature, even though there are three divine Persons in God.   (200)

115. *What are the principal attributes of the one God?*

As professed by the Creed of the Fourth Lateran Council, "We firmly believe and confess without reservation that there is only one true God, eternal, infinite and unchangeable, incomprehensible, almighty, and ineffable, the Father, the Son, and the Holy Spirit; three Persons indeed, but one essence, substance or nature entirely simple" (November 30, 1215).

The occasion for this declaration of faith was the rise of the Albigensian heresy, which claimed there are at least two gods, one the author of what is good and the other the creator of evil.   (202)

116. *Did God reveal His name?*

Yes, God revealed Himself progressively under various names. These names told the Israelites not only who God is, but that He is a personal God and not some impersonal force.   (203-204)

117. *What was the most fundamental divine name revealed by God?*

It was the revelation He made to Moses from the burning bush on Mount Sinai. He declared, "I Am Who Am" (Ex 3:13-15). By this He meant that God's essence is to exist. He is the Being who simply is. He can never not be, or become, or change. He must exist. He is, in the deepest sense of the word, Necessary Being.   (205-206)

118. *Did God also reveal His faithfulness?*

Yes, He told the Chosen People, "I am the God of your fathers," and He promised, "I will be with you" (Ex 3:6,12).   (207)

119. *What are we by comparison with God?*

We are insignificant. In fact, except for God we would be nothing. Yet, God loves us and is merciful to us if we repent of our sins. That is why He told His people that He is "merciful and gracious, slow to anger" (Ex 34:6).

(208, 210)

120. *What title did the Israelites substitute for the name of God?*

The title "Lord," which is also the title that Christians give to Jesus, who is God.   (209)

121. *What is the basic difference between God and His creatures?*

It is the unchangeableness of God. Thus, the psalmist says to the Lord, comparing Him with creatures, "Like clothing, you change them, and they are changed, but you are the same" (Ps 102:26-27).   (212)

122. *What does it mean to say that "God alone is"?*

It means that God is the fullness of being and perfection. He alone is His very Being.   (213)

123. *What is distinctive about God's love for us?*

God's love for us is steadfast, faithful, and constant (Ps 136:2).   (214)

124. *How is God the Truth?*

Since truth is conformity of mind with reality, God is Truth three times over:

- He is Truth because whatever He has made or done conforms with the mind of God.
- He is Truth because whatever God knows conforms with reality.
- He is Truth because whatever He says conforms to the mind of God.

On all three levels, Jesus Christ is the Truth because He is God Incarnate.

(215-217)

125. *How is God Love?*

God is Love in Himself and in His love for us.

- In Himself, the Holy Trinity is the eternal exchange of love among the Father, Son, and Holy Spirit.
- In loving us, His love is everlasting, merciful, and self-revealing in sending us His only Son and the Holy Spirit.   (218-221)

126. *What are the implications of our faith in one God?*

Because of our faith in God:

- we know His greatness and majesty;
- we thank Him for giving us everything we are and have;
- we know the unity and dignity of all people, made in the image and likeness of God;
- we use creatures to bring us closer to God and remove creatures when they turn us away from God;
- we see and trust God in every circumstance of life, knowing there is no such thing as chance with God.   (222-227)

II. "The Father"

127. *On what does the faith of all Christians depend?*

It depends on our belief in the Holy Trinity as the central mystery of Christianity.   (232-233)

128. *How is the Trinity the central mystery of Christianity?*

It is the central mystery because it reveals God as He is in Himself, in His relation to us, who came from the Trinity and are destined to return to the Trinity as our eternal destiny. (234)

129. *What is the difference between "theology" and "economy"?*

Theology is the mystery of God revealing Himself. *Economy* is the mystery of God's relationship with us. (236)

130. *How is the Trinity a strict mystery?*

As a strict mystery, the Trinity could not be rationally conceived before revelation, and cannot be rationally comprehended (fully understood) since revelation. (237)

131. *How is God revealed as Father?*

God is revealed as Father especially in two ways:
- God is the first origin and supreme authority of everything created.
- God is supremely good and loving toward all of His children. (239)

132. *Can we speak of gender in God?*

Absolutely not; and that for two reasons:
- God is Pure Spirit. Not having a body, He cannot have any gender or sex. He is neither male nor female.
- The fatherhood in God is the eternal generation of the Second Person by the First Person of the Trinity. This was revealed by Jesus Christ, the Son of God who became man. (239-240)

133. *What do we believe about Jesus as the Son of God?*

As professed in the Nicene Creed, "We believe in one Lord Jesus Christ, the only Son of God, eternally begotten of the Father; God from God, Light from Light, true God from true God, begotten, not made, one in being with the Father." (242)

134. *What did Christ reveal about the Holy Spirit?*

He revealed two great mysteries:
- that the Holy Spirit is a distinct Divine Person in relation to Jesus and the Father;
- that the Holy Spirit is sent to the Apostles and the Church both by the Father and the Son, and by the Son in a special way once He returned to the Father. (243-244)

135. *What do we believe about the Holy Spirit?*

As professed in the Nicene Creed, "We believe in the Holy Spirit, the giver of life, who proceeds from the Father and the Son. With the Father and the Son, He is worshipped and glorified." (245)

136. *How do the Latin and Eastern traditions differ regarding faith in the Holy Spirit?*

In the Eastern tradition, the original Nicene Creed says, "The Holy Spirit... proceeds from the Father." The Latin version adds the words "... and the Son." Thus, the Latin Church emphasizes the communion "of one being" between Father and Son. If not exaggerated, these additional words do not affect the identity of faith professed by Eastern and Western Christianity.

(246-248)

137. *What were the beginnings of the Church's profession of faith in the Trinity?*

The Church's faith in the Trinity was first found in the administration of Baptism and thus incorporated in the Apostolic writings, religious instruction, prayer, and the Eucharistic liturgy. (249)

138. *How did the Church deepen her understanding of the mystery of the Trinity?*

Under the challenge of prevalent errors, the Church clarified her understanding of the Trinity especially in three ways:
- by speaking of "substance" and "essence" when referring to the divine Being in its unity;
- by speaking of "persons," or "hypostases," when referring to the Father, Son, and Holy Spirit as distinct individuals;
- by speaking of "relation" to bring out the distinction of each Divine Person to the others. (250-252)

139. *How do we profess our faith in the dogma of the Trinity?*

We profess our faith in the Trinity in three ways:
- We confess that there is only one God, that the Trinity is one in being.
- We confess that the three Divine Persons are really distinct among Themselves. The Father is not the Son, nor is the Holy Spirit the Father or the Son. God is not a solitary. He is the Divine Community of the Holy Trinity.
- We confess that the three Persons do not divide God's unity. Rather they express their relationship to one another. (253-256)

140. *How is the divine economy the work of the Holy Trinity?*

Whatever God does outside of His own Trinitarian life is always done by all three Persons of the Trinity. Just as They have only one divine nature, so They have only one divine operation.

Yet, each of the divine Persons also reveals His own distinct properties in the work that is objectively done by the whole Trinity. (257-259)

141. *What is the final goal of the whole divine economy?*

The final goal is that we may enter into the unity of the Trinity in a heavenly eternity. But even now, we are the dwelling place of the Holy Trinity. Our duty is to realize and respond to this marvelous privilege by our faithful love of the Trinity, and grow in God's love in return for His generosity. (260)

III. "The Almighty"

142. *What do we mean by professing that God is almighty?*

We mean that "nothing will be impossible with God" (Lk 1:37). We mean that He is Lord of the universe that He created, which remains totally at His disposal. We mean that He is Lord of history, governing human hearts and events according to His will. (268-269)

143. *How does God especially show His almighty power?*

He does so most clearly by forgiving our sins. (270)

144. *Is the power of God arbitrary?*

No, because God always exercises His power according to His wise intelligence and just will. (271)

145. *How is our faith in God's almighty power especially tried?*

Our faith in God's omnipotence is especially tried by the evil and suffering we see and experience in our lives. (272)

146. *What is our strongest support in coping with evil and suffering?*

Our strongest support in coping with evil and suffering is Christ crucified and glorified. Only this faith can glory in its weakness in order to draw on the power of Christ. Our highest model is the Blessed Virgin Mary, who believed that nothing is impossible with God, who does great things, even miracles, for those who humbly trust in His holy name. (273-274)

IV. "The Creator"

147. *What are the two basic questions of all times?*

They are: "Where do we come from?" and "Where are we going?"

(279-282)

148. *How are these two questions related?*

They are related as condition and consequence. The condition is that we were created *by* God. The inevitable consequence is that we must have been created *for* God. (279-282)

149. *What have been the principal challenges to our faith in creation by God?*

There have been especially five such challenges:
- *pantheism,* which claims that the world is God or is becoming God or is emanating from God;
- *manichaeism,* which claims there are two gods, one the source of all that is good, and the other of everything that is evil;
- *gnosticism,* which claims that at least the material world is evil, even a depravation of the deity, and must, therefore, be rejected or surpassed;
- *deism,* which claims that God made the world like a watch, and then abandoned it to its own power and limitations;
- *materialism,* which claims that the world is merely the interplay of material (nonspiritual) elements that have always existed. (283-285)

150. *Can the existence of God the Creator be known by the light of human reason?*

Yes, that is why St. Paul says the pagans of his day were inexcusable. They were "those men who in wickedness held back the truth of God, seeing that what may be known about God is manifest to them. For since the creation of the world, His invisible attributes are clearly seen—His everlasting power also and divinity—being understood through the things that are made" (Rom 1:18-20). (286)

151. *Has God revealed the truth about creation beyond what we know from reason?*

Yes, He has done so, especially in forming the Chosen People of Israel.

(287)

152. *How is creation related to God's covenant with His Chosen People?*

The truth of creation is the first and most powerful witness to God's all-powerful love. (288)

153. *How important are the first three chapters of Genesis for understanding creation?*

They are most important for relating creation, sin, and God's promise of salvation. (289)

154. *What are we told in the first verse of Genesis?*

We are told that God began everything that exists beyond Himself, that He alone is Creator, and that everything that exists in the world depends on Him who gave it existence. (290)

155. *What do the opening verses of St. John's Gospel tell us?*

They tell us that God created everything by His eternal Word, His beloved Son. (291)

156. *Is creation the work of the entire Trinity?*

Yes, we may say, with St. Irenaeus, that God the Father made all things "by the Son and the Spirit" who are "His hands." (292)

157. *Why did God create the world?*

God created the world "in order to manifest His perfection through the benefits He bestows on creatures" (*First Vatican Council*, 1). (293)

158. *Did God create the world for His glory?*

Yes, He created the world so that His rational creatures might glorify Him by knowing and loving Him and thus sharing in His happiness in time and eternity. (294)

159. *Did God create in perfect freedom?*

Yes, the world is not the product of any necessity, or blind fate, or chance. It proceeds from the free will of God. He wants His creatures to participate in His being, wisdom, and goodness. (295)

160. *Did God create out of nothing?*

Yes, in creating, God needed nothing that already existed, nor did He need any help, nor is creation a necessary emanation from the divine substance. God created freely out of nothing. (296)

161. *What follows from the power of God to create out of nothing?*

Given His almighty power to create, God can also:
- restore sinners to His friendship;
- raise back to life the bodies of the dead on the last day;
- bring into existence that which does not exist;
- give the gift of divine faith to those who do not yet believe. (297-298)

162. *What kind of a world has God created?*

God has created a good and orderly world. It is orderly because it is directed to a divinely ordained purpose. It is good because it comes from God's goodness and is destined for our blessedness. (299)

163. *Is God present in the world?*

Yes, God's presence sustains the world in existence. Yet, God is infinitely superior to the world He created. (300)

164. *How does God sustain the world?*

God sustains the world not only in existence but by giving creatures the power to act and so to reach their appointed destiny. (301)

165. *What is divine providence?*

As expressed by the First Vatican Council, "God, in His providence, watches over and governs all things that He made, reaching from end to end with might and disposing of all things with gentleness" (April 24, 1870). (302)

166. *What do the Scriptures tell us about divine providence?*

They are unanimous in teaching us that God is concretely and practically and immediately exercising His loving care over all creatures and all the events of human history. Thus, "many are the plans in a man's heart, but it is the decision of the Lord that endures" (Prv 19:21). (303)

167. *Why do the Scriptures so often speak exclusively of God doing something?*

The reason is to emphasize that God is the main cause of everything that, as we say, happens. It is also to remind us to trust God always in every event and situation of life. (304)

168. *What does Jesus teach us about providence?*

Our Lord urges us to have childlike confidence in His providence. Our one concern should be to do His will. (305)

169. What is the role of secondary causes in the world?

Secondary causes are the contributions that creatures, especially human beings, make for the fulfillment of God's providential plans. He gives us the privilege of working with Him by freely cooperating in His designs for the universe. (306)

170. Is our free will part of divine providence?

Yes, God gives us the power and the dignity of using our free will for the fulfillment of His designs. Without often realizing it, we are cooperating with Him by our actions, prayers, and sacrifices in the fulfillment of His divine providence. (307-308)

171. What are the two kinds of evil in the world?

They are moral and physical evil. (310-311)

172. What is moral evil?

Moral evil is sin. It is *evil* because it is contrary to the will of God. It is *moral* evil because it is caused by a free created will acting against the will of God. He does not want moral evil as an end or as a means. (311)

173. Why does God permit moral evil?

He permits moral evil out of consideration of human (and angelic) freedom, and because He has the wisdom and the power to cause good to arise from the evil. In the end, moral evil will serve the supreme purpose of the universe, which is the glorification of God, since it reveals His mercy in forgiving and His justice in punishing. (311-312)

174. What is physical evil?

Physical evil is the privation of a natural physical good. It is *evil* because something is lacking in what it should be. It is *physical* because the lack or privation is in the nature (*physis* in Greek) of a thing. The privation may be material, like the size or strength of a body; or it may be spiritual, like ignorance in the mind or courage in the will. When this privation is consciously experienced, it is painful suffering which may also be called a physical evil. (310)

175. Why is there physical evil?

There is physical evil because God willed that there be limitations in the world He created. These limitations provide us with the opportunity to develop the world in which we live. Yet, as the Second Vatican Council reminds us, such "earthy progress... is of vital concern to the Kingdom of God, insofar as it can contribute to the better ordering of human society" (*Gaudium et spes*, 39). (310, 1048-1049)

176. *How did God draw great good from the greatest moral evil?*

The greatest moral evil was the rejection and murder of Jesus Christ. Yet, out of this crime, God brought the greatest blessing, the glorification of the Savior and the redemption of the human race. (312)

177. *What does St. Paul teach about God drawing good out of everything?*

He says, "We know that all things work together for good for those who love God" (Rom 8:28). But note the condition. God draws good out of everything *for those who love Him.* Everything in their lives becomes a grace of God. (313)

178. *When shall we know the mysterious ways of God in our lives?*

We shall know the mysterious ways of God in our lives when we reach our heavenly destiny, when we see God "face-to-face." But while now on earth, we must live by faith and trust in His divine providence. (314)

179. *What do we include when we say that God is "Creator of heaven and earth"?*

In the words of the Nicene Creed, we include "all that is seen and unseen," in other words, everything. (325)

180. *How do we distinguish between "heaven" and "earth"?*

By *heaven* we mean both the abode where God dwells with His angels and saints, and what we popularly call "the sky," including the sun, moon, stars, and planets above the earth. (325)

By *earth* we mean both human beings and the world of our own planet, the Earth which we occupy. (326)

181. *What was the order or sequence of creation?*

In the definition of the Fourth Lateran Council, God "the Creator of all things visible and invisible, spiritual and corporeal...by His almighty power, from the very beginning of time has created both orders of creatures in the same way out of nothing, the spiritual or angelic world and the corporeal or visible universe. And afterwards He formed the creature man" (November 11-30, 1215). (327)

182. *How do we know that angels exist?*

We have the unanimous witness of both Sacred Scripture and Sacred Tradition. (328)

183. *Who are the angels?*

The angels are pure created spirits with intelligence and will. Each is an individual person who is immortal and surpasses all visible creatures in natural perfection. (329-330)

184. *What is the function of the angels?*

Their function is to be servants and messengers of God. (329)

185. *How are the angels related to Christ?*

The angels were created by Christ, the Word of God. They were created for Him as the messengers of His plan of salvation. (331)

186. *How have the angels been active since the dawn of human history?*

The angels have been serving God's salvific providence from the origins of human history. Thus, they closed the earthly paradise to our first parents; they protected Lot, delivered Hagar, saved Abraham, led God's Chosen People, helped the prophets, and finally announced the births of St. John the Baptist and Jesus Christ. (332)

187. *How were the angels associated with the earthly life of Christ?*

The angels announced His birth, protected Him from Herod, served Him in the desert, strengthened Him in His agony, announced His Resurrection, and promised His return after the Ascension. (333)

188. *What is the role of the angels in the life of the Church?*

The life of the Church over the centuries has benefitted from the mysterious assistance of the angels. This is shown in the Church's devotion to the angels, which runs like an angelic theme in the liturgy. There are feast days in honor of the angels, and the faithful are urged to invoke the holy angels. (334-335)

189. *What is the role of the angels in our life?*

In the words of St. Basil, "Beside each believer stands an angel as protector and shepherd for the conduct of life." As believers, we know that the angels are part of our company as people united with God. (336)

190. *How does Scripture present the order of creation?*

Scripture presents the order of creation in symbolic terms as a succession of six days. (337)

191. *What does the Book of Genesis give us?*

It gives us an account of how and when everything in the visible world began. (338)

192. *Does each creature possess its own goodness and perfection?*

Yes, each creature in its own way reflects the infinite wisdom and goodness of God. (339)

193. *What is our duty in the use of creatures?*

We must respect the goodness of all creatures, avoid their disorderly use, and thus avert disastrous consequences on people and the environment. (340)

194. *Are creatures dependent on one another?*

Yes, their interdependence is both for their own perfection and for our benefit. (340)

195. *What is the beauty of the universe?*

Beauty is that which attracts on being seen. It is the result of order and harmony in things. The beauty of the universe is the reflection of the infinite beauty of God, whom we should honor and praise by the submission of our minds and wills to His wisdom and power. (341)

196. *Is there a hierarchy in creatures?*

Yes, there is a hierarchy or gradation in creatures, with some more perfect than others. Yet, God cares for all of them, and above all cares for us. (342)

197. *Who is at the summit of creation?*

Man is the summit of God's creation as shown in the clear distinction the Bible makes between man's origin and that of all other creatures. (343)

198. *Is there solidarity among creatures?*

Yes, all have the same Creator and all are intended by Him to give Him glory as a part of creation. (344)

199. *What is the significance of the Sabbath?*

The Sabbath teaches us many things:
- that we are to be faithful to the laws by which God rules the world He created;
- that our primary duty is to worship the Creator. (345-348)

200. *What is the culmination of creation?*

The culmination of creation is the Redemption. Just as the Sabbath closed the first creation, so the Redemption spurs the new creation. Thus, for us Christians, Sunday became the symbol of a divine work greater than creation. Our salvation was completed when Christ rose from the dead on the first day of the week. (349)

201. *How do we human beings occupy a unique place in creation?*

We are unique because we have been made in the image and likeness of God; we unite in ourselves the spiritual and material world; and we are destined to share in the eternal goodness of God Himself. (355-356)

202. *What is our dignity as human persons?*

As human persons, each of us is capable of knowing, possessing, and giving ourselves to one another. Moreover, we are personally called by divine grace to a covenant with God. He offers us the privilege of believing in and loving Him as our Creator and Lord. (357)

203. *Can we say that God created everything for us?*

Yes, He wants us to use everything according to His will as a means of reaching our eternal destiny. (358)

204. *How are Christ and Adam related?*

Christ is the Creator and the destiny of Adam. He is, therefore, the Second Adam as the one from whom the first Adam came; He is also the goal or purpose for whom the first Adam was made. (359)

205. *What is the unity of the human race?*

The human race forms one family because we were all made by one God;

we all have one human nature; we were all redeemed by one Savior; we all have one heavenly goal; and we all have the same basic means for reaching there. (360-361)

206. *What is a human person?*

A human person is both a bodily and a spiritual being. (362)

207. *How is man a spiritual person?*

Man is a spiritual person because his body is animated by a spiritual principle of life called the soul. This is the main reason why man is created in the image of God. (363)

208. *How does man's body share in the dignity of the image of God?*

The body shares in the image of God for two reasons:
- It is intended to be a temple of the Holy Spirit.
- It is destined to rise on the last day. (364)

209. *How are body and soul united in us?*

Although our body is material (made of quantitative parts), when united with the soul, it is a living body. Body and soul together form one human nature. (365)

210. *What are the main qualities of the human soul?*

The soul is immediately created by God at the time of human conception. It is naturally immortal and will be reunited with the body at the final resurrection. (366)

211. *What is the difference between soul and spirit?*

In the language of St. Paul, the human spirit is the soul animated by supernatural grace and, therefore, capable of the beatific vision of God. (367)

212. *What is the biblical meaning of "heart"?*

The heart often signifies the human will whereby we choose for or against God. (368)

213. *How are the equality and difference between man and woman willed by God?*

God willed man and woman, as human persons, to be perfectly equal in dignity. But each gender reflects distinctive attributes of God's wisdom and goodness. (369)

214. *Is God an image of man?*

Absolutely not. God is a pure spirit, without gender. But men and women somehow reflect the divine attributes of a father, mother, and spouse. (370)

215. *How are man and woman created for each other?*

God made man and woman to complement each other. In Genesis, we read how the first man looked upon the first woman with admiration and a loving sense of unity. In marriage, they are together to cooperate with God for the transmission of human life. (371-372)

216. *How are man and woman to "subdue" the earth?*

They are to do so according to God's will and His all-wise providence, in other words, not arbitrarily or destructively. (373)

217. *What was the condition of our first parents in paradise?*

They were in God's friendship and in harmony with themselves and the world around them. They were in the state of grace, which the Church calls original justice or holiness. (374-375)

218. *What were the main gifts of original justice?*

The main gifts of original justice were bodily immortality, the absence of pain, and the triple harmony of the universe, of peace between man and woman, and of peace between our first parents and the rest of the created world. (376)

219. *Did our first parents have self-mastery before they sinned?*

Yes, before they fell, they had mastery over "carnal allurements, enticement for the eye [and] the life of empty show" (1 Jn 2:16). (377)

220. *Is work a punishment for sin?*

Work, as a distasteful burden, is a punishment for sin. But before the Fall, work was a pleasant collaboration of man and woman with God in the development of the visible world. (378)

221. *What did our first parents lose by their sin?*

They lost all the foregoing peaceful harmony of original justice for themselves and their descendants. (379)

222. *Can we comprehend the mystery of evil in the world?*

We cannot comprehend the mystery of evil as sin and pain. But we can begin to understand it through the eyes of faith in Jesus Christ, who alone has overcome the evil in the world. (385)

223. *What is the basic root of sin?*

The basic root of sin is man's rejection of God and opposition to the divine Will. (386)

224. *What is the reality of sin?*

The reality of sin is the fact that sin is an abuse of the liberty that God has given to persons who were created to love Him and one another. (387)

225. *How do we know the reality of sin?*

Only by the light of revelation can we clearly understand the reality of sin, especially original sin. (387)

226. *Has the New Testament clarified the meaning of sin?*

Yes, immeasurably. With the coming of Christ, His death and Resurrection, and by the light of His Holy Spirit, we can now see the meaning of sin as it could never have been seen before. (388)

227. *How important is the doctrine of original sin?*

Most important. Without the doctrine of original sin, as taught by the Church, you undermine the mystery of Christ. Why? Because we all come into the world as sinners. We all need, and we are all assured, the grace of salvation that comes to us uniquely through Jesus Christ. (389)

228. *What does Genesis teach us about original sin?*

It reveals with the certitude of faith that all human history is marred by the original voluntary sin committed by our first parents. (390)

229. *How was the devil involved in the sin of our first parents?*

Out of envy, the devil (slanderer) seduced our first parents. Also called Satan (adversary), he and his fellow angels were created in God's friendship but became evil by their own self-will. (391)

230. *What was the Fall of the angels?*

The angels fell when they freely chose to rebel against God. As a result, they are irrevocably separated from Him. (392)

231. *Will the devils ever be reconciled with God?*

No, no less than unrepentant human beings who die in their sin, devils will never be reconciled with God. (393)

232. *What is the worst harm caused by the Devil?*

The worst harm is the deceptive seduction of our first parents. (394)

233. *What is the mystery of Satan?*

It is the fact that God allows the evil spirit to tempt human beings to sin and thus cause great spiritual and even physical harm. However, in His providence, God will draw great good out of this satanic evil. (395)

234. *How is man's freedom put to the test?*

Since the origins of the human race, man's freedom is tested by enabling him to recognize and choose to obey the laws of God. (396)

235. *What was the sin of our first parents?*

Tempted by the devil, they abused their freedom by distrusting their Creator and refusing to obey His commandment. All sin, at root, is disobedience of God. (397)

236. *What, in essence, was original sin?*

It was man's preferring himself to God. Destined to be divinized by God in glory, man chose to be like God, but without God and contrary to His will. (398)

237. *How does the Bible describe the result of the sin of Adam and Eve?*

It tells us they lost the grace of God as soon as they acted on their false image of a God who is jealous of His divinity. (399)

238. *What were the results of original sin?*

Original sin deprived man of spiritual control over the body and introduced tensions between men and women, causing their relations to become marked by concupiscence and self-assertion. Visible creation became hostile to humanity. Moreover, death was brought into human history. (400)

239. *What has been the history of the human race since the Fall of our first parents?*

It has been the history of sin. To this day, man is at odds with himself, with others, and with all created things. Why? Because many human beings refuse to acknowledge God as their origin and destiny. (401)

240. *Did Adam's sin affect all mankind?*

Yes, as taught by St. Paul, "through one man, sin entered into the world and through sin, death, and thus death has passed unto all men because all have sinned." That is why Christ had to redeem all mankind: "As from the offense of the one man the result was unto condemnation to all men, so from the justice of the one, the result is unto justification of life to all men" (Rom 5:12,18). (402)

241. *What follows from this universality of sin?*

As a result, all mankind is subject to misery, inclination to evil, and death. Also for this reason, the Church baptizes even infants who have committed no personal sin. (403)

242. *How did Adam's sin become the sin of all his descendants?*

Adam sinned as head of the human race. By sinning, he lost divine grace not only for himself but for all his posterity. Thus, the human nature which Adam and Eve passed on is deprived of God's friendship for their descendants. They contract this original guilt without having personally offended God. (404)

243. *What is the effect of original sin in us?*

We come into the world without the grace that would entitle us to heaven. Moreover, our nature wounded, we become mortal, are ignorant, weakened in our wills, inclined to sin, and subject to suffering. Baptism restores our title to heaven, but the other effects of original sin remain. (405)

244. *Where does the Church teach about the effects of original sin?*

Her teaching is mainly found in two general councils: the Council of Orange (529 A.D.) in response to Pelagianism, which claimed we can live a good moral life without God's grace; and the Council of Trent (1546 A.D.) in response to historic Protestantism, which claimed that original sin depraved human nature and deprived us of freedom of will. (406)

245. *Does everyone believe that we now have a wounded nature inclined to sin?*

No, with disastrous results in education, politics, the social sciences, and morality. (407)

246. *What is the "sin of the world"?*

The "sin of the world" is another name for the fact that everyone has a fallen human nature and has personally sinned. It also means that we are all affected by the sins of society and its sinful structures. (408)

247. *How does this affect all of us?*

As a result, we must "continually fight to ally ourselves with the good, for only with great effort and the help of God's grace can we achieve unity within ourselves" (*Gaudium et spes*, 37, 2). (409)

248. *What is the "First Gospel"?*

This is the promise of a Redeemer, made by God after the Fall of our first parents in the third chapter of the Book of Genesis. The Redeemer would be a descendant of Eve. (410)

249. *Does the "First Gospel" also foretell the Blessed Virgin Mary?*

Yes, this is the interpretation of the "First Gospel" by many Fathers and Doctors of the Church. Mary would be preserved from all stain of original sin and never commit sin. She would be the first and outstanding beneficiary of Christ's redemption. (411)

250. *Why did God allow our first parents to sin?*

He allowed it in order that greater good might result. Christ's redemption brought us more blessings than would have come to the world if our first parents had not sinned. (412)

CHAPTER TWO

"I BELIEVE IN JESUS CHRIST, THE ONLY SON OF GOD"

As announced by the angels on Christmas morning, the Gospel or "Good News" is the fulfillment of the prophecy made to Abraham and his descendants. We believe with St. Peter that Jesus, born of a Jewish mother, is "the Christ, the Son of the living God" (Mt 16:16). It is on this faith that Christ built His Church. (422-424)

Our duty is to proclaim to the world what we believe, namely "the unfathomable riches of Christ" (Eph 3:8).

Jesus Christ, therefore, is at the heart of catechesis. Everything else is taught with reference to Him. Actually, it is He above all who teaches. Others teach only as His representatives. Thus, every catechist should be able to say the mysterious words of Jesus: "My teaching is not mine, but His who sent me" (Jn 7:16).

The implications for us are staggering. We who have been called to teach Christ must know Him and love Him ourselves. Inspired by this loving knowledge, we shall lead others to believe in Jesus Christ. (425-429)

ARTICLE 2: "... AND IN JESUS CHRIST, THE ONLY SON OF GOD, OUR SAVIOR"

I. Jesus

251. What does the name "Jesus" mean?

Jesus means "God saves." Implied in this name is that since God became man, and God alone can forgive sins, Jesus forgives sins because He is God. (430)

252. Did Israel believe in a redeeming God?

Yes, having been redeemed from the bondage of Egypt, Israel gradually came to realize that God was to save everyone from the slavery of sin. (431)

253. How is Christ the Redeemer of all mankind?

He is the Redeemer of all mankind because everyone who believes in Him and invokes His name can be saved. (432)

254. How was the world redeemed by Christ's blood?

God reconciled a sinful world by sending His own Son to become man precisely so that, as man, He could shed His blood for our salvation. All the bloody sacrifices of the Old Law were preludes to the one Sacrifice of Calvary. (433)

255. How important is the name of Jesus?

Most important. It is at once a profession of faith in the incarnation, a petition for mercy, an act of adoration, the most powerful prayer of petition, and a divine promise of working miracles for those who believe in this name.

(434-435)

II. Christ

256. Why was the name "Christ" given to Jesus?

Because Jesus fulfilled the Messianic expectations. He *is* the Messiah foretold to Israel. Messiah, or *Christos* in the Greek, means "Anointed." In the Old Testament, kings, priests, and prophets were anointed to enable them to fulfill their divine mission. Jesus' humanity was "anointed" with the divinity to enable Him as the God-man to carry out the mission of redeeming the human race. (436)

257. Why was Jesus born of the house of David?

In order to fulfill the Messianic prophecies. Both Mary, His virginal mother, and Joseph, His foster father, were of the family of David. (437)

258. What was Jesus' Messianic consecration?

It was twofold: to fulfill the prophecies foretold to Israel; and to accomplish the work of the world's redemption. (438)

259. Did all of Jesus' contemporaries recognize Him as the true Messiah?

No, many saw in Him the fulfillment of their expectations for deliverance from political tyranny. (439)

260. How is the true Messianic kingship of Christ recognized?

It is recognized only through the Cross. This was clearly revealed by Christ, who predicted His passion immediately after Peter professed his faith in Jesus as the Messiah, the Son of the living God. (440)

III. Only Son of God

261. *What is the ordinary meaning of "Son of God"?*

As found in the Old Testament and with many of Christ's contemporaries, it meant a special intimacy as an adopted child of God. (441)

262. *What did Peter mean when he professed Jesus to be the Son of God?*

Under divine inspiration, he professed to believe that Jesus is literally the living God in human form. This, too, was St. Paul's profession that, from the beginning, was the center of the apostolic faith first confessed by Peter to become the foundation of the Church founded by Christ. (442)

263. *Did Jesus claim to be one in being with God the Father?*

Yes, He declared that He was the Son who alone knows the Father. He always knows the Father. He always distinguished between His relation to God as "my Father" and our relation to God as "your Father." In fact, it was on this claim of being uniquely the Son of God that Jesus was condemned by the Sanhedrin. (443)

264. *How do we know that Jesus' divine sonship was absolutely unique?*

From the testimony of the Father at the baptism and transfiguration of Jesus; and from the affirmation by Jesus of His coeternal existence with the Father. (444)

265. *What was the crowning proof of Christ's oneness with God the Father?*

It was Christ's resurrection from the dead. He laid down His life and, by the divine power He shared with the Father, He took it up again, as He had predicted. (445)

IV. Lord

266. *What is the meaning of the word "Lord" as applied to Jesus in the New Testament?*

It means "God." We know this from the Greek Old Testament, which translated the Hebrew term for God as *Kyrios* (Lord). The New Testament regularly refers to Jesus as Lord. (446)

267. *How did Christ's miracles testify to His divinity?*

His miracles were manifestations of His own divine power, even to raising people from the dead. (447)

268. *Did Christ's contemporaries profess their faith in His lordship as God?*

Yes, under divine inspiration, they called Him "Lord," to profess their faith in His dominion over creation. The crowning profession of this faith was that of the Apostle Thomas, who addressed the risen Savior as "My Lord and my God!" (448)

269. *Did the first confessions of the Christian faith speak of Jesus as "Lord"?*

Yes, without exception. This shows the early unanimous Christian faith in Christ's divinity. (449)

270. *What was implied in the early Church's assertion of Christ's lordship?*

Faith was implied in Christ's sovereignty, with God the Father, as Lord of the world and of human history. (450)

271. *Does Christian prayer profess the lordship of Christ?*

Yes, over the centuries, the Church has prayed "through Christ our Lord," and "The Lord be with you," and "Come, Lord Jesus." (451)

ARTICLE 3: "HE WAS CONCEIVED BY THE POWER OF THE HOLY SPIRIT, AND WAS BORN OF THE VIRGIN MARY"

Paragraph 1: The Son of God Became Man

I. Why the Word Became Flesh

272. *Why did the Son of God become man?*

- He became man to reconcile us sinners with God. We were sick and had to be healed; fallen and had to be raised up; dead and had to be brought back to life again. (456-457)
- He became man to teach us the meaning of true love, "for God so loved the world that He gave His only begotten Son, that those who believe in Him may not perish, but may have life everlasting" (Jn 3:16).
- He became man to be our pattern of holiness. By imitating His virtues as a man, we become more and more like Him, the all-holy God.
- He became man to make us sharers in His divine nature. (458-460)

II. The Incarnation

273. *What is the Incarnation?*

It is the enfleshment (Latin *caro* means "flesh") of the Second Person of the Trinity. Although Christ "was by nature God...He emptied Himself, taking the nature of a slave and being made in the form of man" (Phil 2:6-7). As man, Christ could submit His human will to the Father, and thus offer Himself in the sacrifice of the Cross. (461-462)

274. *How important is faith in the Incarnation?*

It is *the* basic mystery of Christianity. It is also the foundation of Christian joy. (463)

III. True God and True Man

275. *How is Christ true God and true man?*

The full explanation is a mystery. What we know is that Christ is not partly human and partly God, nor is He a mixture of humanity and divinity. (464)

276. *What does* homoousios *mean?*

As defined by the Council of Nicea (325 A.D.), Christ is "begotten, not made, one in being (*homoousios*) with the Father." This was a refutation of Arius, who claimed that the Son of God was a creature who came into existence. (465)

277. *What does* Theotokos *mean?*

As defined by the Council of Ephesus (431 A.D.), "If anyone does not profess that Emmanuel is truly God and that the Holy Virgin is therefore Mother of God (*Theotokos*), for she gave birth in the flesh to the Word of God made flesh: let him be anathema." This was directed against Nestorians, who claimed that Christ was two persons, a human person whose mother was Mary, and the divine Second Person of the Trinity. (466)

278. *How many natures and persons are there in Christ?*

As defined by the Council of Chalcedon (451 A.D.), "We confess that one and the same Lord Jesus Christ, the only-begotten Son, is to be acknowledged in two natures without distinction or change, without division or separation. The distinction between His natures was not abolished by their union but the character proper to each of the two natures was preserved as they came together in one person (*prosopon*) and one substance (*hypostasis*)." This was a refutation of the Monophysites, who claimed that Christ's human nature ceased to exist at the Incarnation. (467)

279. *Is everything in Christ's human nature to be attributed to His divine Person?*

Yes, this includes not only His miracles but also His sufferings. As defined by the Fifth Council of Constantinople (553 A.D.), "He who was crucified in the flesh, Our Lord Jesus Christ, is true God, Lord of glory, and one of the Holy Trinity." (468)

280. *Did Christ cease to be God when He became man?*

No, as declared in the Liturgy of St. John Chrysostom, "O Christ, our God, you who by your death have crushed death, you who are one of the Holy Trinity, glorified with the Father and the Holy Spirit, save us!" (469)

IV. How God's Son Is Human

281. *How human is Christ?*

He is like us in all things except sin. Yet, everything that belongs to Christ as man belongs to "One of the Trinity," that is, His divine Person. (470)

282. *Does Christ have a human soul as well as a human body?*

Yes, that is why the evangelist says that Jesus grew in wisdom, stature, and grace. He willed to acquire for Himself what we have to learn from experience. (472)

283. *Did Christ's human knowledge express the divine life of His person?*

Yes, Christ's human nature manifested everything that belongs to God. In His human intellect, He had the immediate knowledge of the Father and of the secret thoughts of men. (473)

284. *Did Christ as man know the eternal plan of salvation?*

Yes, insofar as He came to reveal this plan to mankind. (474)

285. *How many wills does Christ have?*

He has two wills, divine and human. His human will is always conformed to His divine will. (475)

286. *Are images of Christ to be venerated?*

Yes, because He had a true humanity so that His finite body could be seen and can now be portrayed. (476)

287. *Whom do we honor in venerating an image of Christ?*

We are honoring the reality that the image represents. (477)

288. *How does the Sacred Heart signify the love of Christ?*

It signifies Christ's love for His Father and for us because during His life and Passion, He knew and loved each one of us. His human heart, pierced for our salvation, symbolizes this love. (478)

Paragraph 2: "Conceived by the Power of the Holy Spirit, and Born of the Virgin Mary"

I. "Conceived by the Power of the Holy Spirit"

289. *How did the Blessed Virgin conceive her Son?*

As the angel told her, "The Holy Spirit shall come upon you" (Lk 1:35). In other words, the power of the Holy Spirit caused her to conceive the Second Person with a human nature derived from her own. (484-485)

290. *How was Jesus' anointing with the Spirit manifested?*

Gradually, from the shepherds on to His disciples, in fact, through His whole life, Jesus manifested His anointing with the Holy Spirit. (486)

II. "Born of the Virgin Mary"

291. *On what is our Catholic faith in Mary founded?*

It is founded on what this faith believes about Christ. (487)

292. *Was Mary predestined to be the Mother of God?*

Yes, from all eternity God chose the Virgin Mary to be the mother of His Son. (488)

293. *Was Mary's mission anticipated in the Old Testament?*

Yes, many humble and holy women preceded Mary to prepare the world for her mission as the humble handmaid of the Lord who became the Mother of the Most High. (489)

294. *How was Mary prepared to become the Mother of God?*

She was "full of grace" by being endowed with a deep faith to accept her sublime dignity. (490)

295. *Has the Church become increasingly aware of Mary's fullness of grace?*

Yes, so much so that in 1854, Pope Pius IX defined that the Blessed Virgin Mary "from the first moment of her conception [was] preserved immune from all stain of original sin." (491)

296. *How was Mary adorned with such unique holiness?*

She was "preredeemed" in view of her divine Son's merits. (492)

297. *Did Mary ever sin?*

No, as the Fathers of the Church call her, she is "all holy." She was preserved by grace from ever committing any personal sin. (493)

298. *How did Mary respond to the Annunciation?*

She responded with the obedience of faith. In the words of St. Irenaeus, "Through her obedience, she became the cause of salvation both for herself and for the whole human race" (*Adversus Haereses*, 3, 22, 4). (494)

299. *Does the Bible tell us that Mary is the Mother of God?*

Yes. At the visitation, Elizabeth was inspired by the Holy Spirit to address Mary as "the Mother of my Lord" (Lk 1:43). (495)

300. *Did the Church always believe in Mary's virginity?*

Yes, from apostolic times the Church has always professed that Mary conceived Christ only by the power of the Holy Spirit. (496)

301. *Was Mary's virginity foretold in the Old Testament?*

Yes, God promised through the prophet Isaiah that "the virgin shall conceive and bear a son" (Is 7:14). (497)

302. *Is Mary's virginity a historical fact?*

Yes, as attested by St. Ignatius of Antioch (d. 107 A.D.): "The virginity of

Mary and giving birth, like the death of the Lord: three mysteries that were accomplished in the silence of God" (*Letter to the Ephesians,* 19, 1).　　(498)

303. *What is the perpetual virginity of Mary?*

This means that Mary was a virgin before she conceived Jesus, in giving Him birth, and after Jesus was born.　　(499)

304. *What about the "brothers and sisters" of Jesus to which the Gospels refer?*

As was common in the Old Testament, this refers to the near relatives of Jesus.　　(500)

305. *What is Mary's spiritual motherhood?*

Mary conceived and gave birth to Jesus Christ, the Savior of all mankind. She cooperated with Him in His work of redemption. She is, therefore, the spiritual or supernatural Mother of the whole human race.　　(501)

306. *To what does Mary's virginity testify?*

It testifies to the fact that Jesus has only one Father, the First Person of the Holy Trinity.　　(502-503)

307. *How does Christ, conceived by the Virgin Mary, open the new creation?*

He does so by meriting and communicating the graces we need to reach heaven, since from Him "we have received grace upon grace" (Jn 1:16).(504)

308. *What does Mary's virginal conception of Christ signify?*

It signifies Christ's virginal conception of humanity in the new birth of the Holy Spirit. Our supernatural rebirth in the life of grace does not come "from blood or the will of flesh or the will of man, but from God" (Jn 1:13).　(505)

309. *How is Mary's virginity a sign of her faith?*

As expressed by St. Augustine, "Mary is more blessed in perceiving Christ by faith than by conceiving Him in the flesh" (*On Holy Virginity,* 3).　　(506)

310. *How is Mary's maternal virginity a symbol of the Church?*

By preaching the Word of God and Baptism through the Holy Spirit, the Church generates children to a new and immortal life. As a virgin she preserves this faith given by the Holy Spirit.　　(507)

Paragraph 3: The Mysteries of the Life of Christ

The Creed explicitly speaks only of the Incarnation and the paschal mystery of Christ's Passion, Resurrection, and Ascension. Yet, these mysteries are the bedrock of our faith. Our purpose here will be to expand on the basic mysteries of Christmas and Easter. (512-513)

I. The Whole Life of Jesus Is a Mystery

311. *Why were the Gospels written?*

They were written so we might believe that Jesus is the Christ, the Son of God, and by believing, we might have life in His name. (514)

312. *Who wrote the Gospels?*

The Gospels were written by the first believers in Christ, who wanted to share their faith with others. For the evangelists, every human word and action of Jesus was a sacrament or visible sign of His divinity at work in saving the world. (515)

313. *What is a common feature of Christ's whole earthly life?*

Everything in Christ's earthly life is a revelation of God's love for us. (516)

314. *How is Christ's whole life a mystery of Redemption?*

His whole life is a mystery of Redemption above all as the fruit of the blood of the Cross. But this mystery is at work in Christ's whole life from the Incarnation, enriching us by His poverty, to the Resurrection, by which we are justified. (517)

315. *How is Christ's life a mystery of Recapitulation?*

Whatever He did, said, and suffered had the purpose of restoring fallen man to his first vocation. That is why He went through all the stages of human life to bring fallen men back to the friendship of God. (518)

316. *What is Christ's purpose now?*

His purpose is to share with all men the riches of His Redemption. By His Cross we were redeemed; by His Resurrection we were justified. Even now, He continues to make intercession for us before the Father. (519)

317. *How is Jesus our model?*

His whole life on earth invites us to pattern our life on His.   (520)

318. *Are we to share in the mysteries of Christ?*

Yes, He wants us to become an extension and continuation of His mysteries. How? Through the graces He gives us and the effects He wishes to produce in us, both personally and collectively in the Church of which He is the Head.   (521)

II. Infancy and Hidden Life of Jesus

319. *How was the world prepared for Christ's coming?*

By the prediction of the Old Testament prophets and especially by the preaching of St. John the Baptist. All of these are commemorated by the Church in her Advent liturgy.   (522-524)

320. *What is the lesson of Christmas?*

It is the lesson of childlike humility. Jesus was born in the humility of a stable, into a poor family, and first announced to simple shepherds. He lived what He later preached: that we are to become little children, reborn from above to become children of God.   (525-526)

321. *What does Christ's circumcision signify?*

It signifies our Baptism, which is our circumcision in Christ.   (527)

322. *What is the Epiphany?*

It is the manifestation of Jesus as the Messiah of Israel, the Son of God, and the Savior of the world. The Magi represent the pagan nations that are also called to believe the Good News of salvation through Jesus Christ. (528)

323. *What does Christ's Presentation signify?*

It signifies Israel's first encounter with its Savior. It foretells the world's opposition to Christ, and Mary's sorrows in union with her Son's perfect oblation of the Cross.   (529)

324. *What does Christ's flight into Egypt reveal?*

It reveals the opposition of darkness to the Light who is Christ. The return from Egypt symbolizes Jesus as the perfect liberator.   (530)

325. *How did Jesus spend most of His life?*

For most of His life, Jesus lived like the majority of His fellow Jews: in obscurity, working with His hands, and observing the Jewish religious practices of the Law of God. He was obedient to His parents and grew in wisdom, age, and grace. (531)

326. *How important was the obedience of Jesus to Mary and Joseph?*

Most important. It was the perfect observance of the fourth commandment. It was the prelude to Jesus' perfect submission to His Heavenly Father in restoring the obedience destroyed by the disobedience of Adam. (532)

327. *How is the hidden life of the Holy Family in Nazareth a school for all Christians?*

It teaches us the value of silence, the beauty of family life, and the dignity of labor. (533)

328. *What do we learn from the finding of Jesus in the Temple?*

We learn that Jesus professed total dedication to His mission as the Son of God. (534)

III. The Mysteries of the Public Life of Jesus

329. *When did Jesus begin His public life?*

He began His public life when He was baptized by John in the Jordan River. The voice of the heavenly Father proclaimed Jesus as the Messiah of Israel and the Son of God. (535)

330. *What did Christ's baptism signify?*

It signified His acceptance and beginning of the mission given to Him by the Father. The descent of the Holy Spirit on Jesus revealed the outpouring of grace that Christ merited for us by His obedience to the will of the Father.

(536)

331. *How is our Baptism related to that of Jesus?*

Through our Baptism, we are reborn in the likeness of Christ. Our christening makes us partners in the mystery of self-emptying and repentance as a condition for rising with Christ to eternal life. (537)

332. *What did Jesus do after His baptism?*

He was led by the Holy Spirit to the desert for forty days, after which He was tempted by the evil spirit. The devil's intention was to test Jesus' loyalty to the Father. (538)

333. *Why was Jesus tempted by the devil?*

He was tempted by the devil in order to expiate the sin of the first Adam, who was seduced by the devil. Moreover, Jesus' victory over the evil spirit anticipated His final victory over that spirit by His Passion and death on Calvary. (539)

334. *What does Christ's temptation reveal?*

It reveals how Jesus is the true Messiah. Unlike the way Satan proposed, Jesus came to redeem the world by trial and suffering. Each year, during the forty days of Lent, we unite ourselves with Christ's mystery in the desert.

(540)

335. *How did Jesus inaugurate the Church?*

He did so by gathering around Him those who believed in His message of salvation. (541)

336. *How is Jesus the heart of the family of God?*

It was by His word and the miracles He performed that a scattered humanity began to be united. It was especially by His death and resurrection that this reunion of mankind was made possible through the Church that was born when Jesus died on the Cross. (542)

337. *Is everyone called to Christ's kingdom?*

Yes, however it was God's will that this kingdom should first have been proclaimed to the children of Israel. (543)

338. *To whom does Christ's kingdom belong?*

It belongs to the poor and lowly in the eyes of the world. It belongs to the humble of heart. From the manger to the Cross, Christ identified Himself with the hungry and the lonely. (544)

339. *Whom did Christ invite to the table of His kingdom?*

He invited sinners whom He called to be converted from their evil ways and to partake of the mercy of God. (545)

340. *What was Jesus' principal way of teaching?*

It was through parables. At the heart of the parables is Christ's call for detachment from everything in this world. We must use the talents God gave us to give ourselves interiorly to His teaching as expressed in the parables.

(546)

341. *Why did Jesus work miracles?*

He worked miracles to make His teaching credible. Moreover, His miracles are a promise of extraordinary blessings to those who believe in His name. Finally, His miracles were a test of sincerity, since so many refused to believe in Christ, in spite of His miraculous powers. (547-548)

342. *In what sense is Christ our liberator?*

Christ did not come to free us from all evil. He came to deliver us from the slavery of sin. (549)

343. *Did Christ deliver the world from domination by Satan?*

Yes, the exorcisms He performed were a prelude to His conquest of Satan as the prince of this world. (550)

344. *To whom did Christ entrust the keys of the kingdom of Heaven?*

To St. Peter, as head of the Apostles. Although all the Apostles were entrusted with authority in the Church, only Peter was explicitly given the keys of the kingdom of Heaven. This meant supreme authority, under Christ, to forgive sins, pronounce judgment in matters of doctrine, and make disciplinary decisions in the Church. (551-553)

345. *What was the significance of Christ's transfiguration?*

By His transfiguration, Christ confirmed Peter's confession that Jesus is the Son of God; He revealed that He had to suffer to enter into His glory; He manifested His oneness with the Father and the Holy Spirit in the Trinity; and He gave us a preview of His glorious coming on the last day to transform our body to a likeness of His glorified body. (554-556)

346. *Why did Jesus weep over Jerusalem?*

Because Jerusalem had killed the prophets of the Old Testament and, having rejected the Messiah, would also put Him to death. (557-558)

347. *What did Jesus wish to teach us by His triumphal entry into Jerusalem?*

He revealed the coming of the kingdom that He would establish by His death and Resurrection. (559-560)

ARTICLE 4: "JESUS CHRIST SUFFERED UNDER PONTIUS PILATE, WAS CRUCIFIED, DIED, AND WAS BURIED"

348. *How is the paschal mystery at the center of the Gospel proclaimed to the world?*

It was by His Passion and death that Christ redeemed the world. There could be no good news of salvation without the historical sufferings of the Son of God. (571-573)

I. Jesus and Israel

349. *Why was Jesus rejected by some of the leaders of Israel?*

Because they thought He was indifferent to full obedience of their Law, to the centrality of the Temple in divine worship, and to faith in one God whose glory no human being can share. (574-576)

350. *How did Jesus relate to God's Law given on Mount Sinai?*

He not only accepted this Law but He brought it to fulfillment, as He explained in the Sermon on the Mount. (577)

351. *How did Jesus bring the Law of the Old Testament to fulfillment?*

He did so in several ways:

- by subjecting Himself to the Law as the incarnate Son of God;
- by providing the grace for His followers to live the Law beyond anything expected in the Old Testament;
- by giving us the Beatitudes, which are the definitive interpretation of the Mosaic Law;
- by revealing depths of meaning in the Law that only God-become-man could recognize. (578-582)

352. *What was Jesus' attitude toward the Temple?*

It was uniformly reverent and respectful. As a child, He was presented in the Temple. At the age of twelve, He decided to stay on in the Temple. He drove out the money-changers who were desecrating the Temple. In His preaching, He stressed how the Temple was supposed to be a house of prayer. (583-584)

353. *Why did Jesus foretell the destruction of the Temple?*

He did so to predict the dawn of a new age in salvation history. Moreover, He wished to emphasize the fact that He Himself was the perfect dwelling place of God among His people. (585-586)

354. *How did Jesus mainly scandalize His contemporaries?*

It was by His claim to forgive sins on His own authority. In so doing, He professed to possess divine power, since, as His enemies declared, no one but God can forgive sins. (587-591)

II. The Passion

355. *How were the Jews divided regarding Jesus?*

In general, there were two basic attitudes. Many favored Jesus, including Jewish leaders like the Pharisee Nicodemus. Others, especially those in religious authority, not only rejected Jesus but were positively hostile and directly responsible for Christ's crucifixion. (595-596)

356. *Were the Jews, as a body, responsible for Jesus' execution?*

No, neither all the Jews in Christ's time, nor the Jews living today, can be held collectively guilty of Christ's unjust condemnation and death. Consequently, the Jews are not to be considered as somehow rejected by God for what occurred in the Passion of Christ. (597)

357. *Who, then, were the authors of Christ's Passion?*

They are all the sinners who may be called the instruments of the sufferings endured by the Savior. (598)

358. *How is Christ's death part of God's mysterious providence?*

As St. Peter says, Christ was handed over to His enemies "according to the definite plan and foreknowledge of God" (Acts 2:23). Human malice is also part of divine providence, where God allows evil as the occasion for great good, here of our salvation, as a result of the hatred of Christ's enemies.

(599-600)

359. How did Christ "become sin" for us?

He did so by freely assuming the penalty of death for the original sin of our first parents. That is why the Second Person of the Trinity assumed a human nature, in order to expiate the sins of the human race.   (601-603)

360. What are the two main features of God's redemptive love for us?

His love is totally undeserved and universal.

- It is undeserved because, as sinners, we had no claim on His divine mercy.
- It is universal because God wants everyone to be saved.   (604-605)

361. When did Christ sacrifice Himself for our redemption?

It was not only on the Cross but from the first moment of His conception to His death on Calvary. The Crucifixion was simply the consummation of His lifelong sacrifice for our sins.   (606-607)

362. How is Christ the Paschal Lamb?

He is the fulfillment of the centuries of sacrifice of the lamb at the annual Jewish Passover. As the sacrifice of the lamb delivered the Israelites from the avenging angel in Egypt, so the sacrifice of Christ on Calvary delivered the sinful human race from the justice of God.   (608)

363. How did Christ redeem the world by His humanity?

He did so in several ways:

- By His human free will, He submitted Himself to the will of His Father.
- At the Last Supper, He offered His human flesh and blood for our salvation.
- In the agony in the Garden, He surrendered His human will to the divine will of the Father.
- On the Cross, He offered Himself by shedding His human blood for our sins.

- His sacrifice was the supreme oblation that only He could make because He was the God who became incarnate in order to expiate our disobedience.

- By His death on the Cross, He completed the purpose of the Incarnation to redeem us as the God who assumed a human will to make our salvation possible.

(609-616)

364. *How are we to participate in the sacrifice of Christ?*

We do so in three ways:

- by freely uniting our crosses with the Cross of Jesus Christ;

- by following His example of total surrender to the will of God in our lives;

- by uniting our sufferings with those of Jesus, as Mary did all through the life of Christ and especially on Calvary. (617-618)

III. Christ's Burial

365. *What happened when Jesus died?*

His soul separated from His body until it was reunited with the body on Easter Sunday. (624)

366. *Why was Christ's body laid in the tomb?*

For two main reasons:

- to show that it was the same Redeemer who died and rose gloriously from the grave;

- to show that, even though His body and soul were separated, He was still the incarnate Son of God redeeming a sinful human race.

(625-626)

367. *Did Christ's body decay in the grave?*

No, as evidenced by His rising on the third day. The early Christians believed that a dead body begins to decay on the fourth day. (627)

368. *How are we buried with Christ?*

By our Baptism, which restores us to the life of grace lost by the sin of our first parents. (628)

ARTICLE 5: "JESUS CHRIST DESCENDED INTO HELL, AND ON THE THIRD DAY HE ROSE AGAIN"

369. *Why are Christ's resurrection and descent to the dead in the same article of the Creed?*

Because Christ restored life precisely by descending to the depths of the dead. (631)

I. Christ's Descent

370. *What do we mean by Christ's descent?*

We mean three things:

- that in His soul, Christ descended to the "lower regions" to visit the faithful departed of the Old Testament;
- that Christ's salvific mission was completed;
- that Christ descended in order to free those who were awaiting their redemption. (632-635)

II. Christ's Resurrection

371. *How is Christ's Resurrection the crowning mystery of our faith?*

Because by rising from the dead, Christ gave the highest proof of the truth of all His teaching. (638)

372. *Was the Resurrection of Christ both a historical and transcendent event?*

Yes, His resurrection was certainly historical, as all the evidence of Scripture testifies:

- The tomb was empty in spite of the guarded precautions of Christ's enemies.
- Christ appeared to His disciples, who had to be convinced that He really rose from the dead. He spoke to them, ate with them, asked them to touch Him.
- The doubting Thomas was convinced.
- The credibility of Christ's teaching depended on His followers being convinced that He actually rose from the dead. (639-644, 647)

373. *What was the condition of Christ's risen humanity?*

Although He was truly the same Christ, He was now glorified. His body was transfigured, immortal, able to move at will through space. He became, in the words of St. Paul, "a heavenly man." (645-646)

374. *How was Christ's Resurrection the work of the Holy Trinity?*

All three Persons cooperated in the Resurrection of Christ. They exercised Their almighty power no less than in the creation of the world. (648-650)

375. *What is the significance of Christ's Resurrection?*

The resurrection of Christ:

- confirms the truth of His teaching;
- fulfills the Messianic promises of the Old Testament;
- witnesses to His divinity;
- opens the supernatural life to us, even as Christ's death liberates us from sin;
- makes possible our own resurrection from the dead. (651-655)

ARTICLE 6: "HE ASCENDED INTO HEAVEN AND IS SEATED AT THE RIGHT HAND OF THE FATHER"

376. *How was Christ's glorified humanity veiled during the forty days before the Ascension?*

By revealing all of its natural human traits, like eating and drinking and talking with His disciples. (659)

377. *How was Christ's glory elevated by His Ascension?*

It was elevated in its manifestation by vision to the angels and saints in heaven, in contrast to its manifestation by faith to the disciples on earth. (660)

378. *How is Christ's Ascension related to the Incarnation?*

The Ascension completed Christ's mission of salvation. He came from heaven to merit our supernatural destiny. He returned to heaven to communicate to us the graces we need to reach heaven. (661)

379. *What does it mean that Christ is now seated at the right hand of the Father?*

It means three things:

- Christ now glorifies His heavenly Father as the incarnate Son of God.

- Christ is exercising His priesthood by interceding for us with the Father.

- Christ's presence at the right hand of the Father began the fulfillment of His eternal mission, as King of the Universe.   (662-664)

ARTICLE 7: "HE WILL COME AGAIN TO JUDGE THE LIVING AND THE DEAD"

380. *Does the kingdom of Christ already exist?*

Yes, Christ is already Head of the kingdom He came to establish. He is King of the Church Triumphant, Militant, and Suffering. On all three levels, Christ is the Ruler and Judge of His people. We therefore cannot say that His kingdom has yet to come into existence.   (668-670)

381. *Has Christ's kingdom reached its fulfillment?*

No, for several reasons:

- The powers of evil are not yet fully vanquished or subject to Christ.

- There is not yet a new heaven and a new earth.

- The Church Militant and Suffering is still under trial and pain.(671-672)

382. *Are the Jews still to accept the Messiah?*

Yes, over the centuries, the Chosen People have, in large measure, rejected Jesus as the promised Messiah. Sts. Peter and Paul speak of an eventual acceptance of Jesus by the Jews as their Lord and Redeemer.   (673-674)

383. *Will there be a final trial for the Church on earth?*

Yes, this is the teaching of Christ as recorded by the evangelists and St. Paul. The faithful will be tried by opposition and persecution. The final victory over the forces of evil will shake the world to its foundations. (675-677)

384. *By what right will Christ judge the world on the last day?*

It is by the right of His Cross. Having suffered and died for our salvation, Christ has the right to determine our eternal destiny. But He will judge us according to our own free decision to accept or reject the graces of His merciful love. (678-679)

Chapter Three
"I Believe in the Holy Spirit"

The third and last part of the Apostles' Creed is our profession of faith in the Holy Spirit. We believe in the Holy Spirit as the Third Person of the Holy Trinity, as the Spirit by whom Our Lady conceived her Divine Son, as the Spirit promised by Christ to those who profess that Jesus is their Lord and Redeemer, and as the Spirit who animates the Church as the Soul of the Mystical Body of Christ. (683-686)

ARTICLE 8: "I BELIEVE IN THE HOLY SPIRIT"

385. *How do we come to know the Holy Spirit who is dwelling and acting in the Church?*

We come to know the Holy Spirit:

- from the Sacred Scriptures which He inspired;
- from Sacred Tradition;
- from the Church's teaching authority;
- from the sacramental liturgy;
- from prayer and the Church's ministries;
- from the achievement of the Church's apostolate;
- from the witness of the saints by their lives of heroic sanctity.(687-688)

386. *How are the missions of Christ and the Holy Spirit related?*

Both Christ and the Holy Spirit were sent among men but in different ways:

- Christ was sent to redeem a world steeped in sin.

- The Holy Spirit was sent to sanctify those redeemed by Christ by uniting them in a communion of love. (689-690)

387. *What are some of the titles of the Holy Spirit?*

He is known as the Paraclete, "who is near," as the Advocate, who defends and consoles, and as the Spirit of Truth. He is also called the Spirit of promise, of adoption, of Christ, of wisdom, of God, of the Lord, and the Spirit of glory. (692-693)

388. *What are the principal symbols of the Holy Spirit?*

The principal symbols are:

- water, which symbolizes new birth in Baptism;

- oil, by which we are anointed in Confirmation;

- fire, which expresses the transforming power of the Spirit to change ordinary people into zealous apostles of the Gospel;

- cloud and light, where the cloud typifies the obscurity of our faith and the light the illumination that the Spirit gives to those who believe in Christ;

- a seal, which symbolizes especially the indelible change of character produced by the Sacraments of Baptism, Confirmation, and Holy Orders;

- laying on of hands, to indicate the communication of power by the Holy Spirit from one person to another;

- finger of God, or of Christ, which inscribes the will of God on the tablets of human hearts;

- a dove, to testify to the truth of what God wishes to reveal, as in Christ's baptism in the Jordan. (694-701)

389. *Where was the Spirit of promise revealed in the Old Testament?*

In the Law of the first five books of the Bible, in the prophets, and especially in the wisdom literature and the Psalms. (702)

390. *How is the Spirit of promise revealed?*

It is revealed:

- in creation, where God's love is shown in making every creature out of nothing;

- in God's assurance that a sinful human race would be redeemed;

- in theophanies, or manifestations of God, which anticipate the Incarnation of the Son of God;

- in the laws, the observance of which would prepare the Chosen People for the coming of Christ;

- in the earthly kingdom of the Jews as the promise of the heavenly kingdom to be founded by Christ. Even the apparent frustration of this promise became its fulfillment with the establishment of Christ's kingdom, which is the Church built upon a rock. (702-710)

391. *What are some of the promised qualities of the Spirit of the Messiah?*

He shall have the spirit of wisdom and understanding, of counsel and might, of knowledge and the fear of the Lord.

- As the promised Messiah, Jesus proclaimed that "the Spirit of the Lord God is upon me, because the Lord has anointed Me... to bring the good news to the poor" (Lk 4:18).

- As taught by St. Peter, the Spirit of the Messiah actually descended on the disciples on Pentecost Sunday. They then proclaimed how this Spirit would reconcile sinners with God and with one another in peaceful harmony.

- The Psalms predict that the "people of the poor," by their humility and reliance on God's providence, would be the channels of His grace to the whole world. (711-716)

392. *How did the Holy Spirit use John the Baptist as the precursor of Christ?*

He did so in several ways:

- John was filled with the Holy Spirit by Christ when Mary greeted Elizabeth at the Visitation.

- In John, the Holy Spirit closed the age of the prophets foretelling the Messiah.

- John himself testified that the Messiah is the one on whom the Holy Spirit descends.

- Christ's baptism by John was the herald of our Sacrament of Baptism, instituted by Christ. (717-721)

393. *How is the Blessed Virgin full of grace?*

The Blessed Virgin is full of grace because:

- she is the Mother of God, who is the Author of divine grace;

- she was prepared for her divine maternity by being conceived without sin and gifted with unique humility;

- she conceived her divine Son by the grace of the Holy Spirit;

- she became the channel of God's grace by revealing her Son to the poor shepherds and the Magi;

- she brought her Son to be revealed in Bethlehem, at the Presentation, and at Cana in Galilee. (722-726)

394. *How did Jesus promise the Holy Spirit?*

Jesus distinguished between what He openly told His disciples and what He gradually disclosed to the multitudes about the Holy Spirit. When the hour came for His Passion, He clearly made the promise of sending the Holy Spirit, who was to fulfill the mission entrusted to Christ by the Father.
(727-730)

395. *When was Christ's promise of the Holy Spirit fulfilled?*

On Pentecost Sunday, when the Holy Trinity was fully revealed, the Holy Spirit descended on the disciples, who then proclaimed Christ to the world. By believing in Him, the world began to share in the communion of the Holy Trinity. (731-732)

396. *How is the Holy Spirit God's gift to us?*

By His giving us the Holy Spirit:

- we are forgiven our sins;

- we are enabled to love God and others with selfless charity;

- we are given the fruits of the Holy Spirit, which are the supernatural happiness experienced in doing the will of God. (733-736)

397. *How is the Church related to the Holy Spirit?*

- The Church completes the mission of Christ and the Holy Spirit.

- The Church's mission is to proclaim the mission of Christ and the Holy Spirit.

- Through the sacraments, Christ communicates to us the graces of the Holy Spirit.

- The Holy Spirit, in the Church, enables us to pray according to the will of God. (737-741)

ARTICLE 9: "I BELIEVE IN THE HOLY CATHOLIC CHURCH"

Our faith in the Church depends entirely on our faith in Christ and the Holy Spirit. Christ is the light of the Church, even as the Church is where the Holy Spirit is flourishing.

Our faith in the Church as one, holy, Catholic, and apostolic also depends on our faith in God, whose goodness is the source of these gifts of the Church. (748-750)

398. *What does the word "Church" mean?*

Literally, it means "a religious assembly," from the Greek *ecclesia.* Our English word "church" comes from the Greek *kyriake,* meaning "what belongs to the Lord." For Christians, "Church" means the community of Christ's faithful. (751-752)

399. *What are some biblical symbols of the Church?*

Among others, the most important speak of the Church as:

- the sheepfold, whose shepherd and door are Christ;
- the field, with a variety of crops and trees;
- the building, whose cornerstone is Christ and whose synonyms are the home for God's family;
- the Temple, which is the New Jerusalem;
- our Mother, who is the immaculate spouse of the spotless Lamb.

(753-757)

400. *What is the history of the Church's formation and consummation?*

- The Church, as the gathering of God's people, began when our first parents sinned and were promised a Redeemer.
- Her formation started with the call of Abraham and the Chosen People of Israel.
- She was established by Christ when He called the Apostles with Peter as their head, proclaimed His teaching, and instituted the sacraments.
- She was born on Calvary from the heart of Christ, pierced at His death.
- She was manifest to the world on Pentecost Sunday.
- She continues to proclaim the kingdom of Christ to the world.
- She will reach her final destiny in heavenly glory on the last day.

(758-769)

401. *What is the mystery of the Church?*

The Church is a mystery because:

- she is both part of human history and surpasses our human comprehension;
- she is both a hierarchical institution and the Mystical Body of Christ;
- she is both a visible assembly and a spiritual community;
- she is both an earthly society and a heavenly reality;
- she is both human and divine;
- she is the divinely established means for the sanctification of her members. (770-773)

402. *How is the Church the universal sacrament of salvation?*

The Church is the universal sacrament of salvation because she is the visible channel of grace to the whole human race. (774-776)

403. *How is the Church the People of God?*

She is the People of God in seven basic ways:

- Those who belong to the Church are called by God to be "a chosen race, a royal priesthood, a holy nation."
- Her members are born of water and the Spirit of God.
- Her head is Jesus Christ, the Incarnate Son of God.
- Her people have the Holy Spirit dwelling in them as in a temple of God.
- Her law is the New Law given by God-become-man.
- Her mission is that of being the salt of the earth and light of the world as revealed by the Word of God.
- Her destiny is the kingdom of God. (781-782)

404. *How are Christians a priestly, prophetic, and kingly people?*

Basically, by participating in the three offices of Christ as Priest, Prophet, and King.

- By Baptism, they become sharers in Christ's priesthood. They are enabled to offer themselves with Him in His sacrifice to the Father.
- By the virtue of faith, they share in the wisdom of Christ and become witnesses of Christ's truth to the world.

- By their loving service to those in need, they share in Christ's kingship; by their suffering with Christ, they join in His royalty of the Cross. (783-786)

405. *How is the Church the Body of Christ?*

She is the Body of Christ because:

* Her members, although diverse, are united under Christ as their head and by one Spirit, which is the Spirit of Christ. This union is effected by Baptism and sustained by the Eucharist.

* Christ is the head, having founded the Church, by constantly providing varying gifts for her different members and their ministries.

* Christ is the Spouse of the Church, who is His Bride. He loved her even to dying on the Cross to bring her into being, and loves her in that Mystical Marriage which is destined to continue into eternity.

(787-796)

406. *How is the Church the temple of the Holy Spirit?*

The Holy Spirit is the Soul of the Church as her principle of supernatural life, even as the soul is the principle of the natural life of our body. No less than a human soul animates a human body, the Holy Spirit animates the Church and enables her to grow in grace through the sacraments, the virtues He infuses, and the charisms He confers. (797-798)

407. *What are charisms?*

They are special graces that the Holy Spirit gives the Church's members for the building up of the Mystical Body. These charisms are to be humbly accepted but are always subject to discernment by the shepherds of the Church. (799-801)

408. *What are the four basic marks of the Church?*

They are the Church's characteristics, identifying her as the true Church because she is one, holy, catholic, and apostolic. (811-812)

409. *How is the Church one?*

She is one because:

- the one Triune God is the source and pattern of her unity;
- her Founder is the one Jesus Christ, the incarnate Son of God;
- her Soul is the one Holy Spirit;

- her history has been essential unity among a wide variety and diversity of God's people;

- her essence is unity, which has been preserved by the bond of charity.
(813-815)

410. *Where is this one Church of Christ?*

This one true Church of Christ abides in the Catholic Church, governed by the successor of St. Peter and the bishops in communion with him. (816)

411. *Has this unity been wounded?*

Yes, from the Church's beginning to the present day, there have been many dissensions. Yet, all the baptized are incorporated into Christ. Among these separated Christians, there are many elements of sanctification and truth that come from Christ and are calls to Christian unity. (817-819)

412. *How are Catholics to promote Christian unity?*

They must first be convinced that this is the will of Christ. Moreover:

- They must be more faithful to their Christian vocation.

- They must live holier lives, in keeping with the Gospel.

- They must pray with separated Christians.

- They must grow in their mutual knowledge of other Christians.

- They should be ecumenically formed.

- Catholic theologians should dialogue with separated Christians.

- They should collaborate in various services to all people. (820-822)

413. *How is the Church holy?*

- She is holy because her Founder is the all-holy Son of God, who died on the Cross to make her holy.

- She is holy because Christ gave her all the means necessary to sanctify her members.

- She is holy because her members are called to sanctity.

- She is holy because she possesses the life of grace, which is holiness.

- She is holy because she canonizes saints whose heroic virtue is the inspiration for others to imitate.

- She is holy in the perfection of the Blessed Virgin, the Mother of the Church. (823-829)

414. *How is the Church catholic?*

She is catholic because she is universal in two distinct ways:

- She is universal because Christ is present in her in the fullness of His body, with the fullness of the means of salvation, the fullness of faith, sacraments, and ordained ministry by apostolic succession.

- She is universal because her mission is to the whole human race.

(830-831)

415. *How is each particular church catholic?*

By virtue of Christ's presence in every diocese or eparchy. This presence gives each local church a share in the universal Church's unity, holiness, catholicity, and apostolicity. (832-835)

416. *Who belongs to the Catholic Church?*

Everyone who is validly baptized and believes in Christ belongs to the Catholic Church. However, only those belong fully as members of the Church who accept her whole structure and all her means of salvation, and are united by the bonds of faith, sacraments, and obedience to the bishops under the Bishop of Rome. (836-838)

417. *How does the Catholic Church look upon non-Christians?*

While respecting all non-Christians, her estimate differs for different people.

- Judaism is held in special honor because the Jews received the first covenant from God.

- Islam is also highly regarded because Muslims believe in one God.

- All non-Christians are recognized as having one bond of human origin and destiny with the followers of Christ.

- At the same time, the Church sees various limitations and errors in the non-Christian beliefs.

- Finally, she offers the non-Christian world the fullness of God's truth in the one bark of salvation, which is the Roman Catholic Church.

(839-845)

418. *How are we to understand the Catholic doctrine that "outside the Church there is no salvation"?*

It means that whoever reaches heaven is saved through the Catholic Church as the universal sacrament of salvation. (846-848)

419. *What is the Church's mission?*

Her mission is to proclaim the Gospel to all peoples. This is a duty that:

- originates with Christ's commandment to His Apostles;

- expresses God's eternal love to be shared with all mankind;

- is based on God's revelation of the truth and directed by the Holy Spirit;

- requires the practice of penance, acceptance of the Cross, and deep respect for other people by building on the truth in their religious beliefs. (849-856)

420. *How is the Church apostolic?*

She is apostolic in three principal ways:

- She is built on the Apostles whom Christ chose and sent to preach the Gospel.

- She remains faithful to the teaching of the Apostles.

- She continues to be taught, guided, and sanctified by the successors of the Apostles, the bishops of the Catholic Church, united under the Bishop of Rome. (857)

421. *How are bishops successors of the Apostles?*

Bishops trace their heritage, by divine institution, to the original twelve men whom Christ ordained at the Last Supper and commissioned to ordain successors in the episcopate until the end of time. Like the original twelve under Peter, so the bishops are to be united under his successor, the Roman Pontiff. (857-862)

422. *What is the Church's apostolate?*

It is nothing less than to extend the kingdom of Christ to the ends of the earth. Its goal is the heavenly Jerusalem, where the Church will reach her perfection in the City of God. (863-870)

423. *Is there a true equality among the members of the Church?*

Yes, because all are reborn in Christ and united by Christ in His Mystical Body. (874-876)

424. *What is the Church's ministry?*

The Church's ministry was instituted by Christ to provide a means of grace through the sacraments, to give the Church authority and mission, and to enable her to guide her members to their eternal destiny. (874-876)

425. *How important is the sacramental ministry?*

It is the essence of the Church. Thus, without Baptism, there would be no membership in the Church; through the Sacrament of Penance, sinners are reconciled with God; the Sacrifice of Calvary is renewed in the Sacrifice of the Mass. (877-879)

426. *What is the college of bishops?*

It is the bishops of the Roman Catholic Church united under the pope as an episcopal community. This community of pope and bishops, and the bishops among themselves, was created by Christ and therefore belongs, by divine right, to the nature of the Church He founded. (880-881)

427. *What is the position of the pope in the college of bishops?*

As taught by the Second Vatican Council, the pope is Peter's successor and Bishop of Rome. He is the perpetual and visible principle and basis of the unity of both the bishops and the multitude of the faithful. "By virtue of his office as Vicar of Christ, [he] possesses full, supreme, and universal power, which he may always exercise freely over the Church" (*Constitution on the Church*, 22-23). (882)

428. *What is the role of the bishops?*

As an episcopal college or community, bishops exercise their power over the whole Church in an ecumenical council. As individual bishops, they exercise pastoral care over the people in their diocese or ecclesiastical jurisdiction. But in all cases, their authority depends on union with the Bishop of Rome. (883-887)

429. *What is the teaching office of the bishops?*

With priests as co-workers, bishops have as their primary duty to teach the fullness of the Gospel with Christ's authority. (888)

430. *What is the Church's Magisterium?*

It is the Church's teaching authority, which Christ assures will lead God's people to the fullness of the truth without error. (889-890)

431. *When is the Church's Magisterium infallible?*

It is infallible when the pope, as visible head of the Church, pronounces a doctrine in faith or morals as definitive.

"Although the bishops, taken individually, do not enjoy the privilege of infallibility, they do, however, proclaim infallibly the doctrine of Christ on the following conditions: namely, when, even though dispersed throughout the world but preserving for all that amongst themselves and with Peter's successor the bond of communion, in their authoritative teaching concerning matters of faith and morals, they are in agreement that a particular teaching is to be held definitively and absolutely. This is still more clearly the case when, assembled in an ecumenical council, they are for the universal Church, teachers of and judges in matters of faith and morals, whose decisions must be adhered to with the loyal and obedient assent of faith" (*Lumen Gentium*, 3, 25). (891)

432. *What is religious assent?*

This is the acceptance of a doctrine that the Church does not propose definitively. (892)

433. *How do bishops exercise their office of governing the People of God?*

They do so as delegates of Christ. Their power to govern belongs to them as bishops, although regulated by the authority of the pope. Christ, the Good Shepherd, is their model and inspiration. (894-896)

434. *Who are the laity?*

They are all baptized members who are not in sacred orders or in consecrated religious life. (897)

435. *What is the vocation of the laity?*

Their distinct vocation is to promote the kingdom of God in the temporal affairs of life in accordance with the mind of Christ. (898)

436. *Why is the apostolate of the laity necessary?*

Because the laity are directly involved in the social, political, and economic affairs of the world, which they are to influence in accordance with Christian doctrine. (899)

437. *How are the laity entrusted with the apostolate?*

Baptism and Confirmation give them the right and the duty, as individuals and as groups, to bring the teachings of Christ into the world. (900)

438. *How do the laity share in Christ's priestly office?*

By their lives of sacrifice in union with Christ's sacrifice on the Cross, joined with Him in the Sacrifice of the Mass. (901-903)

439. *How do the laity share in Christ's prophetic office?*

By their zealous evangelization and catechesis; by their use of the media to proclaim Christ; and by sharing the faith with their daily contact and conversation with the world in which they live. (904-906)

440. *Should laypeople share their religious views with their pastors?*

Yes, they have the right and sometimes the duty of doing so. They have the same responsibility to make their views known among the faithful. (907)

441. *How do the laity share in Christ's kingly office?*

They are to exercise their influence to improve the structures of secular society that lead people into sin and do all they can to invest the human condition with moral values based on the law of God. All of this presumes that the laity have developed self-mastery according to the mind of Christ.

(908-913)

442. *What is the consecrated life?*

It is a life dedicated to the profession of the evangelical counsels of chastity, poverty, and obedience. (914-915)

443. *What is the religious state?*

It is consecrated life in which the members of a community dedicate themselves to follow Christ more closely, give themselves to God, who is love above all things, and pursue the perfection of charity in the service of the kingdom of God, in order to proclaim in the Church the glory of the world to come. (916)

444. *Why are there different forms of consecrated life?*

In order to glorify the manifold attributes of God and serve the varied needs in the vineyard of the Lord. (917-919)

445. *What is the eremetical life?*

It is a life withdrawn from the world in order to serve God and souls through silent solitude, constant prayer, and penance. Hermits bear witness in a special way to the glory of Christ crucified. (920-921)

446. *What are consecrated virgins?*

They are women who dedicate themselves to a virginal life in the world (or cloister). By prayer, penance, and apostolic service to others, they are consecrated by the bishop as an image of the heavenly bride and of the life of the world to come. (922-924)

447. *What is religious life?*

It is consecrated life characterized by its distinctive worship of God, public profession of the evangelical counsels, community life, and witness to Christ's union with the Church. Over the centuries, religious have been outstanding in spreading the faith and establishing churches throughout the world.

(925-927)

448. *What are secular institutes?*

They are forms of consecrated life whose members sanctify the world (*saeculum*) from within. They serve as a leaven in the world by directing their prayer and union with God to animate the world by the power of the Gospel. (928-929)

449. *What are societies of apostolic life?*

They are associations of the faithful who, without religious vows, pledge themselves to live together according to the evangelical counsels. Their purpose is to engage in the apostolate defined by their constitutions. (930)

450. *What is the mission of consecrated life?*

It is to proclaim the advent of Christ the King. This means first being faithful to one's consecration, and thus cooperating in the Church's apostolate. The final purpose is to witness to Christ's Redemption and His Second Coming, to establish the eternal kingdom of Heaven. (931-933)

451. *What is the Communion of Saints?*

It is the Catholic Church, seen as an assembly of holy persons who share their spiritual possessions. (946-948)

452. *What is the meaning of "communion of spiritual goods"?*

In the early Church, the followers of Christ lived in "fellowship," or community, which we may call "communion of spiritual goods" (Acts 2:44). Thus, they shared:

- in a communion of faith, believing the truths taught them by the Apostles;

- in a communion of the sacraments instituted by Christ;

- in a communion of charisms, or special apostolic gifts;

- everything they owned;

- in a communion of love, as befitted the members of the Body of Christ. (949-953)

453. *What is the communion of the Church of heaven and earth?*

There are three states of the Church: Militant on earth, Suffering in purgatory, and Triumphant in heaven. There is, therefore, a three-way communication among the three states:

- The saints in heaven intercede for persons on earth and in purgatory.

- We on earth foster the memory of the saints in heaven, invoke them, and imitate their virtues.

- We pray for the souls of the faithful departed that "they may be loosed from their sins" (2 Mc 12:45).

Thus, we form the one family of God for the praise of the Holy Trinity. (954-959)

454. *How is Mary the Mother of the Church?*

Mary is Mother of the Church in every conceivable sense:

- She is the Mother of Christ, who instituted the Church and is the Church's invisible head.

- She cooperated with her Son in every stage of His work of redemption, from Christ's virginal conception to His death on Calvary.

- After Christ's Ascension, she assisted the infant Church by her prayers to call down the Holy Spirit.

- After her bodily assumption, because of her immaculate conception, she is the perfect human person for us to imitate. She continually intercedes for us with her Divine Son. In a word, she is our advocate, benefactress, helper, and mediatrix of grace. (963-970)

455. *What should be our devotion to the Blessed Virgin?*

Our devotion to her is:

- to honor her as the Mother of God to whose protection we should fly in all our dangers and needs;

- to see in her what the Church is here on earth by faith and what the Church will be in heavenly glory. In other words, Mary is both the perfect model to imitate and the symbol of our hope in eternity.

(971-972)

ARTICLE 10: "I BELIEVE IN THE FORGIVENESS OF SINS"

The Apostles' Creed associates the forgiveness of sins not only with the Holy Spirit by whose divine power sins are remitted, but also with the Church to which Christ entrusted the authority to reconcile sinners with God.

(976)

456. *What are the two basic sacraments for the forgiveness of sins?*

They are Baptism and Penance. Through Baptism we are restored to God's friendship and provided with grace to resist our sinful inclinations. Penance reconciles the baptized with an offended God. (977-980)

457. *What is the power of the keys?*

It is the power that Christ gave the Church through the Apostles and their successors in the episcopate and priesthood to restore sinners to friendship with God. (981-983)

ARTICLE 11: "I BELIEVE IN THE RESURRECTION OF THE BODY"

As followers of Christ who rose from the dead, we believe that, like Him, we too shall be reunited in body and soul on the last day. Our resurrection, like that of the Savior, will be the work of the Holy Trinity. (988-991)

458. *What was the progressive revelation of the resurrection?*

This was the gradual development of God's revealing the fact of man's final resurrection from the dead. Already in the Old Testament, the Maccabean martyrs professed that "the King of the world will raise us up, who died for His laws in the resurrection of eternal life" (2 Mc 7:9).

In the New Testament, Christ declared that He was the resurrection and the life and that those who eat His Body and drink His Blood will be raised by Him from the dead.

In the early Church, there was strong opposition to faith in the resurrection of the body. Hence the long defense of this truth by St. Paul (1 Cor 15:1-58). (992-996)

459. *How will the dead rise back to life?*

They will rise to life by the almighty power of God reuniting their souls with their bodies. However, these bodies will be transformed. Explaining St. Paul's description (1 Cor 15:42-44), the Church identifies four qualities of the risen body:

- impassibility, which means it will no longer be subject to pain or death;

- brightness, or resplendent beauty;

- agility, or freedom from the present limitations of space and time;

- subtility, which means its being completely under the control of the soul. (997-1000)

460. *When will the resurrection take place?*

On the last day of the present human race. (1001)

461. *What does it mean to be risen with Christ?*

It means that our resurrection is one of the fruits of Christ's death and resurrection; that the risen Christ has been interceding for us in heaven to obtain our resurrection; that our reception of the risen Christ in the Eucharist has gained the graces we need to rise glorious from the dead; that His Resurrection is the guarantee of our rising from the grave; and that already in this life, our bodies and souls belong to Christ. (1002-1004)

462. *What is death?*

In the light of reason, death is separation of the soul from the body. But in the eyes of faith:

- Death is the consequence of sin.

- Death is a share in Christ's death on Calvary.

- Death is the end of our probation on earth. There is no reincarnation.

- Death is God calling us to Himself.

- Death is a precious sacrifice we can make to God.

- Death is the beginning of eternal life. (1005-1014)

ARTICLE 12: "I BELIEVE IN LIFE EVERLASTING"

Our Christian faith enables us to view death not as the end or finish of our life but as the entrance into everlasting life.

In the Prayer of Commendation at a funeral, the Church closes her liturgy with the confident hope: "May you see your Redeemer face to face."   (1020)

463. *What is the particular judgment?*

It is the judgment made by God declaring whether a person who has just died will go to heaven, hell, or purgatory.   (1021-1022)

464. *What is heaven?*

Heaven is the place of perfect happiness where the souls of the just see the face of God even before the resurrection of the body. Heaven is the eternal community of love with the Holy Trinity, Our Lady, the angels, and the saints. Heaven is the kingdom of God, which Christ merited for us by His Passion and death.   (1023-1029)

465. *What is purgatory?*

Purgatory is the state of purification that souls must undergo in order to have the holiness necessary to enter heaven. Infallibly defined by the Church, the existence of purgatory is supported by Sacred Scripture, especially by the Old Testament teaching that "it is a holy and wholesome thought to pray for the dead, that they may be loosed from their sins" (2 Mc 12:46). (1030-1031)

466. *Why do we pray for the dead?*

We pray for the dead because we are not sure they are already in heaven. We believe the souls in purgatory need our prayers, especially through the Sacrifice of the Mass, both to mitigate their suffering and to hasten their entrance into heaven.   (1032)

467. *What is hell?*

Hell is eternal separation from God for those who die unrepentant for their mortal sins.   (1033-1035)

468. *What is the principal lesson of hell?*

It teaches us to use our free will according to the will of God in order to reach our heavenly destiny.   (1036)

469. *Does God predestine anyone to hell?*

No, only a willful persistence in mortal sin can deserve eternal punishment. God wants everyone to be saved; He wants no one to perish in hell.   (1037)

470. *What is the Last Judgment?*

The Last Judgment will come at the end of the world. The whole human race will witness the public manifestation of each person's good and evil actions, and their consequences. The Last Judgment will be a cosmic revelation of God's mercy and justice on the family of mankind. Jesus Christ will make this revelation as King of the Universe.   (1038-1041)

471. *What are the new heaven and the new earth?*

They are the transformations of humanity and of the physical universe that God will produce after the general judgment.

- The human race will finally be united, and all those who are saved will form the Holy City of God.

- The visible universe will be transformed, sharing in the glorification of the just.   (1042)

472. *Do we know the time and manner of these transformations?*

No, except that we know that they will take place, and that the final resurrection refers not only to our human bodies but, in a mysterious sense, to all of visible creation.   (1042-1050)

473. *What is the significance of the word "Amen" at the close of the Apostles' Creed?*

"Amen" literally means "So be it" in Hebrew. It is the last word of the Bible. In the Creed, it means both God's fidelity to us and our confidence in Him. We may say that Christ Himself is the definitive "Amen" of the Father's love for us. Christ is therefore the perfect synthesis of our faith. Whatever else we believe is summarized in Him, our incarnate God.   (1061-1065)

PART TWO

THE CELEBRATION OF
THE SACRED MYSTERY

INTRODUCTION

The liturgy proclaims and celebrates the mysteries professed in the Apostles' Creed, notably the paschal mystery by which Christ redeemed the world.

Liturgy literally means a public service by and for the people. Theologically, the liturgy is both a participation of the Christian faithful in Christ's work of redemption, and Christ's continuing His work of our redemption in, with, and by the Church.

The liturgy is therefore rightly considered the exercise of Christ's priesthood, in which man's sanctification is signified and realized in ways proper to each sensibly perceptible liturgical sign.

Liturgical catechesis is instruction in the liturgy on two levels: as mystery and celebration in general, and as sacraments and sacramentals in particular.

(1066-1075)

SECTION I:
THE SACRAMENTAL ECONOMY

The expression "sacramental economy" simply means the communication or dispensation of the fruits of Christ's paschal mystery through the celebration of the sacramental liturgy.

It is therefore necessary to explain the meaning of this sacramental dispensation and the essential features of liturgical celebration.   (1076)

CHAPTER ONE
THE PASCHAL MYSTERY IN
THE TIME OF THE CHURCH

Our task here is to see how the liturgy is the work of the Holy Trinity. This will be viewed from the perspective of each of the three divine Persons: the Father as the source and goal of the liturgy; Christ's role in the liturgy; and the Holy Spirit working with the Church in the liturgy.

ARTICLE 1: THE LITURGY—WORK OF THE HOLY TRINITY

474. *How is God the Father the source of the liturgy?*

In the same way that He is the source of all creation; the blessings of the liturgy are the words and gifts of God the Father to us. We give Him our blessing as our Creator by responding to His grace.   (1077-1078)

475. *How does the Father manifest His blessings?*

He has done so from the dawn of human history, as recounted in the Old Testament. Noah and Abraham, Isaac and David, the Chosen People, the Law, the Prophets, and the Psalms are all revealed witnesses to how God has blessed those who believed in Him before the coming of Christ. The Christian liturgy preserves the record of these blessings and responds to them in faith and love.   (1079-1083)

476. *What is Christ's work in the liturgy?*

Christ, now at the right hand of the Father, pours out the blessings of the Holy Spirit through the sacraments of the Church. Indeed, the risen Savior communicates the supernatural gifts that He won for us on Calvary by all the channels of His grace, through the Church that He founded on the Apostles. Paramount among these channels is the Holy Eucharist, through the Sacrament of Holy Orders.   (1084-1087)

477. *How is Christ present in the earthly liturgy?*

He is always present in his Church, but especially in her liturgical celebrations. Most especially He is present when He offers Himself to His heavenly Father in the Sacrifice of the Mass. He is fully present in the Holy Eucharist. By His power, He is present in the sacraments as well as in the Sacred Scriptures when they are read in the Church. In fact, He is present whenever two or three are gathered together in His name.   (1088-1089)

478. *What is the heavenly liturgy?*

The heavenly liturgy is the celebration of God's praises by the whole company of angels and saints in the holy city of Jerusalem.   (1090)

479. *How does the Holy Spirit work in the Church's liturgy?*

He is the Teacher whom Christ promised. He enlightens our faith and inspires our response. Provided we respond to His illuminations and inspirations, He unites us in a loving community in the Church and enables us to live the risen life of Christ.   (1091-1092)

480. *How does the Holy Spirit prepare us for Christ?*

He does so by enabling Christ's followers to see the Old Testament as a preparation for the New. He does so by using the Church's liturgy to prepare us to see Christ in one another, to love one another in spite of our differences of race, color, and personality. He does so by the light and strength of His grace to receive the blessings of the liturgy, especially of the Eucharist, which Christ won for us by His paschal mystery.   (1093-1098)

481. *How is the Holy Spirit the Church's memory?*

Mainly in two ways. The Holy Spirit enlightens the minds of the faithful to understand the words of the liturgy, including the inspired words of Scripture. And the Spirit awakens in the hearts of the assembly the memory of the events that the liturgy commemorates, so they can unite themselves with these events in thanking and praising God.   (1099-1103)

482. *How does the Holy Spirit actualize the mystery of Christ?*

He does so by making the liturgy the source of His grace. Most important-ly, it is by the power of the same Holy Spirit that Mary conceived her Divine Son at Nazareth and that the elements of bread and wine are changed at Mass into the living Christ offering Himself to His heavenly Father.
                    (1104-1107)

483. *What is the communion of the Holy Spirit?*

This is the spiritual union, produced by the Holy Spirit, between Christ and his people. Since the Holy Spirit is the Soul of the Mystical Body, it is only logical to see the Holy Spirit, like the juice of the wine that is Christ, invigorating us, the branches, with the supernatural life and making us heirs of heaven and children of God.   (1108-1109)

ARTICLE 2: THE PASCHAL MYSTERY IN THE SACRAMENTS OF THE CHURCH

The Church's whole liturgical life revolves around the Sacrifice of the Eucharist and the sacraments.   (1113)

Our focus here will be on the Church's doctrine on the seven sacraments, namely, Baptism, Confirmation (or Chrismation), the Eucharist, Penance (or Reconciliation), Anointing of the Sick, Orders, and Marriage.

We shall first look at the sacraments in general, and then reflect on each sacrament in particular.

484. *How are the sacraments, sacraments of Christ?*

They are sacraments of Christ because they were all instituted personally by Christ during His visible stay on earth. They are the foundations of the grace that He makes accessible through the Church. They are so many powers flowing from the Body of Christ, as actions of the Holy Spirit at work in this Body, which is the Church. (1114-1116)

485. *How are the sacraments, sacraments of the Church?*

They are sacraments of the Church because they are dispensed by the Church, and they are dispensed for the Church's growth in Christ. Thus, through Baptism and Confirmation, the faithful are enabled to celebrate the liturgy. Those in Holy Orders are to feed the Church with God's word and His grace. That is why these three sacraments confer an indelible character as a permanent seal of assimilation to Christ. Moreover, these three sacraments cannot be repeated. (1117-1121)

486. *Why are the sacraments, sacraments of faith?*

They are sacraments of faith because it is the faith of the Church in the sacraments that Sacred Tradition has preserved the sacraments in her liturgy. Moreover, it is the faith of the Church's believers that underlies their use of the sacraments since apostolic times. The Church's faith in the sacraments makes the sacramental liturgy determined by the authority of Christ. Finally, all progress in the restoration of Christian unity depends on fidelity to Christ's teaching on the sacraments which He instituted. (1122-1126)

487. *How are the sacraments, sacraments of salvation?*

They are sacraments of salvation because they confer the grace they signify. Without grace, there is no salvation. The sacraments actually confer the grace that the liturgical ritual signifies. Invariably, just because a sacrament is properly administered, grace is received. In this light, it is no wonder the Church teaches that for believers, the sacraments are necessary for salvation. (1127-1129)

488. *How are the sacraments, sacraments of eternal life?*

They are sacraments of eternal life twice over.

- Already in this life, those who receive the sacraments possess by anticipation the gift of divine life, which they are to enjoy in a blessed eternity.
- Through the sacraments, the faithful are assured the graces they need on earth in order to enter into eternal glory in the life to come.(1130)

CHAPTER TWO
SACRAMENTAL CELEBRATION OF THE PASCHAL MYSTERY

As we enter the wide field of sacramental celebration, we divide our subject into four logical areas. We ask:

- Who celebrates the sacraments?
- How do we celebrate the sacraments?
- When do we celebrate?
- Where do we celebrate?

Immediately, a pointed question should be answered. Why speak of "celebrating" the sacraments? Why not "administering" or "receiving" the sacraments? Because to "celebrate" includes their conferral and reception. Not only that, "celebration" adds the critical fact that the sacraments are acts of divine worship by which we honor God and in which the Church herself is liturgically involved. (1135)

ARTICLE 1: CELEBRATING THE LITURGY OF THE CHURCH

489. *In the widest sense, who celebrates the liturgy?*

It is all of creation, beginning with the heavenly hosts of angels and saints, and extending to the whole universe, which glorifies the Creator. (1136-1139)

490. *Who celebrates the liturgy on earth?*

It is the whole Church. The basis for this ecclesial celebration is that in every sacrament, Christ is acting as head of the Mystical Body, which is the Church. (1140-1141)

491. *Do all members of the Church have the same function in the sacramental liturgy?*

No, because not all have been called by God to participate in the sacraments in the same way. This is especially true of the Eucharistic Liturgy, which only ordained priests can celebrate. (1142)

492. *What is the role of liturgical ministries outside of Holy Orders?*

Their function is to participate in the liturgy according to the Church's traditions and her pastoral needs. (1143)

493. *Does the whole assembly participate in the liturgy?*

Yes, each according to his office, and all together in the unity of the Holy Spirit, who is active in every participant. (1144)

494. *What is the place of signs and symbols?*

They are sensibly perceptible words, actions, and objects that express the meaning of each sacramental celebration. They are drawn from human experience, where God is constantly speaking to us by means of sensibly perceptible creation. But they have been elevated by Christ to express the mysteries of His work of salvation and sanctification. (1145-1149)

495. *What are the signs of the old covenant?*

They are the symbols the Church has adapted to her own sacramental liturgy. Thus, anointing, laying on of hands, consecrations, and sacrifices in the Old Testament prefigure the corresponding sacramental signs of the new covenant. (1150)

496. *What are the signs used by Christ?*

They are the words and actions of Christ by which He revealed the mysteries of the New Testament. They were at once a fulfillment of the prophetic signs of the Old Law and a preparation for the New. (1151)

497. *What are sacramental signs?*

They are the sensibly perceptible means by which the Holy Spirit sanctifies the people of God through the sacraments. (1152)

498. *What do liturgical actions express?*

They express both God's word and His readiness to bless His people and their faithful willingness to respond to His love. (1153)

499. *How is the Liturgy of the Word related to liturgical actions?*

The Liturgy of the Word includes everything associated with the Scriptures (including books, candles, incense, readings, and the homily). Its role is to serve as a channel of instruction by the Holy Spirit, which leads to the fruitful reception of the sacraments. (1154-1155)

500. *How important are liturgical song and music?*

So important that the Church considers them invaluable treasures and greater than any other art. This, as attested by St. Paul, goes back to the earliest days of the Church and is expressed by St. Augustine's statement that "he who sings, prays twice" (Eph 5:19). It is assumed that both the words to be sung and the music itself are consistent with Catholic teaching. (1156-1158)

501. *What is the significance of sacred images?*

Sacred images are representations in painting or sculpture of Christ, the Blessed Virgin, or the saints. Solemnly defended by the Church's teaching authority, sacred images are a great help in conveying the truths of our faith and inspiring the believing mind with devotion to Christ, His Mother, the angels, and the saints. (1159-1162)

502. *What is liturgical time?*

Liturgical time is a certain day (or other period of time) that already in the Old Testament was specially dedicated to the corporate worship of God. Since the coming of Christ, the Church has consistently set aside certain days or seasons for believers to express their common profession of faith and devotion to the Savior, His Mother, and the holy ones of God. (1163-1165)

503. *What is the Lord's Day?*

The Lord's Day, from apostolic times, celebrates the mystery of Christ's Resurrection. It is, par excellence, the day for liturgical assembly, when the faithful gather together to hear the Word of God and participate in the Holy Eucharist. Called Sunday, after the pagan "day of the sun," it is a weekly commemoration of Christ's Resurrection and special reception of the graces He won for us by His Passion and death. (1166-1167)

504. *What is the liturgical year?*

With Easter, "the feast of feasts," as its center, the liturgical year is the annual cycle of the mysteries of Christianity. It begins with the season of Advent and closes with the thirty-fourth week of Ordinary Time. (1168-1171)

505. *What is the sanctoral cycle?*

This is the annual cycle of feasts of the Blessed Virgin Mary, the martyrs, and saints whom the Church commemorates. They are proposed to the faithful as examples for our imitation, whom we are to ask to intercede for us through Christ our Lord. (1172-1173)

506. *What is the Liturgy of the Hours?*

Also called the Divine Office, it is a group of psalms, hymns, prayers, and biblical and spiritual readings formulated by the Church for chant or recitation at stated times every day. (1174)

507. *How is the Liturgy of the Hours an extension of the Eucharistic celebration?*

Through adoration and worship before the Blessed Sacrament, the Liturgy of the Hours complements the Liturgy of the Eucharist. (1174-1178)

508. *What is a Catholic church?*

It is a house of prayer suited for private devotion and liturgy, where the faithful gather for the Sacrifice of the Mass and where the Eucharist is reserved for adoration. (1179-1181)

509. *What are the principal furnishings of a Catholic church?*

They are:
- the altar, where the Sacrifice of the Mass is offered;
- the tabernacle, situated in a most dignified place for adoration and prayer before the Real Presence;
- the sacred chrism, in the sanctuary, for the holy oils of catechumens and the sick;
- the chair of the bishop (or priest), to express his office of presiding over the assembly;
- the lectern, for reading the Scriptures, homily, and announcements;
- the baptistry and holy water font;
- the confessional, for hearing confessions and giving absolution.

(1182-1186)

ARTICLE 2: LITURGICAL DIVERSITY AND UNITY OF THE MYSTERY

510. *What have always been the two main features of the Church's liturgy?*

Since apostolic times, the Church's liturgy has been one and the same paschal mystery, celebrated in a variety of forms. (1200-1201)

511. *Why have there been so many different liturgical traditions?*

The basic reason is that there are varied cultures in the world. The Church is ready to adapt the liturgy to reflect this cultural variety, but always on one condition: that essential unity is maintained by fidelity to the Apostolic Tradition, by professing the same faith, receiving the same sacraments deriving from apostolic succession, and obedience to the Roman Pontiff.

(1202-1205)

512. *Can liturgical diversity be a source of tension?*

Yes. Always to be kept in mind is that adaptation to different cultures must never endanger unity of faith, or sacramental validity, or submission to hierarchical authority. Moreover, adapting the liturgy to the people's culture requires conversion of their heart and, if need be, surrender of their ancient practices that are incompatible with the Catholic faith. (1206)

SECTION II:
THE SEVEN SACRAMENTS OF THE CHURCH

As we begin our reflection on each of the seven sacraments, it should be noted that they can be classified into three categories:

- The three sacraments of *initiation*—Baptism, Confirmation, and the Eucharist—lay the foundations of our life as Christians.
- The two sacraments of *healing*—Penance and the Anointing of the Sick—provide for the restoration to supernatural life and health.
- The two sacraments of Orders and Matrimony are for the service of the communion and mission of the faithful. (1210-1211)

CHAPTER ONE
THE SACRAMENTS OF CHRISTIAN INITIATION

The name "Sacraments of Initiation" has been given to Baptism, Confirmation, and the Eucharist because they correspond to the foundations of our natural life. We must first be born in the supernatural life through Baptism, strengthened in this life by Confirmation, and nourished in the life of God by the Holy Eucharist. (1212)

ARTICLE 1: BAPTISM

513. *What is the Sacrament of Baptism?*

It is the foundation of the whole Christian life, the gate to our life in the Spirit, and the door to the other sacraments. "Baptism is the sacrament of regeneration through water in the word," as declared by the ecumenical Council of Florence (1438-1445 A.D.). (1213)

514. *What are some of the names for Baptism?*

It is called Baptism from the Greek *baptizein*, which means "to immerse." The one baptized is plunged into water to symbolize being buried into Christ's death and then rising up as a new creature. It is also called the washing of rebirth, renewal by the Holy Spirit, and enlightenment. (1214-1216)

515. *What are some pre-Christian figures of Baptism?*

- water, as the source of life and fruitfulness;
- Noah's Ark, in which eight persons were saved from the deluge;
- water of the sea, as an emblem of death, signifying Christ's death on the Cross;
- the Red Sea, which the Israelites crossed miraculously in escaping from the Egyptians;
- the Jordan River, which the People of God crossed to enter the Promised Land. (1217-1222)

516. *What is the meaning of Christ's baptism?*

Christ allowed Himself to be baptized in order to teach us:
- the primacy of Baptism, since He began His ministry by being baptized and ended it by commissioning His disciples to baptize others;

- the necessity of "self-emptying," since Christ submitted Himself to being baptized as though He were a sinner;
- we were redeemed by the Cross of Christ, since the efficacy of Baptism comes from Christ's death on Calvary.   (1223-1225)

517. *What is the history of Baptism in the Church?*

From the day of Pentecost to the present, Baptism has been the door of the Church. It is through Baptism that a person is purified, justified, and sanctified by the Holy Spirit.   (1226-1228)

518. *What is the preparation for Baptism?*

In the early Church, this preparation involved several stages to ensure adequate understanding of the faith. Over the centuries, we have distinguished the preparation of adult converts from the training of children who are baptized in infancy.

Today the Church provides a formal catechumenate, called the Rite of Christian Initiation of Adults (RCIA). Also in mission countries, the Church allows the use of such initiation elements as are compatible with the Catholic faith.

One major difference between Eastern and Western rites is that Eastern Churches confer all three Sacraments of Initiation in infancy. In the Roman rite, there are years of preparation of children before receiving First Confession and Communion as well as Confirmation.   (1229-1233)

519. *What are the principal aspects of the liturgy for Baptism?*

- The Sign of the Cross on the candidate symbolizes the grace of redemption through Christ's crucifixion.
- Announcing of God's word typifies the faith necessary for Baptism.
- Anointing with the oil of catechumens, or laying on of hands, declares the renouncing of Satan and readiness to profess the true faith.
- By the blessing of the baptismal water, the one to be baptized is to be "born of water and the Spirit."
- Actual Baptism with immersion or pouring of water follows two different rites:
  — In the Latin Church: "[Name], I baptize you in the name of the Father, and of the Son, and of the Holy Spirit."
  — In the Eastern liturgies: "The servant of God, [name], is baptized in the name of the Father, and of the Son, and of the Holy Spirit."

- Anointing with chrism declares that the baptized person has been christened to share in Christ's triple anointing as Priest, Prophet, and King.
- In the liturgies of the East, the anointing is the Sacrament of Confirmation.
- The white garment symbolizes that the newly baptized has been clothed in the vesture of Christ, that is, risen with Christ to supernatural life.
- In the Eastern Churches, Holy Communion is given to the baptized, even infants, recalling Christ's words, "Let the little children come to me." In the Latin rite, the baptized person is brought to the altar for the *Pater Noster,* which precedes Communion at Mass.
- There is a solemn blessing of the one baptized. In the case of infants, the mother also receives a special blessing.   (1234-1245)

520. *Who can receive Baptism?*

Every nonbaptized person, whether adult or child:
- In places recently evangelized, the normal procedure is to have adults go through the catechumenate. This is an extensive formation in the Catholic faith.
- Children are baptized, even in infancy, on the premise that Baptism removes the stain of original sin. Infant Baptism was certainly practiced since the second century, and most probably already in apostolic times.   (1250-1252)

521. *How important is faith for Baptism?*

It is indispensable. Either the one to be baptized or, in the case of infants, the parents and sponsors must believe. No doubt the faith in the one receiving Baptism has to be developed. This is a grave responsibility for the parents and sponsors, to provide the necessary instruction and nurture of the virtue of faith received at Baptism.   (1253-1255)

522. *Who can baptize?*

Bishops and priests and, in the Latin rite, also deacons. But in case of necessity, anyone can baptize who has the intention to do what the Church does, and uses the Trinitarian formula and water.   (1256)

523. *How necessary is Baptism?*

Absolutely necessary for salvation, since the Church does not recognize any other sure way of being saved.

At the same time, the Church teaches that those who suffer for the faith and catechumens are saved even without Baptism of water.

Moreover, the Church believes that since God wants everyone to be saved, there is such a thing as Baptism of desire. We may hold that those will reach heaven who want to do God's will and who would have been baptized had they known of its necessity.

Finally, the Church cannot but trust in God's mercy that He will bring to heaven the children who die without Baptism. Yet, she does not cease insisting on the urgency of Baptism for children.   (1257-1261)

524. *What graces are received in Baptism?*

The two basic graces are remission of sin and the new birth in the Spirit.

- The purification from sin means the remission of all the guilt, or estrangement from God, and all the penalty, or suffering due to sin. The inclination to sin, or concupiscence, remains, but grace is received to overcome this sinful inclination and be crowned with victory over the struggle.
- The new birth in the Spirit means becoming a new creature, being incorporated into the Church, acquiring a sacramental bond of Christian unity, and receiving an indelible spiritual mark. (1262-1274)

525. *Explain in more detail this new birth in the Spirit.*

- As a new creation, baptized persons receive sanctifying grace, the theological and moral virtues, and the gifts of the Holy Spirit.
- Incorporation into the Church makes them members of the Church, gives them the rights of a Christian, including the right to receive the other sacraments, and places on them corresponding responsibilities, especially the duty to profess and share their faith in the Church's missionary apostolate.
- The sacramental bond includes all the baptized, even those who are not professed Catholics. They acquire a certain, albeit imperfect, communion with the Catholic Church.
- The indelible mark (character) means that no one can be rebaptized. There is an irradicable seal that binds those who receive Baptism and gives them a special title to God's grace and a special accountability for assimilation to Christ in living a holy life.   (1265-1274)

ARTICLE 2: CONFIRMATION

Confirmation binds the baptized more perfectly to the Church, endows them with special strength from the Holy Spirit, and thus obliges them more strictly to be true witnesses of Christ to spread and defend the Catholic faith by their words and actions.   (1285)

526. *What is the role of Confirmation in the economy of salvation?*

In the Old Testament, the coming of the Messiah was foretold, as was a special coming of the Spirit of the Lord. However, as Christ made clear, this Spirit was to be shared by those upon whom the Apostles laid their hands. In the early Church, there were two titles by which this sacrament was named: it was *chrismation* (or anointing with chrism) in the East, and *confirmation* (or ratification and strengthening) in the West.   (1286-1289)

527. *How do the Eastern and Western traditions differ?*

In the Eastern tradition, the stress has been on the unity of Christian initiation, hence the conferral of all three sacraments—Baptism, Confirmation, and the Eucharist—at the same time.

In the Western or Roman tradition, the increase in infant baptisms occasioned the separation of Confirmation from Baptism. However, when adults are baptized, they are commonly confirmed by the bishop or priest who has just baptized them.   (1290-1292)

528. *What is the ritual of Confirmation?*

- Anointing with the oil of chrism symbolizes cleansing and making flexible, healing and soothing, beautifying and strengthening. The anointing imparts a spiritual seal that marks the confirmed person as totally committed to Christ, enrolled in His service, and assured of His special grace of protection and care.
- When separated from Baptism, the rite of Confirmation includes the renewal of the promises of faith and the profession of faith. Also, when adults are confirmed, they assist at Mass and receive the Eucharist after Confirmation.
- Also in the Roman rite, the bishop extends his hands over the persons being confirmed. In doing this, he says the following prayer: "All-powerful God, Father of our Lord Jesus Christ, by water and the Holy Spirit you freed your sons and daughters from sin, and gave them new life. Send your Holy Spirit upon them to be their Helper and Guide. Give them the spirit of wisdom and understanding, the spirit of counsel and fortitude, the spirit of knowledge and filial affection; fill them with the spirit of the fear of God. Through Christ our Lord."
- The essential rite for Confirmation differs between the East and West. In the Latin ritual, it consists of anointing with chrism on the fore-

head with the hand and pronouncing the words: "Be sealed with the gift of the Holy Spirit." In the Eastern Churches, after a prayer of *Epiclesis* (invocation of the Holy Spirit), the body's important parts are anointed. Each anointing is accompanied by the words: "The seal of the gift that is the Holy Spirit."

- After Confirmation a sign of peace is exchanged with the bishop and with all the faithful. (1293-1301)

529. What are the effects of Confirmation?

The basic effect is an outpouring of the Holy Spirit, similar to what the Apostles received on Pentecost. Specifically, the Holy Spirit:

- deepens our sense of adoption by God;
- joins us more firmly to Christ;
- increases the gifts of the Holy Spirit;
- makes our union with the Church more perfect;
- enables us to spread and defend our faith as witnesses of Christ and never to be ashamed of the Cross. (1302-1303)

530. Can Confirmation be received more than once?

No, it imprints a permanent character on our souls. We are able to testify to our faith in Christ because we are, in his own words, clothed with power from on high" (Lk 24:49). (1304-1305)

531. Who can receive the Sacrament of Confirmation?

Everyone who is baptized should be confirmed. In the Latin rite, the person should have reached the age of discretion. But in danger of death, even infants should be confirmed. (1306-1308)

532. What is the preparation for Confirmation?

There should be adequate instruction in the faith and the responsibilities of belonging to the Church of Christ. Those to be confirmed are to be in the state of grace. Also, there should be a sponsor, preferably the same as for Baptism, to show the unity of the two sacraments. (1309-1311)

533. Who is the minister of Confirmation?

The originating minister is the bishop. In the Eastern Churches, the bishop or priest who baptizes also confirms. But the chrism used in both East and West must have been consecrated by the bishop (or patriarch).

In the Latin rite, the ordinary minister of Confirmation is the bishop, although for serious reasons he may delegate a priest. Any priest should confirm even the youngest children who are in danger of death.   (1312-1314)

ARTICLE 3: THE EUCHARIST

The Holy Eucharist completes the Christian initiation. As described by the Second Vatican Council, "At the Last Supper, on the night He was betrayed, the Savior instituted the Eucharistic Sacrifice of His Body and Blood. He did this in order to perpetuate the Sacrifice of the Cross throughout the centuries until He should come again. So He entrusted to His beloved Spouse, the Church, the memorial of His death and Resurrection: a sacrament of love, a sign of unity, a bond of charity, the paschal banquet in which Christ is received in nourishment, the soul is filled by grace, and the pledge of future glory is given to us" (*Constitution on the Sacred Liturgy*, 47).   (1322-1323)

534. *How is the Eucharist the source and summit of the Church's life?*

Where the other sacraments give the grace they signify, the Eucharist contains the Church's spiritual treasury, who is Christ Himself. That is why the other sacraments are directed to the Eucharist and the eucharistic celebration is already the heavenly liturgy by anticipating eternal life.   (1324-1327)

535. *What are some of the names by which the Eucharist is called?*

Each of the following names expresses a different aspect of this treasure of faith. It is called:

- the Eucharist, as our highest act of thanksgiving to God;
- the Lord's Supper, because it reenacts what the Savior did on the night before His Passion;
- the Breaking of the Bread, by which is indicated our communion with Christ and one another;
- the Christian Assembly (*synaxis*), as a visible expression of the Church;
- the Memorial of the Lord's Passion and Resurrection;
- the Holy Sacrifice, or Sacrifice of the Mass, Sacrifice of Praise, Spiritual and Holy Sacrifice—which all proclaim synonymously the presence of the sacrifice of Christ and the Church;
- Communion, because the Eucharist unites us in one body by receiving the Body and Blood of Christ;

- Holy Mass, because the Eucharistic Liturgy closes with the sending (*missio*) of the faithful to fulfill the will of God in their daily lives.

(1328-1332)

536. *What is the significance of the bread and wine in the Eucharist?*

- Bread and wine become Christ's Body and Blood. Even so, bread and wine express the goodness of creation. They also witness the fulfillment of the Priest Melchizedek's offering in the Old Law.
- The bread commemorates the Passover of the Israelites; the manna in the desert; and the pledge of God's fidelity to feed His people.
- The cup of blessing symbolizes the New Jerusalem at the end of time.

(1333-1334)

537. *When did Christ promise the Eucharist?*

After He worked the miracle of multiplying the loaves to feed the multitude. His promise to give His own flesh to eat and blood to drink divided the disciples. But instead of retracting the promise, He asked the Apostles if they, too, wished to go away.

(1335-1336)

538. *When did Christ institute the Holy Eucharist?*

At the Last Supper, as narrated in the Gospels of Matthew, Mark, and Luke, and in the letters of St. Paul. Jesus chose the Passover to institute the Eucharist, saying to His disciples, "This is my Body, which is given for you. Do this in remembrance of me." And again, after supper, "This cup is the New Covenant in my Blood, that will be poured out for you" (Lk 22:19-20).

By this action, Christ gave the Passover its ultimate meaning and anticipated the final Passover of the Church in the glory of His kingdom.

(1337-1340)

539. *What is the significance of Christ's words, "Do this in memory of me"?*

By giving this command to the Apostles, Christ gave them the power to do what He had done, and of communicating this power to their successors, the bishops, until the end of time. Thus was ensured the preservation of the Eucharist in the Catholic Church. Thus, too, was preserved the celebration of Mass every day, especially on Sunday. Thus, finally, the Eucharist became the center of the Church for the obvious reason that the Eucharist is Christ.

(1341-1344)

540. *What is one of the earliest records of the Mass in the Catholic Church?*

It occurs in the letter of St. Justin, written about 155 A.D., in which he

describes the full sequence of the eucharistic celebration. There is even pro-
vision for deacons bringing Holy Communion to the faithful who could not
attend the Mass. What stands out in this historic document is that there were,
and are, two fundamental parts to every Mass: the Liturgy of the Word and
the Liturgy of the Eucharist. (1345-1347)

541. *Explain the sequence of the eucharistic celebration.*
- The gathering of the faithful for Mass is the precondition for having a
  eucharistic assembly.
- The Liturgy of the Word draws on the Old and New Testaments, and
  includes petitions for all the people.
- The Offertory makes clear that the Holy Eucharist is first of all a sacrifice. Along with the bread and wine, from earliest times, the faithful
  brought their own gifts to the altar.
- The Eucharistic Prayer is both a prayer of thanksgiving and consecration. By the Words of Institution, bread and wine are separately consecrated to become the Body and Blood of Christ. Thus, the sacrifice
  He offered once for all on Calvary is reenacted on the altar.
- The intercessions that follow show that the Eucharist is offered
  everywhere throughout the world.
- In Communion, the faithful are nourished on the living Christ. But
  they must be truly faithful, who believe in the Savior and are in communion with the pope and pastors of the Church. (1348-1355)

542. *How is the Eucharist a sacramental sacrifice?*

The Eucharist is the sacramental sacrifice in which the Church offers to
God the Father what He Himself has created. She gives Him the bread and
wine, which by His power become the living Jesus Christ. (1356-1358)

543. *How is the Eucharist a sacrifice of praise and thanksgiving?*

It is a sacrifice of thanksgiving to the Father as an act of gratitude for the
blessings of His creation, redemption, and sanctification. It is a sacrifice of
praise by which the Church glorifies the Father *through* Christ, *with* Christ, as
an acceptable sacrifice *in* Christ. (1359-1361)

544. *How is the Eucharist the sacrificial memorial of Christ?*

The Eucharist is a memorial (Greek *anamnesis*) as both the recollection of
past events and the proclamation of the marvels that God has done for men.
These events become present and actual. Christ is now carrying out His
Sacrifice of the Cross.

The Eucharist is a sacrifice because Christ is now offering the same Body and Blood that He offered on Calvary. What He does now is make Himself present in order to apply the fruits of Calvary by communicating to us the graces He merited on the Cross.

The Mass and Calvary are one sacrifice. It is the same Victim who offered Himself then, in a bloody manner, who now offers Himself in an unbloody manner through the ministry of priests. (1362-1367)

545. *How is the Eucharist the sacrificial memorial of the Church?*

In the Eucharist, the Church offers herself with Christ by giving to the Father all the praise, suffering, prayer, and labor of her members.

In the Eucharist, the Church is united as one Body in communion with the Bishop of Rome and the bishop of the place where Mass is offered. She intercedes for all the priestly ministers who offer their Masses for and in union with the Church.

In the Eucharist, the Church's offering is united with those in heavenly glory. She is with Mary at the foot of the Cross, joined in Christ's offering and intercession.

The Eucharist is finally offered for the faithful departed, that they may enter into the light and peace of Christ.

In the words of St. Augustine, "The Church does not cease to reproduce [this sacrifice] in the sacrament of the altar, so well-known to the faithful, where it is shown that in what she is offering she herself is being offered" (*The City of God*, 10:6). (1368-1372)

546. *How is Christ present in the Eucharist?*

Christ's presence in the Eucharist is unique. In the Eucharist, the Body and Blood, together with the soul and divinity of our Lord Jesus Christ and, therefore, the whole Christ, is truly, really, and substantially contained. (1373-1374)

547. *How does the bread and wine become the Body and Blood of Christ?*

In the language of the Council of Trent, "By the consecration of the bread and wine, there takes place a change of the whole substance of the bread into the substance of the Body of Christ our Lord, and of the whole Christ our Lord, and of the whole substance of the wine into the substance of His Blood. This change the holy Catholic Church has fittingly and properly called transubstantiation" (October 11, 1551). (1375-1376)

548. *Is the whole Christ present in each of the species or physical properties of bread and wine?*

Yes, He is wholly present in each species and in every particle. Thus the breaking of the host does not divide Christ. (1377)

549. *How are we to worship the Eucharist?*

During Mass, we are to express our faith in the Real Presence of Christ by genuflecting or profoundly bowing as a sign of our adoration of the Lord. After celebration of Mass, the consecrated hosts are to be preserved with the greatest reverence for veneration by the faithful and for carrying in procession. (1378)

550. *What is the role of the tabernacle in the veneration of the Eucharist?*

Originally used to reserve the Eucharist for the sick and imprisoned, the tabernacle is now an integral part of a Catholic church. Here the Eucharistic Lord is reserved for silent adoration and prayer. (1379)

551. *Why is Our Lord with us in the Eucharist, also outside the Sacrifice of the Mass?*

He remains in the Eucharist to provide us the same privilege enjoyed by His contemporaries in Palestine: to express our love for Him and receive the blessings of His love in return. (1380-1381)

552. *What does the altar signify?*

It signifies both the Eucharistic sacrifice and communion. In fact, it symbolizes Christ Himself, who now offers Himself for our sins and invites us to receive Him at His holy table. (1383)

553. *How should we prepare for Holy Communion?*

We are to make sure there is no grave sin on our souls. The prescribed fast should be observed. Our bodily deportment, including our clothes, should reflect our interior dispositions. (1384-1387)

554. *How often should Holy Communion be received?*

Assuming the necessary dispositions, Communion should be received at the very least once a year, especially during the Easter season. However, Communion is recommended at every Mass attended, even every day.
(1388-1389)

555. *Should Communion be received under both forms?*

In the Eastern Churches, this is the established custom. In the Latin rite, the chalice may also be given according to the norm of the Church's liturgical laws, or even the chalice alone in case of necessity. (1390)

556. *What are the effects of Holy Communion?*

The most fundamental effect is the deepening of our union with Christ. From this follow many other spiritual benefits. It also:

- increases and renews our supernatural life;
- cleanses the soul of venial sins, as to both guilt and penalty;
- strengthens our soul to resist sin in the future;
- deepens our love for God and others;
- joins us more intimately with the Church, which is the Mystical Body of Christ;
- directs our concern for the physically and spiritually poor;
- impels us to Christian unity to pray and work for the day when all Christians will believe in and receive the living Christ in Holy Communion. (1391-1400)

557. *When may Communion be received by Christians who are not Catholic?*

They may be given Holy Communion under the following conditions:

- when in the bishop's judgment, there is a grave necessity;
- when the people ask for communion of their own free will;
- when they profess the Catholic faith in the Holy Eucharist;
- when they are properly disposed. (1401)

558. *How is the Eucharist the pledge of future glory?*

It is the pledge of future glory on the promise of Christ. Why? Because the graces communicated by Christ in the Eucharist assure us of reaching heavenly glory. Even on earth we have a foretaste of heaven in the measure that we avail ourselves of the light and strength that the Eucharistic Christ confers on those who believe in Him. (1402-1405)

CHAPTER TWO

THE SACRAMENTS OF HEALING

Jesus Christ came into the world to heal the sick and restore to life those who were spiritually dead. He therefore instituted the two sacraments of Penance and Anointing of the Sick. Their purpose is to continue His mission of restoring to health, and back to life, those who have been even mortally wounded by sin. (1420-1421)

ARTICLE 4: PENANCE AND RECONCILIATION

559. *What are the names by which the first sacrament of healing is called?*
- It is the Sacrament of Conversion because it restores sinners to friendship with God.
- It is the Sacrament of Penance because it consecrates the three steps required by the Church, namely, conversion, penance, and satisfaction.
- It is the Sacrament of Confession because auricular, spoken and heard, telling of one's sins to a priest is essential for this sacrament.
- It is the Sacrament of Pardon because the sacramental absolution by a priest gives pardon (forgiveness) and peace to the penitent.
- It is the Sacrament of Reconciliation because it restores God's merciful love to the penitent. (1422-1444)

560. *Why did Christ institute the Sacrament of Penance?*

Because He knew that, although baptized, His followers would fall into sin. They would have to struggle for conversion if they were to become holy and reach eternal life. (1425-1426)

561. *What are the two conversions of Christ's followers?*

In the words of St. Ambrose, there are two conversions: "There is water and tears: the water of Baptism and the tears of Penance." (1427-1429)

562. *What is interior penance?*

Interior penance is a radical reorientation of one's whole life. It is a return to God in the depths of one's heart; firm resolve to amend one's life, with trust in His mercy and sorrow for having offended Him. (1430-1433)

563. *What are some forms of penance in the Christian life?*
- The Bible and the Church Fathers identify the three basic forms of penance as fasting, prayer, and almsgiving.
- Regular examination of conscience, spiritual direction, and suffering opposition to the true faith are recognized penitential practices.
- The daily carrying of the cross in union with our Lord is the most assured kind of penance.
- Reception of the Eucharist is a most effective way of expiating sin and preserving oneself from the contagion of sin.

- Scripture reading, the Divine Office, and all the forms of Catholic worship deepen our spirit of conversion.
- The Church's seasons (such as Lent), days of penance (such as Fridays), pilgrimages, and voluntary sacrifices are all recognized ways of making reparation. (1434-1439)

564. *Who alone forgives sin?*

Only God forgives sins. Christ forgives sins because He is God. He instituted the Church to forgive sins in His name through the Apostles and their successors in the priestly ministry. (1440-1442)

565. *What is reconciliation with the Church?*

This is the restoration of communion with the Body of the faithful. Sin alienates, forgiveness reunites. Thus, reconciliation with the Church is inseparable from reconciliation with God. (1443-1445)

566. *How is the Sacrament of Penance the second plank of salvation?*

It is God's way of providing forgiveness of sins committed after Baptism. (1446)

567. *Has there been a development of discipline in the Sacrament of Penance?*

Yes, mainly in a lessening of the rigor and publicity, and an increase in the frequency, along with confessing just venial sins. (1447)

568. *What are the unchangeable elements in the practice of this sacrament?*

They are mainly two: on the part of the penitent, sorrow, confession, and satisfaction; on God's part, the absolution through the Church by her bishops and priests. (1448)

569. *What is the formula of absolution in the Latin rite?*

It is: "God, the Father of mercies, through the death and resurrection of His Son has reconciled the world to Himself and sent the Holy Spirit among us for the forgiveness of sin. Through the ministry of the Church, may God give you pardon and peace, and *I absolve you from your sins, in the name of the Father, and of the Son, and of the Holy Spirit.*" (1449)

570. *What is contrition?*

Contrition is sorrow of soul over one's sins, the detesting of sins committed, and the resolution not to sin in the future. This is the first duty of a penitent. (1450-1451)

571. *What is perfect contrition?*

It is sorrow for sin mainly motivated by the love of God, which removes the guilt of venial sins. If joined with the intention to receive the Sacrament of Penance, mortal sins are also remitted. (1452)

572. *What is imperfect contrition?*

It is sorrow for sin motivated by fear of eternal punishment or of other sufferings due to sin. By itself, imperfect contrition does not obtain pardon for mortal sins, although it disposes a person to obtain this pardon in the Sacrament of Penance. (1453)

573. *What is an examination of conscience?*

It is a prayerful reflection on the sins we have committed since our last confession. This examination should be made in the light of God's revealed Word, for example the Sermon on the Mount. (1454)

574. *What sins must be confessed?*

All mortal sins of which a person is aware after making a serious examination of conscience. (1456)

575. *Is the confession of sins necessary?*

Yes, by Christ's command, the confession of sins is essential to the Sacrament of Penance. (1457)

576. *What sins may be confessed?*

The Church encourages the confession of our daily faults or venial sins. Regular confession of such sins sensitizes our conscience, helps us to overcome temptations, heals our souls, and enables us to grow in the spiritual life. (1458)

577. *How do we make satisfaction for our sins?*

We do so by returning what was stolen, restoring the reputation of persons we have injured, and making compensation for injuries. Sacramental absolution does not remove all the penalties due to forgiven sins. (1459)

578. *What is the penance imposed by the confessor?*

It is part of the required satisfaction and should correspond to the gravity of the sins confessed. (1460)

579. *Who has the power to absolve sins?*

Only bishops, as successors of the Apostles, and priests (*presbyters*) who have received this power in the Sacrament of Orders. (1461)

580. *Must priests have faculties to exercise their power of absolution?*

Yes, they must receive these faculties from their bishop, religious superior, or the pope, according to the law of the Church. According to Canon Law, "Those who enjoy the faculty of hearing confessions habitually... can exercise the same faculty everywhere unless the local ordinary denies it in a particular case" (Canon 967, no.2). (1462)

581. *What is excommunication?*

It is the penalty imposed by the Church for certain grave sins. Its effect is to forbid the reception of the sacraments and the exercise of certain ecclesiastical acts. It is removed only by the pope, the bishop, or priests authorized by them. (1463)

582. *What is the responsibility of priests?*

As ministers of this sacrament, priests should be faithful to the Church's teaching, direct the penitents to moral healing and spiritual maturity, pray and do penance for their penitents, encourage the faithful to confess their sins, and make themselves available to hear the confessions of the faithful.

(1464-1466)

583. *What is the seal of confession?*

It is the absolute prohibition against the priest revealing anything that he learns in confession. He remains "sealed" by the sacrament, and there is no exception to this secrecy. (1467)

584. *What are the effects of the Sacrament of Penance?*

The Sacrament of Penance reconciles the sinner with God, bringing peace of conscience, spiritual consolation, and a restoration of the graces belonging to the children of God. Moreover, this sacrament reconciles a person with the Church by restoring communion with all the members of Christ's Mystical Body and regaining the exchange of their spiritual goods. (1468-1469)

585. *How does the Sacrament of Penance anticipate our judgment at death?*

By our conversion and absolution from mortal sin, we remove the one obstacle that would prevent us from entering heaven. (1470)

586. *How are indulgences related to the Sacrament of Penance?*

An indulgence is the remission before God of the temporal punishment still due to forgiven sins. Plenary indulgences remove all of this punishment, and partial indulgences remove some of this punishment. Indulgences may be applied to the living or the dead. (1471)

587. *What are the two consequences of sin?*

They are losing divine grace and incurring a debt of punishment. Mortal sin deprives a person of sanctifying grace and incurs the debt of eternal punishment. Venial sin deprives us of some of God's grace and requires temporal punishment. These two consequences follow on the very nature of sin. (1472)

588. *What are the consequences of forgiveness of sin?*

They are the restoration of sanctifying grace and the remission of eternal punishment when mortal sin is forgiven. The forgiveness of venial sin brings a greater or lesser restoration of lost grace and the remission of some of the temporal punishment. (1473)

589. *What is the Communion of Saints?*

The Communion of Saints is the bond of spiritual unity among all the faithful in heaven, on earth, and in purgatory. It is the interchange of prayers and spiritual goods; the sharing of graces and blessings; and the communication of holy thoughts and inspirations among the members of the Church Triumphant, Militant, and Suffering, which constitutes the Mystical Body of Christ. (1474-1477)

590. *How do we obtain God's indulgence through the Church?*

We obtain the divine indulgence of the temporal punishment from the Church's treasury of Christ's merits and those of His saints. As members of the Church, the souls of the faithful departed in purgatory profit from the indulgences we gain for them. (1478-1479)

591. *What is the liturgy of the Sacrament of Penance?*

The main parts are confession of sins by the penitent and absolution with assigned penance by the priest. Secondary parts are a greeting and blessing by the priest, reading from Scripture, and exhortation before confession, followed by the priest's blessing and dismissal after confession, along with the penitent's prayer of thanks. (1480)

592. *What is distinctive about the Byzantine form of absolution?*

Several formulas of absolution are recognized; the mercy of God in biblical history is recalled; and the absolution is given in an exhortatory form, such as, "May God forgive you through me." (1481)

593. *What is the communal form of the Sacrament of Penance?*

Individual confession by each penitent and individual absolution by the priest is inserted into a communal liturgy. This consists of Scripture readings, a homily, examination of conscience, and communal prayers. (1482)

594. *When are general confession and absolution permissible?*

In cases of grave emergency. A large gathering of the faithful is not a grave emergency. Moreover, the penitents must intend to confess their grave sins individually in due time in order for a general absolution to be valid. (1483)

595. *How necessary are the complete confession and personal absolution of the individual?*

They are the only ordinary means for the faithful to be reconciled with God after they have committed mortal sin. (1484)

ARTICLE 5: ANOINTING OF THE SICK

The Second Vatican Council identifies the power which Christ gave to His priests for their ministry to the sick and the dying.

By the sacred anointing of the sick, and the prayer of the priests, the whole Church commends those who are ill to the suffering and glorified Lord, that He may raise them up and save them. And indeed she exhorts them to contribute to the good of the People of God by freely uniting themselves to the Passion and death of Christ (*Constitution on the Church II,* 11). (1499)

As painful as sickness can be, in God's providence it can bring a person closer to God or even be the occasion for reconciling a sinner with God. (1500-1501)

596. *What was the focus on sickness in the Old Testament?*

The focus was the mysterious relation between sickness and sin. Sin and pain are related as condition and consequence. Among the prophets, Isaiah foretold that in His own time, God would pardon every sin and heal every human pain. (1502)

597. *How is Christ the divine Physician?*

He is the divine Physician on both levels of human suffering.

- He is the Physician of bodily illness and disease. During His public ministry, He miraculously healed multitudes of their illness of body. He did so out of love for those who were suffering and to witness to His power of healing souls estranged from God.
- He is the Physician of spiritual sickness and even Restorer of supernatural life to persons who are in deadly sin.

By His Passion and death, Jesus Christ gave suffering a new meaning. His followers can unite their sufferings with His and thus enable them, through love, to become like Him and cooperate with Him in the redemption of the world. (1503-1505)

598. *Did Christ commission His disciples to heal the sick?*

Yes, when He told them, "Cure the sick" (Mt 10:8) and foretold that "in my name... they shall lay hands on the sick, and they shall get well" (Mk 16:17-18). (1506-1507)

599. *Why did Christ confer the power to heal the sick?*

In order to confirm His mission as the divine Healer of human bodies and souls. (1602)

600. *How does Christ exercise His ministry of healing?*

He exercises His ministry of healing:

- through the Church's care for the sick and her prayers of intercession;
- through the special charism of healing that He gives certain people, as we read in the lives of the saints;
- through the sacraments, especially the Holy Eucharist;
- through the Sacrament of the Anointing of the Sick. (1508-1510)

601. *Did the apostolic Church recognize a distinct sacrament for the sick?*

Yes, as attested by the Letter of St. James: "Is anyone sick among you? Let him bring in the presbyters (priests) of the Church, and let them pray over him, anointing him with oil in the name of the Lord. And the prayer of faith will save the sick man, and the Lord will raise him up, and if he be in sin, they shall be forgiven him" (Jas 5:14-15). (1511)

602. *What has been the Church's tradition on anointing?*

In both the East and West, the Church has always practiced anointing of the sick with blessed oil. As the practice became more limited to those near death, it came to be called Extreme Unction. (1512)

603. *What is the discipline of the Church, established by Pope Paul VI?*

The seriously sick person is anointed on the forehead and hands with blessed olive oil, or when necessary, with another blessed plant oil. The one who anoints says only once, "Through this holy anointing, may the Lord in His love and mercy help you with the grace of the Holy Spirit. May the Lord, who frees you from sin, save you and raise you up." (1513)

604. *Who receives the Sacrament of Anointing?*

Baptized persons who are in danger of death from sickness or old age. (1514)

605. *May this sacrament be repeated?*

Yes, if there is a relapse in the sickness after anointing, or if the same illness becomes more serious. The sacrament may be repeated also before a serious operation, or if an elderly person becomes notably weakened. (1515)

606. *Who can administer this sacrament?*

Only priests (bishops and presbyters). Pastors should instruct the faithful on the benefits of the Sacrament of Anointing. (1516)

607. *What is the liturgy of anointing?*

If circumstances indicate, the anointing should be preceded by the Sacrament of Penance and followed by Holy Communion. (1517-1519)

608. *What are the effects of the Sacrament of Anointing?*

The spiritual effects of this sacrament are:

- the grace to accept the trials experienced by the sick person;
- forgiveness of sins, including grave sins and eternal punishment, requiring only imperfect contrition even before a person has lapsed into unconsciousness;
- the grace to unite oneself with the Passion of Christ;

- the gift of sharing in the merits and of contributing to the holiness of the Church;
- the supernatural strength needed to prepare for eternity. The bodily effects are a curing of the sickness, if this is God's will.   (1520-1523)

609. *What is Viaticum?*

Viaticum is the Holy Eucharist received as a preparation for the close of our earthly life and entrance into eternal life.

(1524-1525)

CHAPTER THREE
THE SACRAMENTS IN THE
SERVICE OF COMMUNION

The first three sacraments—Baptism, Confirmation, and the Eucharist—provide the foundation for the Christian life. Through them we are grounded in the life of Christ and given the mission to evangelize the world.

The last two sacraments—Holy Orders and Matrimony—are directed to the salvation and sanctification of others. Certainly those who receive these sacraments are sanctified. But their divinely instituted purpose is mainly apostolic, to reach out to other people. Those who are ordained are to nourish the Church with the Word and grace of God. Those who are married are to cooperate as husband and wife in the spiritual propagation of the human race.   (1533-1535)

ARTICLE 6: HOLY ORDERS

The Sacrament of Holy Orders is the sacrament of apostolic ministry. Its purpose is to continue the work of the Apostles until the end of time.

There are three degrees of this sacrament, namely, the episcopacy, the presbyterate, and the diaconate.   (1536)

610. *Why is this called the Sacrament of "Orders"?*

The reason is because in the first century of Christianity, the Latin word *ordo*, or order, meant an organized civil body of persons under authority. The Church adopted this name to identify the religious body of persons established by Christ for the sanctification of the People of God. Also called consecration, the Sacrament of Holy Orders sets certain persons apart and empowers them to sanctify others. The laying on of hands by the bishop along with the prayer of consecration is the visible sign of sacramental ordination. (1537-1538)

611. *What was the priesthood of the Old Testament?*

It was instituted to proclaim God's Word and to restore communion with God through prescribed prayers and sacrifices. (1539-1540)

612. *Was the Old Testament priesthood able to bring about salvation?*

No, this could be done only by the sacrifice of Jesus Christ. The Old Testament prefigured the ordained ministry of the new covenant, exercised through the Sacrament of Orders. (1540-1541)

613. *What is the Church's prayer at the ordination of bishops?*

In the Latin rite, the following prayer is recited:

God, the Father of our Lord Jesus Christ... by your gracious word you established the plan of your Church. From the beginning, you chose the descendants of Abraham to be your holy nation. You established rulers and priests and did not leave your sanctuary without ministers to serve you. (1541)

614. *What is the Church's prayer at the ordination of priests?*

In the ordination of priests, the Church prays:

Lord, holy Father... when you had appointed high priests to rule your people, you chose other men next to them in rank and dignity to be with them and help them in their task.... you extended the spirit of Moses to seventy wise men... and you shared among the sons of Aaron the fullness of their father's power. (1542)

615. *What is the Church's prayer at the ordination of deacons?*

In the ordination of deacons, the Church prays:

Almighty God... you make the Church, Christ's Body, grow to its full stature as a new and greater temple...As ministers of your tabernacle, you chose the sons of Levi and gave them your blessing as their everlasting inheritance. (1543)

616. *Is there only one priesthood of Christ?*

Yes, Christ is the one Mediator between God and man. His sacrifice on the Cross merited all the grace for the salvation of the human race. Through His ministerial priesthood, He communicates the grace that He merited on Calvary. (1544-1545)

617. *What are the two participations in the one priesthood of Christ?*

They are the ministerial and common priesthood. They differ in essence and not only in degree.

- The ministerial or hierarchical priesthood is received by bishops and priests through the Sacrament of Orders.
- The common priesthood of the faithful is received at Baptism and deepened by Confirmation. (1546-1547)

618. *What is the essence of the ministerial priesthood?*

It is the conferral of sacred powers, which Christ exercises through bishops and priests for the service of the Church. (1548-1551)

619. *Are bishops and priests mere delegates of the community?*

No, they exercise their priestly powers for the Christian community and in union with the members of the Mystical Body of Christ. (1552-1553)

620. *What are the three grades of the Sacrament of Orders?*

As previously explained, they are the episcopate, the presbyterate, and diaconate. The Church now uses the following terms:

- the priesthood, which includes bishops and presbyters. In Latin, the generic word is *sacerdos* for both bishops and presbyters.
- the diaconate, which identifies the first level of the sacrament of Orders but is not a participation in the priesthood or sacerdotal powers of bishops and presbyters. (1554)

621. *What is the episcopate?*

It is the fullness of the Sacrament of Orders, the high priesthood, the summit of the sacred ministry. (1555-1557)

622. *What office and powers are conferred by the episcopate?*

The episcopate makes the bishop a member of the college of bishops as a successor of the Apostles. He is empowered to ordain bishops, presbyters, and deacons. He has authority over his own diocese and shares with his fellow bishops in responsibility for the whole Church.   (1558-1560)

623. *What is the presbyterate?*

This is the second level of the priesthood. In ordaining men to the presbyterate, bishops hand on a share in the priestly consecration and mission.

(1563)

624. *What is the principal power of the presbyterate?*

It is to offer the Sacrifice of the Mass. Their whole priesthood is sustained by this one sacrifice, in which they unite the prayers of the faithful with the sacrifice of Jesus Christ their head.   (1564-1566)

625. *How are priests collaborators with their bishops?*

Priests cooperate with their bishops in serving the People of God. They may exercise their priestly ministry only by depending on the bishop and being in faithful communion with him.   (1567)

626. *What is the diaconate?*

It is the third level of the Sacrament of Orders, by which the bishop ordains men to be of service to the Church in the ministry of Christian charity. (1569)

627. *What are the main forms of service of deacons?*

They are to assist bishops and priests in the celebration of the liturgy, especially the Eucharist; distribute Holy Communion; witness and bless marriages; proclaim and preach the Gospel; celebrate funerals and perform the various ministries of Christian charity.   (1570)

628. *What is the permanent diaconate?*

It is the ordination to a lifetime commitment to serve the Church as a deacon. Always retained by the Churches of the East, it was restored in the Latin Church since the Second Vatican Council. Married men may serve as permanent deacons as a distinct and permanent rank in the hierarchy.   (1571)

629. *What is the ritual for the conferral of the Sacrament of Orders?*

The essential rite is the bishop's laying of hands on the head of the one being ordained and the recitation of the consecrating prayer proper to each order. Among other rites of ordination in the Latin Church are the presentation and election of the one to be ordained; the instruction by the bishop; examination of the candidate; litanies of the saints for bishops and priests;

anointing with holy chrism; presentation of the Gospel ring, miter, and staff to the new bishop; presentation of paten and chalice to priests and the book of the Gospels to deacons. (1574)

630. *Who can confer the Sacrament of Orders?*

Only validly ordained bishops, as successors of the Apostles, can validly confer the three degrees of the Sacrament of Orders. (1575-1576)

631. *Who can receive the Sacrament of Orders?*

Only baptized males can validly receive the Sacrament of Orders. Since Christ chose men to form the college of the Apostles, the Church considers herself bound to follow the choice made by Christ. Women, therefore, cannot be validly ordained. (1577)

632. *Does any man have a right to be ordained?*

No, because a man must be called to this sacrament by a special vocation from Christ. It is therefore a privilege, but only for those who have been thus called by the Master. (1578)

633. *What is the duty to celibacy for the reception of sacred orders?*

Deacons may be either celibate or married. In the Latin Church, priests are normally chosen from the faithful who live and promise to live in celibacy. In the Eastern Churches, priestly celibacy is highly honored, but married men are also ordained to the priesthood. However, in both the Latin and Eastern Churches, bishops must be celibate. (1579-1580)

634. *What is the indelible character conferred by the Sacrament of Holy Orders?*

It is the permanent share in Christ's triple office of priest, prophet, and king. This character remains no matter how unfaithful a cleric may be. The unworthiness of a particular bishop, priest, or deacon does not prevent Christ from communicating divine grace through him. (1581-1584)

635. *What is the grace of the Holy Spirit proper to the Sacrament of Orders?*

In general, it is assimilation to Christ as priest, teacher, and pastor. However, this grace differs according to each of the three degrees of ordination.

- The bishop receives the power to govern the flock of Christ committed to his care. He is enabled to be a model to the faithful and care for his sheep, even to laying down his life for them. Also, the bishop alone can confer the Sacrament of Orders.

- The presbyter or priest is empowered to offer the Sacrifice of the Eucharist, to reconcile sinners, and to prepare the people for their eternal destiny.
- Deacons receive the grace to serve the people in the ministry of the liturgy, the word, and charity. (1585-1588)

636. *What have the saints said regarding the dignity and responsibility of the priesthood?*

St. Gregory Nazianzen stressed the duty of priests to be holy if they are to sanctify others. St. John Vianney declared that the priest continues Christ's redemption on earth. "If we really understood the priest on earth, we would die, not of fright but of love. The priesthood is the love of the heart of Jesus."
(1589)

ARTICLE 7: MATRIMONY

By its very nature, marriage was instituted by God as a lifelong covenant. Its purpose is the well-being of the spouses and the procreation and upbringing of their children. Christ elevated marriage to the dignity of a sacrament. The official Latin title, as in the documents of the Second Vatican Council, is *matrimonium*, matrimony.

637. *Who is the author of matrimony?*

God Himself is the Author of matrimony. It was He who established conjugal life and love, and He who determined its structure, its laws, and the marital covenant. (1603)

638. *Why did God institute matrimony?*

He instituted matrimony as a covenant of love: the love of husband and wife are to be an image of God's love for the human race. Their fruitfulness in begetting children is an expression of God's creative love in propagating the human family. (1603-1605)

639. *Why do we speak of matrimony under the sway of sin?*

We speak this way to recognize the natural tendency to discord, a spirit of domination, infidelity, jealousy, and conflicts between husband and wife. These struggles are the result of sin. They can be healed only by the grace of God. (1606-1608)

640. *What do we mean by matrimony under the pedagogy of the law?*

By this we mean the marital norms and directives that God gave to the Chosen People in the Old Law. Without yet rejecting the polygamy of the patriarchs and kings, God elevated marriage far beyond what it was among the pagans. The unity and indissolubility of marriage began to be recognized. To this day, the Song of Songs is a unique revelation of human love as a reflection of God's selfless love that is as strong as death. (1609-1611)

641. *What do we mean by "matrimony in the Lord"?*

By this we mean the fulfillment of the Old Testament prophecies. Christian marriage is a symbol of Christ's unfailing love of His Spouse, the Church. The Savior restored marriage to its original state before the fall of our first parents. It is now to be an indissoluble, lifelong union of one man and one woman until death. The followers of Christ are given the grace to deny themselves, take up their cross, and remain faithful to each other out of love for the Savior and with the assurance of His supernatural light and strength.
(1612-1616)

642. *How is Baptism a nuptial mystery?*

It is a nuptial mystery because it entitles baptized persons to receive the Sacrament of Matrimony. Their marriage both signifies and confers the graces they need for life, as a sign of the covenant between Christ and His Church.
(1617)

643. *What is consecrated virginity?*

Consecrated virginity is the lifetime sacrifice of marriage for the sake of the Kingdom of Heaven. (1618-1619)

644. *Why is consecrated virginity pleasing to God?*

It is pleasing to God because it is the answer to Christ's invitation to some men and women to follow His example. They renounce the great good of marriage to follow the Lamb wherever He goes. (1618-1619)

645. *How are the Sacrament of Matrimony and consecrated virginity related?*

They both come from the Lord. Moreover, consecrated virginity and matrimony reinforce and support each other. (1620)

646. *Why is the Sacrament of Matrimony celebrated at Mass?*

In this way, the spouses seal their mutual covenant by offering their married lives in union with Christ's sacrifice of Himself for His Church. Moreover, the married spouses receive special graces from the Savior, who becomes present in the Mass, and whom they receive in Holy Communion.

(1621)

647. *What are the conditions for receiving the Sacrament of Matrimony?*

To receive the Sacrament of Matrimony, a man and woman must both be baptized. They must be free to marry and to express their mutual consent. This means they are under no constraint, nor impeded by any natural or ecclesiastical law. The exchange of consent brings their marriage into being. Natural intercourse after marriage consummates their union and makes it indissoluble. (1625-1628)

648. *Can the Church declare the nullity of a marriage?*

Yes, provided sufficient grounds exist, the competent Church authority can declare that a marriage never existed. (1629)

649. *What is the role of the bishop, priest, or deacon who assists at a sacramental marriage?*

He receives the consent of the marrying partners in the name of the Church and imparts the Church's blessing. However, it is the man and woman marrying who confer the sacrament on each other by their mutual exchange of vows. (1630)

650. *What is the canonical form of matrimony?*

This is the set of norms that the Church requires for the validity and liceity of a marriage in which at least one party is a professed Catholic. Behind this form is the Church's understanding that matrimony is a liturgical action that creates certain rights and responsibilities, and requires the certification of witnesses. The public character of their mutual consent protects their agreement and ensures its permanent fidelity. (1631)

651. *How important is preparation before marriage?*

It is most important in order to ensure that the marriage is entered into freely and responsibly. Parents and families have the primary duty to provide this preparation by their example and teaching. Pastors and the Christian community are especially to help when the marrying people come from broken homes. What young people need is to develop the virtue of chastity in order to make the transition through an honorable engagement at a suitable age. (1632)

652. *What is the Church's law on mixed marriages?*

A mixed marriage is a marriage between a Catholic and a baptized non-Catholic. A dispensation is necessary from ecclesiastical authority for the liceity of a mixed marriage. Such dispensations assume that the Catholic partner will be free to practice his or her faith, that all the children will be raised Catholic, and that both parties do not exclude the divinely revealed purposes and properties of a valid marriage. (1633-1635)

653. *What is disparity of cult?*

A disparity-of-cult marriage is a marriage between a Catholic and a non-baptized person. Dispensation in this case is necessary for the validity of the marriage. The same conditions apply here as in a mixed marriage. In disparity-of-cult marriages, neither partner receives the Sacrament of Matrimony. However, as St. Paul explains, "The unbelieving husband is made holy through his wife, and the unbelieving wife is made holy through her husband" (1 Cor 7:14). The Church's great wish is that the holiness of the Catholic spouse will lead to the conversion of the other spouse to the Catholic faith. (1636-1637)

654. *What are the effects of the Sacrament of Matrimony?*

There are mainly two effects:

- The matrimonial bond established by God Himself. Consummated sacramental marriage is indissoluble by any human authority. The Church herself cannot pronounce against this disposition of divine wisdom.
- The married partners are assured a lifetime of God's grace, by which their marital love is perfected and their indissoluble unity is strengthened. Christ Himself becomes the source of this grace. (1638-1643)

655. *What does marital love require of the spouses?*

It requires an inviolable fidelity between the spouses and binds them to an indissoluble unity. (1646)

656. *Is this fidelity naturally impossible?*

Yes, but this is precisely why Christ instituted the Sacrament of Matrimony. This sacrament enables the married spouses to do the humanly impossible. They are thus empowered to witness to God's selfless love for the human race. (1647-1648)

657. *What is the Church's position on divorce and remarriage?*

The Church is sympathetic toward those of the faithful whose marriage is in trouble. They may even be separated "from bed and board." But the Church remains firm in obedience to the teaching of Christ. A valid, sacramental, consummated marriage cannot be dissolved, with the right to remarry, by any authority on earth. Catholics who are thus married and yet are cohabiting with someone who is not their spouse may not receive the Holy Eucharist. They should, however, pray and assist at Mass in order to be reconciled with God. They cannot be absolved in the Sacrament of Penance until they give up their sinful cohabitation. Nevertheless, they remain members of the Church and benefit from their membership in the Mystical Body of Christ. (1649-1651)

658. *What is the fruitfulness of conjugal love?*

According to the will of God, conjugal love is ordained to the procreation and education of children. Moreover, the fruits of this procreative marital love extend beyond the powers of human nature. As the first principal teachers, parents become channels of divine grace for the moral, spiritual, and supernatural life of their offspring. (1652-1654)

659. *What is the domestic Church?*

The domestic Church is the Christian family in which parents and children exercise their priesthood of the baptized. They worship God, receive the sacraments, and witness to Christ and His Church by their lives of holiness, self-denial, and active charity. (1657)

660. *How necessary is the domestic Church in our day?*

Indispensably necessary in today's world, which is alien and even hostile to Christ and His teaching. In the first centuries of the Christian era, believing families were the catalyst by which the Church became established in the Roman Empire. (1655-1656)

661. *What is the first school of the Christian life?*

It is the believing Christian home. Here the family learns endurance and the joy of work, generous love and forgiveness, the practice of prayer, and the meaning of sacrifice as a lifetime surrender of oneself to the will of God. (1657)

662. *Is anyone without a family in this world?*

No, childless couples and those without a natural family, through poverty or for other reasons, all belong to the great family which is the Church. In the words of Pope John Paul II, "The Church is a home and family for everyone, especially those who 'labor and are heavily burdened'" (*Familiaris Consortium*, 85). (1658)

CHAPTER FOUR
OTHER CELEBRATIONS OF THE LITURGY

ARTICLE 1: SACRAMENTALS

The Church's liturgy is primarily the sacraments, which directly confer the grace they signify. Besides the sacraments, however, there are also sacramentals. Both should be seen together, because both are sources of divine grace. But sacramentals were not immediately instituted by Christ. They were, and are, instituted by the Church, which is guided by her Founder, Jesus Christ.

663. *What are sacramentals?*

Sacramentals are sensibly perceptible prayers, and often actions or things, which resemble the sacraments and which signify spiritual effects obtained through the intercession of the Church. (1667)

664. *How do sacramentals differ from the sacraments?*

They differ from the sacraments in not being instrumental causes of grace. Rather, they arouse the faith of believers to better dispose themselves for the reception of grace from the sacraments.

665. *What is characteristic of all the sacramentals?*

They always include a prayer and normally an object or action that signifies some profession of faith, such as the Sign of the Cross recalling Christ's crucifixion, or holy water recalling our baptismal incorporation into the Church. (1668)

666. *How do sacramentals arise from the priesthood of the baptized?*

Baptism empowers every baptized person to bless and be blessed.

However, the more intimately a blessing is related to the Church's sacramental life, the more likely a blessing is reserved to the ordained bishops, priests, and deacons. (1669)

667. *How do the sacramentals confer grace?*

They confer grace indirectly, that is, by preparing us to recognize a source of grace and then to cooperate with the grace that the sacramental signifies. Consequently, we may say that almost every respectable object can be used to give praise to God and can be a source of grace to those who believe.

(1670)

668. *What are some of the main forms of sacramentals?*

- The primary sacramentals are the blessings of persons and places, objects and meals. These are normally given by invoking the name of Jesus and making the Sign of the Cross.
- Some blessings are intended to have a lasting effect, such as the blessing of an abbot, a consecrated virgin, or an altar.
- Finally, the Church authorizes the solemn exorcisms to drive the evil spirit out of persons possessed by the devil. Exorcisms may be performed only by priests and with the authorization of the bishop.

(1671-1673)

669. *What do we mean by popular piety?*

Popular piety is the vast arena of devotions and religious practices of the faithful that are not strictly liturgical or sacramental but yet are approved by the Church. This includes the veneration of relics, sanctuaries, pilgrimages, processions, Stations of the Cross, the rosary, and medals.

Such expressions of piety do not replace the sacred liturgy. They are to support and harmonize with the liturgy, and are to be practiced with the Church's approval. Properly exercised, these forms of piety serve to combine the divine and the human, Christ and Mary, spirit and body, person and community, faith and homeland, intelligence and emotion. (1674-1676)

ARTICLE 2: CHRISTIAN FUNERALS

All the sacraments have as their final purpose to bring the faithful to eternal life. In the Christian perspective, physical death is the gateway to life in the kingdom that Christ went to prepare for us. This is what we profess whenever we recite the Nicene Creed: "I believe in the resurrection of the dead and the life of the world to come." (1680)

670. *What is the Christian understanding of bodily death?*

It marks the end of our sacramental life of grace, and the beginning of our new life of glory. This presumes that we are in Christ Jesus. It may require purification of the soul in purgatory before we are finally clothed with the wedding garments of heaven. (1681-1682)

671. *What is the distinctive feature of the Church's funeral services?*

These ceremonies surrounding the Sacrifice of the Mass are sacramental, focusing on the Church's hope that the body being buried is the seed that will one day be raised in resplendent glory. (1683)

672. *Why does the Church conduct funerals for the deceased?*

She does so to express her effective communion with the departed, to enable the faithful to share in that communion, and to proclaim her faith in eternal life. (1684)

673. *What are the principal features of the Church's funeral liturgy?*
- The Roman liturgy provides for three forms of burial service: at the home of the deceased (or funeral parlor), in the church, and at the cemetery.
- There are four stages in the liturgy. Relatives and friends of the deceased are welcomed with the New Testament encouragement of hope in eternal life. The Liturgy of the Word illuminates the mystery of Christians in the light of the risen Christ.
- The Eucharistic Sacrifice is the heart of the funeral ceremony, stressing the hope of the resurrection and the need of prayer for the deceased that God might "cleanse his child of sin." In the closing farewell, the deceased is commended to God by the Church (*Order of Christian Funerals,* 57). (1685-1690)

PART THREE

THE LIFE IN CHRIST

INTRODUCTION

As Christians, we know that our faith is not just another religion. We know that Christianity is more than a set of moral regulations or a prescribed form of worship. This is made clear in *The Catechism of the Catholic Church.*

Before the coming of Christ, there was one divinely revealed religion, Judaism, whose members were the Chosen People of God. With the Incarnation, Judaism was replaced by Christianity, whose believers became the New Israel, the New Chosen People, or, in the language of the Second Vatican Council, *the* People of God.

As we continue our reflections on *The Catechism,* we enter on its third part, which is called *The Life in Christ.* This section includes a detailed treatment of the Ten Commandments, or the *Decalogue.* The foundation for the Decalogue is what *The Catechism* calls "Man's Vocation: The Life in the Spirit," in which Pope Leo the Great declares:

Christian, remember your dignity. Now that you share in God's own nature, do not return by sin to your former base condition. Bear in mind who is your Head, and of whose Body you are a member. Do not forget that you have been rescued from the power of darkness and brought into the light of God's Kingdom.

674. *How does the Apostles' Creed express our dignity as Christians?*

In the Apostles' Creed we profess the greatness of God's gifts to us. We are His creatures, whom He brought into being out of nothing. Even more, He redeemed us by the Blood of His divine Son. And most of all, He sanctified us by giving us the indwelling of His own Spirit. (1692)

675. *How do the sacraments enable us to live our Christian faith?*

What the Apostles' Creed confesses, the sacraments communicate. Through the sacraments, we are literally reborn as children of God and become sharers, by grace, in the very nature of God. (1692)

676. *How is Jesus Christ our teacher?*

He is our teacher because we are His disciples. Christ Jesus always did what was pleasing to His heavenly Father. He always lived in perfect communion with Him. As Christ's disciples, we, too, are expected to live in the presence of the Father, who sees in secret. In Christ's words, we are to become perfect "as your heavenly Father is perfect" (Mt 5:48). (1693)

677. *How do we become incorporated into Christ?*

By Baptism. Through this sacrament, we acquire sanctifying grace, which is the supernatural soul of our natural soul. No less than we become human beings through the soul, so we become divinized beings through sanctifying grace. (1694)

678. *What is our responsibility as partakers of the divine nature through Baptism?*

It is nothing less than to become dead to sin and alive to God in Christ Jesus. We are to follow Christ. In union with Him, we are to "imitate God, as beloved children, and live in love" (Eph 5:1-2). (1694)

679. *How do we imitate God?*

We imitate God by *conforming* our thoughts, words, and actions to the mind of Christ, and by *following* His example. (1694)

680. *How are we temples of the Holy Spirit?*

We are temples of the Holy Spirit because He dwells in our souls:
- to heal the wounds of our sin;
- to renew us by a transformation of our spiritual life;
- to enlighten our minds and strengthen our lives as children of the light through "goodness, justice, and the truth" in everything (Eph 5:9). (1695)

681. *How is the Holy Spirit the Spirit of Christ?*

By His Passion and death, Christ merited for us the gift of the Holy Spirit. Just as the Father sent His Son to redeem the world, so the Son with the Father sent the Holy Spirit to sanctify the world. (1695)

682. *What are the two basic ways of making moral decisions?*

They are the way of Christ and the way independent of Christ. The way of Christ leads to life, the contrary leads to perdition. (1696)

683. *What are the qualities of every authentic Catholic moral teaching or catechesis?*

Catholic moral instruction must:
- be clear about the joys of following the way of Christ;
- be equally clear about the demands that following Christ places on us;

- be a catechesis of the Holy Spirit, which recognizes Him as the inner Master of our life;
- recognize the absolute necessity of grace, without which we could not reach heaven;
- teach us the Beatitudes as the only way of reaching eternal happiness;
- convince us that we are sinners, yet protect us from despair by offering us the merciful forgiveness of God;
- make the practice of virtue attractive and show us the beauty of living a good moral life;
- inspire us to follow the saints as models of faith, hope, and charity;
- show us how to live the Ten Commandments by observing the twofold love of God and our neighbor;
- enable us to see the Church as the indispensable means of exchanging our spiritual gifts with others, and they with us, in the Communion of Saints. (1697)

684. *What is the first and last point of reference in Catholic moral teaching?*

It is always Jesus Christ, our way, our truth, and our life. (1698)

685. *How is Jesus Christ at the center of authentic Catholic moral teaching?*

In three ways:

- Our faith in Jesus Christ is the intellectual foundation for the whole of Christian morality.
- Our hope that Christ will fulfill the promises He made enables our wills to want to follow in His ways.
- Our love of Jesus Christ inspires us to give Him our hearts in return for His selfless love for us. (1698)

686. *How is Jesus Christ our true head, and we His members?*

He belongs to us as the head belongs to the body. All that is His is ours: breath, heart, body and soul, and all His faculties.

All of these we must use as if they belonged to us so that in serving Him we may give Him praise, love, and glory as our God. We belong to Him as a member belongs to the head.

That is why Christ wants us to use all our faculties as if they were His, for the service and glory of His Father. (1698)

SECTION I:
THE VOCATION OF MAN: LIFE IN THE SPIRIT

There are three fundamental aspects to our life in the Spirit. This life fulfills our vocation as human persons. It is at once a work of divine charity and of human solidarity. And by God's grace, it leads to our salvation.　　　(1699)

CHAPTER ONE
THE DIGNITY OF THE HUMAN PERSON

The dignity of human beings is rooted in man's creation in the image and likeness of God. This dignity is fulfilled in his vocation to divine happiness. It belongs to a human being to reach this destiny by the exercise of his free will. By these deliberate actions, the human person is either conformed or not to the good promised by God and attested by the moral conscience. Human beings thus grow and develop themselves from within. Their whole sentient and spiritual life is involved in this growth. With the help of divine grace, they advance in virtue, avoid sin, and, if they have sinned, are like the prodigal son, forgiven by the mercy of their heavenly Father. Thus they attain the perfection of charity.　　　(1700)

ARTICLE 1: MAN, THE IMAGE OF GOD

We have all been created in the image and likeness of God. This means that, like God, we are spiritual beings with a mind that can know and judge, and a will that can choose and love.　　　(1701)

687. Who has fully revealed what it means to be human?

It was Jesus Christ who fully disclosed the meaning of man and revealed the sublimity of his vocation.　　　(1701)

688. *What else has Christ done?*

He restored humanity, damaged by sin, to its original beauty and ennobled it by God's grace. (1701)

689. *Where is God's image present?*

It is present in every man. It shines forth in a communion of persons by its resemblance to the Divine Persons in the Holy Trinity. (1702)

690. *What do we mean when we say the human person has been willed by God for its own sake?*

We mean that, having spiritual and immortal souls, we ourselves are destined from conception for an eternal destiny. (1703)

691. *Why do we have reason and a free will?*

We have reason so that we might know what is good, because it leads to our heavenly destiny, and what is evil, because it leads away from the end for which God created us. We have free will in order to direct ourselves toward the true good, which is to reach heaven. (1704)

692. *What then is the foundation of our human dignity?*

It is the conduct of our moral life. (1706)

693. *What does it mean to abuse our human freedom?*

It means to use our free will to choose what is contrary to the will of God. (1707)

694. *When did man begin to abuse his freedom?*

At the dawn of human history, through seduction by the Evil One. As a result, we retain our basic desire for what is good, but our nature has been wounded by original sin. We are therefore inclined to evil and subject to error. (1707)

695. *What did Christ do by His Passion and death?*

He did three things:
- He delivered us from the power of Satan.
- He merited for us the new life in the Holy Spirit.
- By His grace, He restored to us what had been damaged by sin.

(1708)

696. *What does faith in Christ enable us to do?*

Most fundamentally, it enables us to become children of God. We are thus empowered to follow the example of Christ. In union with Him, we can reach the perfection of charity. As we mature in grace, our moral life grows as eternal life, reaching its summit in heavenly glory. (1709)

ARTICLE 2: OUR VOCATION TO HAPPINESS

The Beatitudes are at the heart of Jesus' preaching. Their proclamation expresses the promises made to the Chosen People since Abraham. They fulfilled these promises by directing the People of God not only to happiness here on earth but to the Kingdom of Heaven. (1716)

697. *Where in the Gospels do we find the text of the Beatitudes revealed by Christ?*

In the Gospels of St. Matthew and St. Luke. (1716)

698. *How does the narrative of the Beatitudes differ between the two Gospels?*

In Matthew's Gospel, there are eight Beatitudes, with the last Beatitude having a further detailed explanation. In Luke's Gospel, there are four Beatitudes and four woes. Each of the woes corresponds to the Beatitudes and predicts the dire consequence that follows for not living the Beatitude.

699. *What are the Beatitudes accepted by the Church's Tradition?*

They are the eight Beatitudes recounted in the Gospel of St. Matthew, as follows:
- Blessed are the poor in spirit, for theirs is the Kingdom of Heaven.
- Blessed are those who mourn, for they will be comforted.
- Blessed are the meek, for they will inherit the earth.
- Blessed are they who hunger and thirst for righteousness, for they will be filled.
- Blessed are the merciful, for they will receive mercy.
- Blessed are the pure in heart, for they will see God.
- Blessed are the peacemakers, for they will be called children of God.
- Blessed are those who are persecuted for righteousness' sake, for theirs is the Kingdom of Heaven. (Mt 5:3-12). (1716)

700. *How are the Beatitudes an epitome of the New Testament?*

They epitomize the New Testament in many ways:
- They portray the countenance of Jesus Christ and describe His charity.
- They express the vocation of the faithful associated with the glory of Christ's Passion and Resurrection.
- They clarify the characteristic actions and attitudes of the Christian life.
- They are paradoxical promises that sustain hope in the midst of tribulations.
- They proclaim the blessings and rewards acquired, however dimly, by Christ's disciples here on earth.
- They are lived out by the Blessed Virgin Mary and all the saints.

(1717)

701. *How do the Beatitudes respond to the natural desire for happiness?*

Our desire for happiness is of divine origin. God has placed it in the heart of man in order to draw us to Him, who alone can satisfy this desire. In the words of St. Augustine, "God alone satisfies." Since Christ is the incarnate God, His Beatitudes are the formula for reaching God and thus becoming truly happy. (1718)

702. *To whom is Christ's call to happiness addressed?*

To each one of us personally, and to all the People of God who accept Christ's promise of happiness and live it out by faith. (1719)

703. *How does the New Testament describe the beatitude to which we are called?*

It is called the coming of the kingdom of God, the vision of God, the entrance into the joy of the Lord, the entrance into the rest of the Lord.(1720)

704. *How does beatitude enable us to share in the divine nature and in eternal life?*

God has placed us in this world to know, serve, and love Him and thus enter Paradise. Once entered, we participate in God's nature, which is perfect happiness for all eternity. (1721)

705. *Why is beatitude supernatural?*

Beatitude is supernatural because only God has a natural right to the vision of Himself. Like divine grace, which leads to beatitude, it is a totally free gift of God. (1722)

706. *How do moral decisions depend on the promise of beatitude?*

Beatitude is the promise of living a Christian moral life. Christian morality purifies our evil inclinations and leads us to seek the love of God above all things. It teaches us that true happiness does not reside in riches or comfort or human glory or power or in any human achievement, no matter how useful, but in God alone, the source of all good and of all love. (1723)

707. *Where do we find the norms for Christian morality?*

In the Ten Commandments elevated by Christ's Sermon on the Mount and in the preaching of the Apostles. Following these norms and with the help of God's grace, we gradually bear fruit in the Church for the glory of God. (1724)

ARTICLE 3: HUMAN FREEDOM

God created us as rational beings who are to reach our destiny by our own free choice. We are therefore to seek our Creator without coercion and, freely embracing Him, are to attain full and blessed perfection. (1730)

708. *What is human freedom?*

Based on reason and the will, freedom is the power to act or not act, to do this or that: in other words, to perform deliberate actions by ourselves. (1731)

709. *When does freedom reach perfection?*

When it is directed to God, our Beatitude. (1731)

710. *Is our freedom definitely fixed on God as our final end?*

Not necessarily. We can choose either good or evil, either to grow in perfection or to fail and commit sin. Freedom identifies truly human acts, which deserve either praise or blame, either merit (reward) or demerit (punishment). (1732)

711. *What is true freedom?*

True freedom is at the service of what is good and just. The choice to disobey is an abuse of freedom and leads to the slavery of sin. (1733)

712. *How responsible are we for the acts we perform?*

To the extent that our actions are voluntary. (1734)

713. *How do we grow in the mastery of our will?*

By progress in virtue, the knowledge of what is good, and the asceticism of self-denial. (1734)

714. *What can diminish or even remove our responsibility or imputability?*

Ignorance, inadvertence, violence, fear, habitual dispositions, inordinate affections, and other psychological or social factors can reduce or even remove our culpability. (1735)

715. *Is every directly willed action imputed to its author?*

Yes, as we see already in the Book of Genesis, where God asks Adam and then Cain, "What have *you* done?" (1736)

716. *When is an action indirectly voluntary?*

When it results from negligence with regard to what should have been known or done. (1736)

717. *Can the effect of an action be tolerated without being willed?*

Yes, when I permit something to happen from an action that I voluntarily perform. (1737)

718. *What is the imputability for tolerated effects?*

The evil effect is not imputable if it is not willed, as either the means or purpose of an action—for example, the death of a rescuer in time of danger. The evil effect is imputable if it is foreseeable and could have been avoided.

(1737)

719. *Does every human person have the natural right to be recognized as a free and responsible being?*

Yes, it is essential to human dignity. Especially in moral and religious matters, it should be protected by civil laws within the limits of public order and the common good. (1738)

720. *Can man refuse God's plan of love?*

Yes, he has the power to choose what is contrary to the will of God, even though he has no right to do so. He can deceive himself and become a slave of sin. His first alienation from God at the dawn of human history has engendered a multitude of others. History testifies to the evils and enslavements of the heart born of the misuse of freedom. (1739)

721. *What are some of the threats to human freedom?*

Distorted ideas and unjust practices in society can pose grave obstacles to the right use of freedom in the practice of Christian charity. (1740)

722. *How has Christ set us free?*

Christ, by His death, has redeemed us from the slavery of sin. (1741)

723. *How does God's grace benefit our freedom?*

By our cooperation with divine grace, we become more docile to God's will, more free to respond to His Spirit, and more ready to collaborate with His work in the Church and in the world. (1742)

ARTICLE 4: THE MORALITY OF HUMAN ACTS

We must distinguish between what are called "acts of man" and human acts. Acts of man are the physical or spontaneous actions of a human being that are independent of the free will. The metabolism of the body, circulation of the blood, and instinctive impulses of feeling or emotion are examples of these "acts of man."

Human acts, on the contrary, are freely chosen as a result of a previous judgment of conscience. They are also called *moral acts*. Moral acts can be good or bad. (1749)

724. *What are the basic sources of morality?*

They are mainly three: the object chosen, the end or intention for which the choice was made, and the circumstances of the moral action. We may say the sources of morality are the *what*, the *why*, and the *how* of our behavior. (1750)

725. *When is the object of a human act good?*

The object is good if it conforms to the true good. The true good is that which leads to our heavenly destiny. (1751)

726. *When is the intention of a human act good?*

The intention is also good when the reason I choose to do something is because God wants it. My intention is good when it is inspired by the desire to please God. In general, my intention is good when it agrees with the purpose of my existence, which is to serve God and save my soul. (1752)

727. *Can a good intention justify a bad action?*

No, the end or intention does not justify a bad means. Thus, we may not lie or calumniate in order to help someone in need. Conversely, a bad intention corrupts an otherwise good act. For example, it is wrong to give alms simply to impress others with one's generosity. (1753)

728. *How are the circumstances secondary to the morality of our human acts?*

They do not directly make our actions morally good or bad. But they do increase or diminish the moral goodness or evil of what we freely do. Thus, in general, the more difficult a morally good action is, the more meritorious it is before God. Also the more emotional pressure to do something wrong, the less responsible or culpable a person becomes. (1754)

729. *When is a human act morally good?*

It is morally good when the object, intention, and circumstances are all good. (1755)

730. *If the object of my choice is morally bad, can anything make that choice morally good?*

No, no matter what motives for the action and no matter what the circumstances, if an act is objectively wrong, it is a sin to do it. Why? Because this implies a disorder of the will. Therefore, contraception or fornication, perjury or adultery is always morally wrong. (1756)

ARTICLE 5: THE MORALITY OF PASSIONS

As human beings, we all have passions or feelings. In God's providence, we are directed to happiness by the deliberate actions we perform. Our passions or feelings are to dispose us to happiness and contribute to its achievement. (1762)

What needs mentioning, as noted before, is that we have a fallen human nature. As a result, we do not have a built-in control of our passions.

731. *What are the passions?*

They are emotions or movements of sensibility which incline to do or not do something in view of what is felt or imagined to be good or evil. (1763)

732. *How are the passions natural?*

They are natural because they connect our sensible (or bodily) life and the life of the spirit (or mind and will). (1764)

733. *What is the most fundamental passion?*

The most fundamental passion is love, aroused by its attraction to the good. The apprehension of evil causes fear, or aversion from a future evil.

(1765)

734. *What does it mean to love?*

To love is to will the good for someone. All other affections have their source in this original movement of the heart of man toward the good. We can love only the good. The passions are evil if the love is evil, and good if the love is good. Of course, we can love what is apparently good but in reality evil. (1766)

735. *How do the passions take on a moral character?*

They take on a moral character to the extent that they effectively assist reason and the will. It is part of moral perfection for the passions to be guided by reason enlightened by faith. (1767)

736. *What determines whether the passions are good or bad?*

They are morally good when they lead to a good action; they are bad when they lead to a morally bad action. (1768)

737. *What is the difference between an orderly (upright) will and an evil will?*

It all depends on how the will responds to the passions. An orderly will directs the passions to beatitude and the good. An evil will gives in to disorderly passions and even makes them worse. (1768)

738. *How does the will contribute to the formation of virtues or vices?*

It depends on how the will deals with the passions. If the will develops the good passions, it contributes to the formation of virtues. But if the will fosters the disorderly passions, it contributes to the formation of vices. (1768)

739. *Did Christ have any passions?*

He did not have any disorderly passions or sinful inclinations, but He did have the natural emotions and movements of sensibility that enabled Him to be human like us in everything except sin. (1769)

740. *When did Christ especially reveal His human feelings?*

It was especially during His agony, when His human feelings could reach their fulfillment in the charity and happiness of God. (1769)

741. *Does moral perfection consist only in the will choosing the good?*

No, moral perfection is more than merely willing or choosing the good. It also involves the fulfillment of our bodily or sensible desires. This is dramatically illustrated in the statement of the psalmist who says, "My heart and my flesh sing for joy to the living God" (Ps 84:2)   (1770)

ARTICLE 6: THE MORAL CONSCIENCE

Deep within his conscience, man discovers a law which he did not make for himself, but which he is bound to obey. This voice is always calling him to love, to do good, and to avoid evil. As needed, it echoes in the depths of his heart. It is a law inscribed by God in the heart of man. Conscience is the most intimate and most secret core of a human being, where he is alone with God and where God's voice can be heard within.   (1776)

742. *What is the function of the moral conscience?*

It has two main functions: to opportunely enjoin a person to do good and avoid evil; and to make specific choices, approving those which are good and rejecting those which are bad.   (1777)

743. *What is the moral conscience?*

It is a judgment of reason by which a human person recognizes the moral quality of a specific act that he faces, is in the process of doing, or has already done.   (1778)

744. *Must the conscience always be followed?*

Yes, man is always obliged to follow his conscience in what he knows to be right and just.   (1778)

745. *How is the conscience related to the divine law?*

By the judgment of conscience, man perceives and recognizes the prescriptions of the divine law. In the words of Cardinal Newman, "Conscience is the first of all the vicars of Christ."   (1778)

746. *How are we to develop our moral conscience?*

We must take time out regularly for reflection and self-awareness. In the words of St. Alphonsus Liguori, "Turn within yourself and in everything you do, see God as your witness."   (1779)

747. *What is an upright conscience?*

An upright conscience is one that has these qualities:
- It knows the sound principles of morality.
- It can apply these principles in the practical circumstances of life.
- It makes good decisions about specific actions already done or to be done. (1780)

748. *How does our conscience stand as a pledge of mercy and hope?*

When we have sinned, our conscience bears witness to what we have done wrong. At the same time, it reminds us that God is merciful and that we should repent and grow in virtue with the help of His grace. (1781)

749. *Is everyone free to follow his conscience?*

Yes. In fact, no one is to be forced to act against conscience, nor impeded from acting according to conscience, especially in religious matters. (1782)

750. *What is formation of conscience?*

Formation of conscience is educating the conscience in keeping with the true good as willed by the wisdom of the Creator. It should begin from the earliest years of infancy, and it is a lifelong task. (1784)

751. *How is the conscience to be educated?*

Through study of the Word of God, prayer, practice, examination of conscience, the witness or advice of others, and guidance by the Church's authoritative teaching. (1785)

752. *What are some basic rules for choosing according to one's conscience?*
- Evil may never be done to produce a good result.
- The Golden Rule, "In everything you want others to do to you, do the same to them" (Mt 7:12).
- Charity always works with respect for the neighbor and his conscience. (1786-1789)

753. *Are we always to obey the certain judgment of conscience?*

Our judgment of conscience is certain when we have no positive doubt that something should be done or not done. A certain (not doubtful) conscience must always be followed. Otherwise, we would be condemning ourselves. (1790)

754. *Can the conscience be certain and yet incorrect?*

Yes, through ignorance. (1791)

755. *Are we obliged to have a correct conscience?*

Yes. Failure to enlighten the conscience through seeking the true and good as well as habits of sin blind the conscience. In these cases a person is guilty of the evil committed through what is called vincible or culpable ignorance. (1791)

756. *What are some causes of a blinded conscience?*

They are many. Among others there are:
- ignorance of Christ and His Gospel;
- the bad example given by others;
- slavery of the passions;
- the pretense of a misunderstood autonomy of conscience;
- refusal to accept the Church's authority and teaching;
- lack of moral conversion;
- lack of charity toward God and one's neighbor. (1792)

757. *Does invincible ignorance excuse a person of moral responsibility?*

We must distinguish. If the ignorance is truly invincible, that is, not culpable, the person does not sin in acting on a certain but erroneous conscience. However, as stated before, the erroneous conscience should be corrected. Nevertheless, *the evil consequences of acting on an erroneous conscience remain evil.* This emphasizes the duty we have to make sure our moral conscience is correct. (1793)

758. *Does the conscience have to be enlightened by the true faith?*

Yes, for two reasons:
- because our natural reason has been darkened by sin—original, personal, and social sin;
- because Christ came into the world to reveal mysteries that are beyond the comprehension of reason. These mysteries are to be believed and put into practice. Hence, true faith is needed to enlighten our natural conscience. (1794)

ARTICLE 7: THE VIRTUES

Virtue, in general, is a firm and habitual disposition to do good. It allows a person not only to perform good actions but to give the best of himself. The virtuous person tends toward the good with all his bodily and spiritual powers. He pursues and chooses this good in the concrete actions of daily life.

(1803)

759. *What are the virtues?*

Human virtues are firm attitudes, stable dispositions, and habitual dispositions of the intellect and will that regulate our actions, direct our passions, and guide our conduct according to reason and faith. They confer the facility, self-control, and joy needed to lead a good moral life. (1804)

760. *What are the four cardinal virtues?*

They are prudence, justice, fortitude, and temperance. All other human virtues are expressions of these four. (1805)

761. *What is prudence?*

Prudence disposes our practical reason to recognize our true good in every circumstance of life and to choose the correct means of achieving it. Prudence is called the guide or pilot of the virtues because it guides them by directing them to choose the proper means for achieving a predetermined good end. (1806)

762. *What is justice?*

Justice is the virtue that guides the human will to give to God and to others what is their due. (1807)

763. *What is justice toward God?*

Justice toward God is the virtue of religion. God has a right to be known and obeyed. He has a right to be spoken to and listened to. God has a right to deal with us as He wills. In all these cases, our justice toward God implies our submission to God, His laws, and His providence in our lives. Our humble response to His divine rights as His creatures is the practice of religion. (1807)

764. *What is our justice toward others?*

Justice toward others recognizes their rights as human beings. Always in view of the common good, a just person considers the good of a commu-

nity and how his own interests are to be subordinated to the welfare of
others.   (1807)

765. *What is fortitude?*

Fortitude is the virtue that regulates our fears. It assures stability and con-
stancy in doing what is good even in the face of difficulties. The virtue of fortitude enables us to resist fear, even the fear of death, and to suffer everything in the defense of our practice of the faith. We are sustained by the
promise of Our Lord, who told us, "In the world you will face persecution.
But take courage, I have overcome the world" (Jn 16:33).   (1808)

766. *What is temperance?*

Temperance moderates our desires. It moderates the attraction of pleasure—bodily, emotional, and spiritual. In the words of St. Paul, we are "to
live lives that are self-controlled, upright, and godly" (Titus 2:12). Always this
control of our appetites is to be guided by right reason but illumined by the
light of faith, in which Christ is our model of temperance. We surrender not
only pleasures that are sinful but even legitimate pleasures out of love for
God and in imitation of His Son, Jesus Christ.   (1809)

767. *What is the relation of grace to the practice of human virtues?*

Grace is indispensable. With regard to the human virtues:

- grace elevates the human virtues from the natural to the supernatural plane;
- grace forges the virtues and gives us a facility or ease in their practice;
- grace enables us to persevere in the practice of virtue;
- grace prompts us to pray, receive the sacraments, and respond to
  God's call to an ever greater practice of the human virtues.
                                                                (1810-1811)

768. *What are the theological virtues?*

The theological virtues refer directly to God (*Theos*) by enabling Christians
to live in relation to the Holy Trinity. They are the virtues of faith, hope, and
charity. They have God as their origin, motive, and object. They give life to
the moral virtues.   (1812-1813)

769. *What is faith?*

Faith is the virtue by which we assent with the intellect to everything that
God has revealed, not because we understand but because of the authority

of God revealing, who can neither deceive nor be deceived.   (1814)

770. *What is our duty toward the virtue of faith?*

As followers of Christ, we have a series of responsibilities:

- We are to preserve the faith.
- We are to live the faith.
- We are to profess the faith.
- We are to courageously bear witness to the faith.
- We are to spread the faith.
- We are to be ready to confess Christ before others and follow Him along the way of the Cross.
- We are to be ready to suffer persecution for the faith.
- We are to be willing to die for the faith.   (1815-1816)

771. *What is the virtue of hope?*

Hope is the virtue by which we desire our happiness and the Kingdom of Heaven. It is the virtue by which we place our trust in Christ's promises. It is the virtue that enables us to rely not on our own powers but on the grace of the Holy Spirit to remain faithful to Jesus Christ.   (1817)

772. *How does hope protect us?*

It protects us from discouragement, sustains us in our abandonment by creatures, and rejoices our heart in anticipation of the heavenly glory that awaits us. It preserves us from selfishness.   (1818)

773. *What is the foundation of our hope?*

It is nothing less than our faith in the merits and Passion of Jesus Christ.   (1820)

774. *Are we to hope to reach eternal glory?*

Emphatically. We are to trust confidently in the mercy and love of God, that He will bring us to the heavenly destiny to which He has called us and for which He endured His Passion and death on Calvary.   (1821)

775. *What is charity?*

Charity is the theological virtue by which we love God above all things and everyone else out of love for God.   (1822)

776. *What is Christ's new commandment of love?*

He told us, "As the Father has loved me, so I have loved you…. This is my commandment, that you love one another as I have loved you" (Jn 15:12).

(1823)

777. *Is love the norm for keeping the commandments of Christ?*

Yes. In His own words, "Abide in my love. If you keep my commandments, you will abide in my love" (Jn 15:9-10). (1824)

778. *What are the qualities of true Christian charity?*

They are spelled out in the famous first letter of St. Paul, in which he says, "Charity is patient, charity is kind, charity is not envious or boastful or arrogant or rude, it does not insist on its own way, it is not irritable or resentful, it does not rejoice in wrongdoing, but it rejoices in the truth. Charity believes all things, hopes all things, and endures all things" (1 Cor 13:4-7). (1825)

779. *What is Christian charity?*

It is the practice of all the virtues animated by love. It is more than natural love because it is a supernatural virtue that enables a person to love beyond the powers of human nature. It purifies our human ability to love and raises it to the superhuman perfection of divine love. (1827)

780. *How is Christian charity the bond of unity?*

In the words of St. Paul, it "binds everything together in perfect harmony" (Col 3:14). Without charity there could be no Christianity. And Christianity is only as vital and vibrant as the members of Christ's Mystical Body are united in the practice of selfless charity. (1827)

781. *What are the fruits of Christian charity?*

They are joy, peace, and mercy. Charity begets fraternal correction, friendship, and communion. Charity, says St. Augustine, is the fulfillment and goal of all our good works. Charity is not only the means but the goal of all our efforts. And once we have reached it, we have entered our eternal repose.

(1829)

782. *What are the gifts of the Holy Spirit?*

They are the supernatural impulses by which the Holy Spirit urges us to the practice of the Christian virtues. They correspond to the instincts of our human nature. There are four of these supernatural instincts for the mind, namely, wisdom, understanding, knowledge, and counsel. There are three for the will, namely, fortitude, piety, and fear of the Lord. (1830-1831)

783. How do the gifts and fruits differ from their natural counterparts?

They differ in their cause and effect. Their cause is the supernatural power of grace coming from the indwelling Holy Spirit. Their effect is to assist Christian believers to serve God in spite of a natural reluctance to embrace the Cross in the following of Christ. (1832)

784. What are the fruits of the Holy Spirit?

They are the supernatural enjoyment (Latin *frui*, "to enjoy") that the Holy Spirit gives in the practice of the virtues. As with the gifts, the fruits correspond to the satisfaction we derive from putting our natural powers of body and soul into practice. (1832)

ARTICLE 8: SIN

If there is one focus in the New Testament, it is that God became man to redeem us from sin.

The very name "Jesus" means "Savior." As the angel directed St. Joseph regarding the child that Mary had conceived, "You are to name Him Jesus, for He will save His people from their sins" (Mt 1:21).

Corresponding to this focus on Christ as man's Redeemer is the necessity on our part to repent and be sorry for having sinned.

St. Augustine sees two great gifts that Christ brought to the world. His Spirit of truth enables us to recognize that we have sinned and at the same time to believe in the certainty of our redemption. (1846-1848)

785. What is sin?

Sin is a deliberate offense against a law of God. It is the selfish indulgence of our own will against the known will of God. In the words of St. Augustine, sin may be defined as "a word, an act, or a desire contrary to the eternal law." (1849)

786. What are the causes of sin?

The basic cause of sin is the love of oneself even to the rejection of God. Pride, therefore, or proud self-exaltation is at the root of sin. (1850)

787. What are the effects of sin?

Sin turns the heart of the sinner away from the love of God. It wounds human nature and injures the solidarity of the human race. (1849-1850)

788. *How is Christ's Passion related to sin?*

In two ways. During His Passion, sin reached a peak of intensity, seen in the hatred and violence of His enemies against the incarnate Son of God. By His Passion, Christ opened for us the inexhaustible treasure of divine mercy.

(1851)

789. *What are the different kinds of sin?*

Sins are variously classified. The most fundamental classification is according to the commandments of God. In Sacred Scripture, St. Paul identifies the works of the flesh in contrast with those of the Spirit. "The works of the flesh," he says, "are obvious: fornication, impurity, licentiousness, idolatry, sorcery, enmities, strife, jealousy, anger, quarrels, dissensions, factions, envy, drunkenness, carousing. Those who commit these sins," he concludes, "will not inherit the Kingdom of God" (Gal 5:19-21). (1852-1853)

790. *How do sins differ according to gravity?*

They differ according to whether the sinner loses his state of sanctifying grace or merely weakens his friendship with God. They are, therefore, either mortal or venial. (1854)

791. *What is mortal sin?*

It is a serious disobedience of a law of God. It destroys the virtue of charity in a man's heart and turns him away from God. (1855-1856)

792. *What is venial sin?*

Venial sin allows the virtue of charity to remain, but it injures and wounds the supernatural life of the soul. (1855)

793. *What are the conditions for a mortal sin?*

They are three:

- The matter or action itself must be gravely offensive to God.
- The person knows that it is gravely forbidden by God.
- The person deliberately consents to the sinful action. (1857)

794. *How are mortal sins forgiven?*

The person must repent by conversion of heart, which is normally obtained through the Sacrament of Reconciliation. On God's side, it requires a new initiative of divine mercy. (1856)

795. *What is the grave matter required for a mortal sin?*

It is determined by the Ten Commandments, as illustrated in Christ's response to the rich young man: "You shall not murder; you shall not commit adultery; you shall not steal; you shall not bear false witness; you shall not defraud; honor your father and your mother" (Mk 10:19). These examples reflect different degrees of gravity. It is up to the Church's Magisterium to specify what sinful actions are mortal. (1858)

796. *What are the full knowledge and consent required for a mortal sin?*

A person should be mentally aware that a given action is seriously forbidden by God and must make a personal choice to commit what is known to be a serious sin. (1859)

797. *Can ignorance reduce or even remove the responsibility for a grave sin?*

Yes, provided the ignorance is not voluntary. Moreover, emotions, passions, external pressures, or pathological conditions can reduce the voluntary and free character of grave sins. The worst sins are those of malice and the deliberate choice of evil. (1860)

798. *What are the effects of mortal sin?*

As a radical choice of human freedom, mortal sin deprives a person of the state of grace. Unless repented and forgiven by God, it causes exclusion from Christ's kingdom and the eternal death of hell. Of course, we must always leave the final judgment of grave sinners to the justice and mercy of God.

(1861)

799. *When are venial sins committed?*

When the matter is gravely sinful, but there is not full awareness or consent. Also when the action committed is less serious, venial sins are committed. (1862)

800. *What are the effects of venial sins?*

They weaken the virtue of charity, lead to disorderly love for creatures, interfere with the soul's progress in moral goodness, and merit temporal punishment. Persistent venial sins dispose a person to sin mortally. (1863)

801. *What is blasphemy against the Holy Spirit?*

It is the hardening of heart in which a sinner refuses to repent and accept God's mercy. It can lead to final impenitence and eternal damnation. (1864)

802. *How does sin reproduce itself?*

Sin creates an attraction to sin. Every sinful act naturally tends to repeat itself. The repetition of sin becomes a vice, or a habit of sin. (1865)

803. *What are the capital sins?*

They are pride, lust, anger, covetousness, envy, sloth, and gluttony. They are the root cause of all other sins. (1866)

804. *What are the "sins that cry to heaven"?*

They are specially grievous and are commonly identified as the sin of the Sodomites; the oppression of the Israelites in Egypt; the cry of the stranger, the widow, and orphan; and injustice in wages. (1867)

805. *How do we cooperate in the sins of others?*

We cooperate in other persons' sins by:
- direct and voluntary participation;
- command, counsel, praise, and approval;
- not revealing or stopping sins when we are bound to do so;
- protecting those who do evil. (1868)

806. *What are social sins?*

They are the sinful structures in society created by the multiplication and organization of personal sins. (1869)

Chapter Two

The Human Community

The vocation of humanity is to manifest the image of God and to be transformed to the image of the only Son of the Father. This vocation assumes a personal form, since each individual is called to enter into divine beatitude. But this is also a vocation for the entire human community. (1877)

ARTICLE 1: THE PERSON AND SOCIETY

All men are called to the same end, God Himself. Indeed, there is a certain resemblance between the union of the Divine Persons in the Trinity and the fraternity of truth and love that men should establish among themselves. Love of one's neighbor is inseparable from love for God. (1878)

807. *What is a society?*

A society is an association of persons bound together organically by a principle of unity that surpasses each of its members. It is natural for human persons to live in a society. (1879-1880)

808. *What is the principal subject and end of all social institutions?*

It is and should be the human person. (1881)

809. *What societies are necessary to human nature?*

They are the family and the state. (1882)

810. *What is socialization?*

It is the formation of voluntary associations which foster economic, cultural, political, and other such goals in a society. (1882)

811. *What are the dangers of socialization?*

Socialization becomes dangerous when the state intervenes to threaten personal liberty and initiative. According to the Church's teaching of subsidiarity, a society of a higher order should assist but not intervene in the internal life of a society of a lower order. (1883)

812. *How is God's government of the world the model for governing human communities?*

God respects human freedom. So in human societies, those in authority should act as ministers of divine providence. (1884)

813. *How does subsidiarity oppose all forms of collectivism?*

It does so by setting limits to state intervention, harmonizing relations between individuals and societies, and seeking to establish a true international order. (1885)

814. *What is the primary meaning of life in society?*

Life in society should be seen as primarily a reality of the spiritual order. In other words, all other functions are to be subordinated to interior and spiritual values. (1886)

815. *What is the inversion of means and ends in society?*

This is to confer ultimate value on what is only a means. It is also to use persons as merely a means for attaining the purpose of a society. Such inversion makes Christian obedience to God's laws difficult or even impossible.

(1887)

816. *What must be done to accomplish truly beneficial changes in society?*

There must be permanent interior conversion. This means cleansing society of such institutions and conditions as give rise to sin and reforming them according to the norms of justice and the common good. (1888)

817. *Is divine grace necessary for this reformation?*

Yes, because only God's grace enables human beings to practice supernatural charity. Thus, the love for God and neighbor, inspired by Christ's teaching, is necessary for finding the narrow path between the cowardice that gives in to the evil and the violence that believes it is fighting the evil but only aggravates it. (1889)

ARTICLE 2: PARTICIPATION IN THE SOCIAL LIFE

It is impossible to speak about participation in the life of a society without recognizing the need for authority in that society.

As understood by the Church, authority in a society is the quality by which persons or institutions provide the laws and directives and expect obedience from the people in that society. (1897)

818. *What is the basis for authority in a human community?*

It is human nature. In the state, this authority is necessary to preserve unity and to provide for the common good. (1898)

819. *From whom does civil authority come?*

It comes from God to ensure moral order in civil society. (1899)

820. *Are civil authorities to be obeyed?*

Yes, everyone in a civil society is to obey those in authority and treat them with the honor, respect, and gratitude they deserve. (1900)

821. *Who determines the form of government?*

The form of government and the appointment of its rulers depend on the free will of its citizens. However, to be legitimate, the form of government may not be contrary to the natural law, the public order, or the fundamental rights of the people. (1901)

822. *What is the basis for moral legitimacy of civil authority?*

It is the eternal law of God and therefore does not derive from itself. Human laws, therefore, are true laws only if they correspond to right reason, based on divine law. Otherwise, they are wicked laws and are rather a form of violence. (1902)

823. *When is authority exercised legitimately?*

When it seeks the common good and uses morally licit means to attain this good. Otherwise, the authority ceases to be legitimate and degenerates into oppression. (1903)

824. *What is balance of power in government?*

It is the equilibrium of powers in a government to ensure the sovereignty of the law and prevent domination by the arbitrary will of individuals. (1904)

825. *What is the common good?*

The common good is the sum total of social conditions that enable groups and individuals within the group to achieve perfection more readily and completely by belonging to it. (1906)

826. *What are the essentials of the common good?*

As explained by the Second Vatican Council and Pope Paul VI, the common good must:

- respect each person as such. This means that each person is enabled to follow the correct norms of his conscience, his private life is protected, and his just freedom, especially religious freedom, can be exercised.
- provide for the social well-being and development of the group itself. The means for leading a truly human life are made available in food, clothing, health, work, education and culture, suitable information, and the right to found a family.
- ensure peace, which means the stability and security of a just order. This includes the right to legitimate personal and collective defense. (1907-1909)

827. *What is the universal common good?*

This is the development of international organizations to promote the unity of the human family, provide for people's needs, and alleviate their distress in various places throughout the world. (1911)

828. *How is the common good related to the progress of persons?*

The common good should be oriented to the progress of persons and not the reverse. It must be based on truth built on justice and animated by love. (1912)

829. *What responsibility do we have to participate in public life?*

We have a serious responsibility to promote the common good according to our ability and position. This first means to fulfill the duties a person has freely assumed, such as raising a family. It also means engaging in conscientious work. It finally means laboring for the continued conversion of the members of a society, especially through sound education in moral values. (1913-1917)

ARTICLE 3: SOCIAL JUSTICE

Society assures social justice to its people by allowing associations and their members to obtain what is due to them, according to their nature and vocation. Social justice is associated with the common good and the exercise of authority. (1928)

830. *Why does society exist?*

The ultimate purpose of society is for the good of the person to which it has been ordained. (1929)

831. *What is respect for the human person?*

It is respect for his rights as a creature. Without such respect, authority can obtain obedience from its subjects only by force or violence. (1930)

832. *What is the basis for respect of the human person?*

It is seeing one's neighbor as another self. This includes respect for his existence and for the means necessary to preserve his human dignity. (1931)

833. *When are we especially to serve the needs of others?*

When people are in any way disadvantaged. This follows from Christ's teaching, "As long as you did it to one of these my least brethren, you did it to me" (Mt 25:40). (1932)

834. *Do we have the same duty toward those who think or act differently from us?*

Yes, in fact, Christ commands us to love even our enemies. We may not hate a person, even when we hate the evil that he does. (1933)

835. *How are all human beings equal?*

They are equal because each has been created by God, possesses an immortal soul, has been redeemed by Christ, and is destined for the same divine beatitude. All, therefore, enjoy an equal dignity. (1934)

836. *What follows from our equal dignity?*

As a result, every discrimination affecting a person's basic human rights is contrary to the plan of God. (1935)

837. *Why are human beings so different?*

These differences are willed by God to enable people to practice love for one another. Those who have can share with those who lack. (1937)

838. *Are there also unjust inequalities?*

Yes, in the words of the Second Vatican Council, "The excessive economic and social inequalities...are a scandal... at variance with social justice, equity, the dignity of the human person, and, not least, civil and international peace" (*Gaudium et spes*, 29, 3). (1938)

839. *What is human solidarity?*

Human solidarity is the divinely willed unity and interdependence of the human race. As a law of human and Christian fellowship, it is sealed by the sacrifice of Jesus Christ for the redemption of a sinful humanity. (1939)

840. *How is solidarity first of all manifested?*

By the distribution of goods and remuneration for labor. (1940)

841. *How can socioeconomic problems be solved?*

Only by the help of all forms of solidarity. (1941)

842. *Does the virtue of solidarity go beyond material goods?*

Yes. While promoting the faith, the Church never failed to promote the development of temporal goods. She has pioneered in advancing farmers, liberating slaves, healing the sick, and creating social conditions worthy of Christian and human dignity. Over the centuries, she has proved the truth of Christ's teaching, "Seek first the kingdom of God and his justice, and all these things will be given you as well" (Mt 6:33). (1942)

Chapter Three
Divine Salvation: Law and Grace

Called to beatitude but wounded by sin, the human race is in need of salvation. Divine help comes in Christ by means of the law that guides us and the grace that sustains us. (1949)

ARTICLE 1: THE MORAL LAW

The moral law is the work of divine wisdom. It is at once a paternal instruction and a divine pedagogy. It prescribes for man the ways and rules of conduct that lead to the promised beatitude. (1950)

843. *What is law?*

Law is a rule of conduct decreed by the competent authority in view of the common good. (1951)

844. *What does the moral law presuppose?*

It presupposes the rational order established among creatures for their good and in view of their destiny by the power, wisdom, and goodness of the Creator. (1951)

845. *Where does all law find its truth?*

All law finds its first and last truth in the eternal law. (1951)

846. *What are the expressions of the moral law?*

They are varied and yet all interrelated. Thus, there are:

- the eternal law, the source in God of all laws;
- the natural law;
- the revealed law, which includes the Old Law and the New Law of the Gospel;
- the civil and ecclesiastical laws. (1952)

847. *Where does the moral law find its fullness and unity?*

In the person of Jesus Christ. He is at once the end or purpose of the law and the way of perfection. He alone teaches and confers the justice of God.
(1953)

848. *What is the natural law?*

It is the law written in the soul of all men because our human reason orders us to do good and forbids sin. Its binding power comes from a higher Reason, which we are to obey. (1954)

849. *Where do we find the principal commandments of the natural law?*

We find them in the Decalogue, or the Ten Commandments, given to Moses and elevated by Christ in His Sermon on the Mount. (1955)

850. *What are some notable features of the natural law?*

The natural law is universal; its authority extends to all human beings. Its applications vary, but its basic principles unify the whole human race. It is unchangeable over the centuries of history, and even when denied or rejected, its basic principles cannot be destroyed. (1956-1958)

851. *What are the benefits of the natural law?*

The natural law provides a solid foundation for guiding the human community in moral living. It gives the necessary grounds for civil laws and wise judicial decisions. (1959)

852. *Are the precepts of the natural law perceived clearly and immediately by everyone?*

No, because of the darkening of man's intellect by sin. That is why God provided revelation and grace, so that the basic truths of religion and morality would "be known by everyone, with facility, with firm certitude, and with no admixture of error" (First Vatican Council, *Dei Filius*, 2). (1960)

853. *What is the first stage of the revealed law?*

It is the Old Law summed up in the Ten Commandments, given to Moses on Mount Sinai. (1961-1962)

854. *How is the Old Law imperfect?*

It is imperfect because already before the coming of Christ it had to be completed by the prophetic and wisdom revelation of the Old Testament. But it is mainly imperfect because it had to be fulfilled by the teaching and life of Jesus Christ. (1963)

855. *How is the Law of Moses a preparation for the Gospel?*

It foretells the work of redemption of the Savior, and provides the New Testament with images, types, and symbols for expressing the life of the Spirit. (1964)

856. *What is the New Law of the Gospel?*

The New Law of the Gospel is the perfection here below of the natural and revealed divine law. Moreover:

- It is the grace of the Holy Spirit given to believers by their faith in Christ.
- It surpasses the Old Law, as seen in the Beatitudes, which direct God's promises beyond this world to the kingdom of Heaven.
- In the Sermon on the Mount, it does not add new external precepts but reforms our actions in the heart.
- It directs our acts of religion to the Father, who sees in secret. Its prayer is the Our Father.
- It is summed up in Christ's teaching to do everything to others as we would have them do to us.
- It is expressed in Christ's new commandment that we should love one another as He has loved us. (1965-1970)

857. *How is Christ's Sermon on the Mount amplified?*

By the moral catechesis of the apostolic teaching, for example, the letters of St. Paul to the Romans, Corinthians, Colossians, and Ephesians. This catechesis shows that we are to treat cases of conscience in the light of our relation to Christ and the Church. (1971)

858. *Why is the New Law called the law of love, grace, and freedom?*

- It is called the law of love because it is animated by the love infused by the Holy Spirit, rather than by fear.

- It is called the law of grace because it confers the supernatural power of grace to observe the New Law by means of faith and the sacraments.
- It is called the law of freedom because it frees us from the ritual and juridical observances of the Old Law; it inclines us to act spontaneously under the impulse of charity; and it leads us from the state of servants to that of Christ's friends.   (1972)

859. *What are the evangelical counsels?*

They are invitations extended by Christ to His followers not only to avoid sin, or whatever is incompatible with love, but to choose ways that are more direct and means that are more effective expressions of love. The counsels seek to remove whatever would impede the development of charity.

(1973-1974)

860. *Are the followers of Christ to practice the counsels?*

Yes, but according to each person's grace from God and vocation in life. In the words of St. Francis de Sales, God wants us to observe "only those appropriate to the diversity of persons, times, opportunities, and strengths, as love requires" (*Love*, 8, 6).   (1974)

ARTICLE 2: GRACE AND JUSTIFICATION

The grace of the Holy Spirit has the power to justify us. We are thus cleansed from our sins. Through faith in Jesus Christ and Baptism, we receive a share in the very justice or holiness of God. We become members of His Body, which is the Church.   (1987-1988)

861. *What are the effects of justification?*

Most fundamentally, justification not only frees us from sin but sanctifies us in the depths of our being. Moreover:
- Justification pours into our souls the virtues of faith, hope, and charity.
- Justification conforms us to the justice of God and enables us to attain eternal life.
- Justification establishes cooperation between the grace of God and the freedom of man. We are thus able to merit before God.

(1989-1995)

862. *What is divine grace?*

Divine grace is the favor or undeserved help that God gives us to respond to His call of becoming children of God, adopted sons, sharers in the divine nature and of eternal life. Grace is what we need beyond what we have by nature to reach our heavenly destiny. (1996)

863. *How is our vocation to eternal life supernatural?*

It is supernatural because it is beyond the powers of any created nature either to know or to reach. God alone had to reveal it, and His grace alone makes it possible to attain. (1997-1998)

864. *How does sanctifying grace differ from actual grace?*

Both are totally free gifts of God enabling us to reach the beatific vision of God. Sanctifying grace is the habitual, stable disposition of soul that makes us children of God and heirs of heaven. Actual graces are the transient illuminations of mind and inspirations of will that enable us to obtain, retain, or grow in sanctifying grace. (1999-2000)

865. *Do we need grace to accept grace?*

Yes, God must provide the light for the mind and strength for the will even to first accept His grace. He must also continue giving us His grace in order that we might respond to the graces we receive. But we must cooperate with our free will. In the words of St. Augustine, "Indeed, we also work, but we only collaborate with God who does the work" (St. Augustine, *On Nature and Grace*, 31). (2001)

866. *How does God's free initiative require our free response to grace?*

God made us in His own image and likeness. Like Him, we have a mind and a free will. He wants to bring us to eternal life as intelligent and free human beings. This means that His freedom in giving us His grace must be met by our intelligent freedom in responding to His grace. His gratuitous love for us must be met by our generous love in return. (2002)

867. *Are all graces directed only to our own sanctification?*

No, there are also special graces that St. Paul calls charisms. These are both ordinary and extraordinary. But they are given by the Holy Spirit as apostolic graces, directed to the common good of the Church. They are at the service of the charity that builds up the Church. (2003)

868. *What are the graces of state?*

They are graces given for exercising responsibilities in the Christian life and ministries within the Church. (2004)

869. *How can we know that grace is active in our lives?*

We can know this by the spiritual good that we experience in our lives. As Christ tells us, "By their fruits you shall know them" (Mt 7:20). (2005)

870. *What is merit?*

Merit is the reward received from God for voluntarily cooperating with His grace. (2006)

871. *To whom should merit be attributed?*

It should first be attributed to God, without whom we would not even exist or do any good work. Only then should merit be attributed to the faithful who use their free will to freely cooperate with the free gift of God's grace. (2007-2009)

872. *What can we merit?*

In general, we can merit God's grace in this life and heavenly glory in the life to come. The grace we merit can be a growth in God's life, an increase of the virtues and gifts of the Holy Spirit, and even temporal blessings like health and friendship. The eternal glory we merit is the "right" to enter heaven and an increase in celestial happiness according to our generosity in cooperating with God's grace here on earth. (2010-2011)

873. *What is holiness?*

Holiness or sanctity is fullness of the Christian life and the perfection of charity. (2013)

874. *Are all Christians called to sanctity?*

Yes, all the faithful of whatever rank or state of life. In the words of Christ, "Be perfect as your heavenly Father is perfect" (Mt 5:48). (2012-2013)

875. *What is the mystical union with Christ?*

It is an intimate union with Christ that is the fruit of progress in the spiritual life. It is called mystical because it means a sharing in the mystery of Christ and through Him in the mystery of the Trinity. Moreover, it is attained through the sacred mysteries or sacraments of the Church. (2014)

876. *Are extraordinary experiences or phenomena essential to a mystical union with Christ?*

No, they are special graces that are granted to some people in order to reveal God's grace to all. (2014)

877. *What is necessary to attain Christian perfection or sanctity?*

The road to perfection is the way of the Cross. There is no holiness without renouncement and spiritual conflict. (2015)

878. *Are we to be confident of our salvation?*

Yes, as children of the Church, we should justly hope for the grace of final perseverance and of God's reward for the good works we have done with His grace in union with Jesus. (2016)

ARTICLE 3: THE CHURCH, MOTHER AND TEACHER

It is in the Church that the Christian fulfills his vocation. It is from the Church that he receives the Word of God, which contains the teachings of the law of Christ. From the Church he receives the grace of the sacraments to sustain him on the way. From the Church he learns the example of holiness, and recognizes its source and model in the most holy Virgin Mary. (2030)

The moral life is spiritual worship. Moreover, like the whole of the Christian life, the moral life finds its source and summit in the Eucharistic Sacrifice. (2031)

879. *Does the Church have the right to teach moral matters?*

Yes, she has received from Christ the solemn commandment to preach the truth of salvation. She therefore has the duty always to proclaim the principles of morality, even in the social order, and to pass judgment on any human issue as required by the basic personal rights and the salvation of souls. (2032)

880. *How is the Church's Magisterium ordinarily exercised in moral matters?*

Through catechesis and preaching, with the help of theologians and spiritual authors. (2033)

881. *What is the ordinary and universal Magisterium?*

It is the teaching authority of the Roman Pontiff and the bishops in communion with him, which is intended for all the faithful.   (2034)

882. *Is this ordinary and universal Magisterium infallible in moral matters?*

Yes, based on divine revelation, it includes all those elements of doctrine, including morals, without which the saving truths of salvation could not be safeguarded, explained, or observed.   (2035)

883. *Does the Church's Magisterium extend to specific precepts of the moral law?*

Yes, because their observance, demanded by the Creator, is necessary for salvation.   (2036)

884. *Are the faithful to be instructed in their moral duties?*

Yes, because these duties are the law of God, which Christ entrusted to the Church. Even when the Church's moral teachings concern disciplinary matters, the faithful are to accept them from the legitimate authority of the Church.   (2037)

885. *Are the faithful to contribute to the Church's understanding of the moral law?*

Yes, the Holy Spirit can use the most humble of the faithful to enlighten even the learned and those in the highest dignity.   (2038)

886. *Can there be any real conflict in moral matters between reason or a person's conscience and the moral law or the Church's teaching authority?*

No, because the same Spirit of God who guides the moral law and the Church's Magisterium also enlightens all persons of good will and the faithful of the Catholic Church.   (2039)

887. *What is a true filial spirit toward the Church?*

It is the spirit received at Baptism that inspires us to see the Church as our loving mother. We trust her in teaching us the Word of God, forgiving our sins, and feeding our souls with the Eucharist of the Lord.   (2040)

888. *What are the precepts of the Church?*

They are the indispensable minimum that the faithful are expected to obey as members of the Church. Six precepts are universally binding:
- Participate at Mass on Sundays and feast days.
- Receive the Sacrament of Confession at least once a year.

- Receive Holy Communion at least during the Easter season.
- Keep holy the feast days of obligation.
- Observe the prescribed days of fast and abstinence.
- Support the Church in her material needs according to one's ability.

(2041-2043)

889. *How is a moral life a missionary witness to the Church?*

Fidelity in living out their faith is a basic witness to the Gospel of all the baptized. The believer's holiness of life, more than anything else, contributes to the increase, growth, and development of the Church founded by Christ.

(2044-2046)

SECTION II:
THE TEN COMMANDMENTS

Jesus did not eliminate the Ten Commandments; he elevated them. This is especially clear in the Gospel of St. Matthew, written for the converts from Judaism.

In this Gospel, the Savior does several things:

- He shows that following Him means obeying the commandments, since He is the Master of the law.
- He shows how the evangelical counsels are inseparable from the commandments.
- He restates the Ten Commandments in such a way as to show that the Spirit elevated the letter of the law beyond anything preached by the Scribes and Pharisees or taught by the Gentiles.
- He explains how the Decalogue is really the twofold commandment of love for God and our neighbor.   (2052-2055)

INTRODUCTION

890. *What does the word "Decalogue" mean?*

It means "Ten Words," referring to the Ten Commandments given by God to Moses, who wrote them down. They are found in the books of Exodus and Deuteronomy.

(2056)

891. *How are the Ten Commandments an exodus?*

They are an exodus, or deliverance, because they are the way to be delivered from sin. (2057)

892. *How do the Ten Commandments summarize and proclaim the law of God?*

They contain the basic covenant between God and His people. That is why they were to be kept in the Ark of the Covenant. (2058)

893. *How are the Ten Commandments a theophany, or self-revelation, of God?*

Because they manifest the will of God to His people. (2059)

894. *How does the text of the Decalogue differ in Exodus and Deuteronomy?*

In Deuteronomy, the Decalogue brings out the covenant or agreement by which the Chosen People bind themselves to obey whatever the Lord has previously commanded them. (2060)

895. *How are the Ten Commandments related to original sin?*

Original sin enslaved the human race to this world. The Ten Commandments liberate mankind from this punishment for sin. This is symbolized in the deliverance of the Israelites from the slavery of Egypt. (2061)

896. *How do the Ten Commandments express our worship of God?*

By telling us how God wants us to cooperate with His plan in human history. (2062)

897. *How does the Decalogue express God's covenant with each human being?*

The Ten Commandments are preceded by the singular pronoun "I," which indicates that God is speaking personally. Each commandment is expressed in the singular pronoun "you" to indicate that He is addressing each of us personally. (2063)

898. *What has been the Church's tradition regarding the Decalogue?*

From the beginning, the Church has given the Ten Commandments a preponderant place in her catechetical instruction before Baptism and of the baptized faithful. (2064-2065)

899. *What is the division of the Decalogue in the present catechism?*

It is the division of St. Augustine and has been traditional in the Catholic Church ever since. (2066)

900. *What do the Ten Commandments express?*

They express our duties to love God in the first three commandments, and to love our neighbor in the last seven. (2067)

901. *What is our duty to observe the Ten Commandments?*

The Council of Trent teaches that all Christians are obliged to observe the Ten Commandments. The Second Vatican Council confirms this obligation by reminding the bishops, as successors of the Apostles, that their mission from Christ is "to preach the Gospel so that all may be saved through faith, Baptism, and the observance of the commandments" (*Lumen Gentium*, 24).
(2068)

902. *What is the unity of the Decalogue?*

The commandments are so united that each precept depends on the others. Most important, the first three commandments on the love of God determine the last seven on loving our neighbor. (2069)

903. *How is the Decalogue related to the natural law?*

We may say the Decalogue is the divine revelation of the natural law. The revelation was needed because human reason has been darkened by sin.
(2070-2071)

904. *Is the Decalogue irreversible?*

Yes, it applies to all human beings, everywhere, at all times, and no one can be dispensed from obeying it. (2072)

905. *Are all the commandments equally binding?*

No, as explained before, the gravity of a sin depends on the seriousness of what is done, the intention, and the circumstances. (2073)

906. *Can we keep the commandments without divine grace?*

No, as Christ tells us, "Without me you can do nothing" on the way to heaven. We therefore need the grace that only He can give. (2074)

907. *What are the Ten Commandments as found in the Church's tradition?*

They are:

1. I am the Lord your God. You shall have no other gods before me.
2. You shall not take the name of the Lord your God in vain.
3. Observe the Sabbath day, and keep it holy.
4. Honor your father and mother as the Lord your God commanded you.
5. You shall not kill.
6. You shall not commit adultery.
7. You shall not steal.
8. You shall not bear false witness against your neighbor.
9. You shall not covet your neighbor's wife.
10. You shall not covet anything which belongs to your neighbor.

CHAPTER ONE

"YOU SHALL LOVE THE LORD YOUR GOD WITH ALL YOUR HEART"

Jesus synthesized man's duties toward God in one sentence. "You shall love the Lord your God with your whole heart, and with your whole soul, and with your whole mind" (Mt 22:37).

God has first loved us. We may call this the first of God's "ten words" to us. The commandments then spell out how man is to give his love to God in return. (2083)

ARTICLE 1: THE FIRST COMMANDMENT

"I am the Lord your God, who brought you out of the land of Egypt, out of the house of slavery. You shall have no other gods before me. You shall not make for yourself an idol, whether in the form of anything that is in heaven above, or that is on the earth beneath, or that is in the water under the earth. You shall not bow down before them or worship them" (Ex 20:2-5).

908. *What is distinctive about the First Commandment?*

It professes absolute monotheism. There is and can be only one true God. (2084)

909. *To whom did God first reveal himself?*

To the people of Israel. (2085)

910. *What virtues does the First Commandment embrace?*

It embraces the virtues of faith or believing in God; hope or trusting in God; and charity or loving God. (2086)

911. *How is our moral life based on our faith in God?*

Faith in God reveals His love for us. Our moral responsibility is to respond to God's love by keeping His commandments. (2087)

912. *What are the principal sins against faith?*

They are voluntary doubt, unbelief, heresy, and apostasy. Voluntary doubt is deliberately suspending judgment about the certitude of any truth revealed by God. To be noted is that difficulties about the faith are not positive doubts.

Unbelief is either apathy toward revealed truth or the refusal to assent.

Heresy is obstinate denial after Baptism to believe a truth that must be believed with divine and Catholic faith, or an obstinate doubt regarding such a truth.

Apostasy is the total rejection of the Christian faith. Schism is the refusal of submission to the Sovereign Pontiff or communion with the members of the Church who are subject to him. (2088-2089)

913. *What is hope?*

Hope is the confident expectation of God's grace in this life and the beatific vision of God in eternity. It is also the fear of offending God's love and provoking His punishment. (2090)

914. *What are the two principal sins against hope?*

They are despair and presumption.
- Despair is giving up hope in God for one's salvation, for the means of reaching heaven, and for pardon of our sins.
- Presumption is either assuming that I can reach heaven without divine grace, or assuming that God will forgive me without repentance for my sins, or give me eternal glory without my voluntary merit with His grace. (2091-2092)

915. *What is charity?*

Charity is the divine commandment that obliges us to love God above all things and to love creatures for Him and because of Him. (2093)

916. *What are the sins against the love of God?*

- Indifference either ignores or refuses to pay attention to God's love.
- Ingratitude refuses either to recognize God's love or to render love to Him in return.
- Tepidity is either hesitation or negligence in responding to divine love.
- Spiritual sloth goes so far as to reject the joy that comes from God.
- Hatred of God comes from pride, denies His goodness, and presumes to curse Him because He forbids sins and inflicts punishment. (2094)

917. *What is the virtue of religion?*

It is the virtue that disposes us to render to God what He justly deserves from us creatures. It is the virtue of justice toward God. (2095)

918. *What is adoration?*

To adore God is to recognize, with respect and submission, the creature's worthlessness apart from God. To adore God is to praise Him, exalt Him, and humble oneself before Him, as Mary did in the *Magnificat.* (2097)

919. *Why is prayer prescribed by the First Commandment?*

Because without prayer we would not receive the grace we need to keep the commandments. (2098)

920. *What is a sacrifice?*

In the words of St. Augustine, "A true sacrifice is every action performed to be happy and to cling to God in holy fellowship" (*The City of God,* 10:6). In more technical language, a sacrifice is the voluntary surrender of something precious to God. (2099-2100)

921. *How can we make our whole life a sacrifice to God?*

By uniting our daily sacrifices with Christ's sacrifice on Calvary. (2100)

922. *What is a promise to God?*

It is either part of the liturgy, as in the Sacraments of Baptism and Marriage; or an act of personal devotion in which a Christian promises God to do some good work, such as saying a certain prayer or giving a donation to some worthy cause. (2101)

923. *What is a vow?*

A vow is a deliberate and free promise made to God concerning something that is both possible and better than its omission. Moreover, a vow is made as an act of the virtue of religion. (2102)

924. *What are the vows of religion?*

They are lifetime commitments to follow Christ more closely in the practice of the evangelical counsels of consecrated chastity, poverty, and obedience. (915, 2103)

925. *Are all people obliged to seek the truth?*

Yes, especially in what concerns God and His Church. They are further bound to embrace this truth once it is found. The reason is that the grace necessary for salvation is communicated only through faith in the truth revealed by God. (2104)

926. *Are Catholics obligated to spread their faith?*

Yes, they have the duty to make known the worship of God in the one true religion and the unique Church of Christ. (2105)

927. *Does everyone have a right to religious freedom?*

Yes, even those who do not fulfill their obligation to seek and adhere to the truth. However, where special recognition is given to a particular religion, the equal right of all citizens and religions must be recognized. (2106-2107)

928. *Is the right to religious liberty unlimited?*

No, its limits must finally be determined by the objective moral order.
(2108-2109)

929. *What are the principal sins against the First Commandment?*

They are:

- superstition, which may be called a perverse excess of religion, such as attributing religious benefits to merely external actions;

- idolatry, which gives a creature divine honors;
- divination, which seeks to know the future by having recourse to the evil spirit, or the spirits of the dead, or alleged hidden powers, instead of trusting in the providence of God;
- magic and sorcery, which claim to evoke occult forces in order to have power over other people.   (2110-2117)

930. *What are the principal sins against the virtue of religion?*

They are:

- testing God by demanding that He prove Himself in word or deed. This is what Satan did when he told Jesus to throw Himself from the pinnacle of the Temple, thus forcing God to act.
- sacrilege, which means profaning or misusing the sacraments or other liturgical actions, or sacred persons, places, or things.
- simony, which is buying or selling spiritual things. It is named after Simon Magus, the magician, who tried to buy from St. Peter the spiritual power that the Apostle possessed. Those who administer the sacraments may not ask for more than the Church's authority permits and never deprive the poor of the sacramental services they need.   (2118-2122)

931. *What is atheism?*

Atheism denies or rejects the existence of God. It takes on different forms:

- practical atheism, where people think and act as though there were no reality beyond space and time;
- atheistic humanism, which considers man to be his own end, the sole maker and agent of his own history;
- atheistic liberalism, which looks for man's liberation by merely social or economic means, independent of religion and God.

(2124)

932. *What are the causes of atheism?*

Basically, atheism is the result of a false idea of human autonomy. In practice, it is often due to believers not having been educated in their faith, or taught erroneous doctrine, failing to live good religious, moral, or social lives.

(2125-2126)

933. *What is agnosticism?*

It refuses to affirm or deny God's existence, which it claims cannot be proved. It is often simply a form of practical atheism.   (2127)

934. What are the causes of agnosticism?

It can be the result of a search for God. But more often it is an escape from the ultimate question of existence and a laziness of one's moral conscience. (2128)

935. What is the Church's teaching on the veneration of sacred images?

The Church teaches that the Old Testament did not absolutely forbid the veneration of sacred images but only the idolatrous representation of God by the hand of man. With the Incarnation, Christ introduced a new understanding of images. Consequently, we are justified in venerating images of Christ, Our Lady, the angels, and saints. Our worship goes beyond the image to the reality we venerate. (2129-2132)

ARTICLE 2: THE SECOND COMMANDMENT

"You shall not make wrongful use of the name of the Lord your God" (Ex 20:7; Dt 5:11).

"You have heard that it was said to them of old, you shall not forswear yourself.... But I say to you not to swear at all" (Mt 5:33-34).

936. What does the Second Commandment prescribe?

It prescribes respect for the name of the Lord and regulates our use of words in speaking of sacred things. (2142)

937. To whom does God entrust the use of His name?

To those who believe in Him and to whom therefore He reveals His personal mystery. (2142)

938. How is the believer to witness to the Lord's name?

By professing his faith without fear. Preaching and catechesis are to be permeated with respectful adoration of the name of our Lord Jesus Christ. (2145)

939. What does the Second Commandment forbid?

It forbids every irreverent use of the names of God, Jesus Christ, the Virgin Mary, and of all the saints. It also forbids the magical use of God's name. (2146, 2149)

940. *What are promises made to others in God's name?*

They are pledges of God's honor. Not keeping such promises makes God a liar. (2147)

941. *What is blasphemy?*

Blasphemy is speaking either inwardly or outwardly against God. It can be uttering words of hatred, reproach, defiance, or evil against God. It is likewise blasphemous to speak evil against the Church of Christ, the saints, and sacred things. And finally, it is blasphemy to use God's name for such criminal practices as enslaving, torturing, and killing people. Blasphemy is a grave sin by its very nature. (2148)

942. *What is perjury?*

It is a promissory oath that a person either does not intend or fails to keep. It is a grave sin. (2150-2152)

943. *Is it permitted to take an oath?*

Yes, when it is taken to witness to the truth for serious reasons and when the oath is made with discernment and in the service of justice. (2153-2154)

944. *May an oath ever be refused?*

Yes, whenever demanded for purposes contrary to a person's dignity or communion with the Church. (2155)

945. *What is the baptismal name?*

It is the name given at Baptism, which can be the name of a saint or of a Christian faith or mystery. It should never be alien to Christian sentiment. (2156)

946. *Why does a Christian make the sign of the Cross?*

To begin his day, his prayers and actions "in the name of the Father, and of the Son, and of the Holy Spirit." Moreover, the sign of the Cross strengthens us in trials and temptations. (2157)

947. *Why is each person's name sacred?*

Because God calls each of us by name (Is 43:1). Consequently, a person's name is his icon, and must be respected as a sign of his dignity. (2158)

948. *Does each person have a distinct name for all eternity?*

Yes, in the kingdom, the mysterious and unique character of each person will shine in full light, marked with God's name. (2159)

ARTICLE 3: THE THIRD COMMANDMENT

"Remember the Sabbath day, to keep it holy. Six days shall you labor, and do all your work; but the seventh is a sabbath to the Lord your God; in it you shall not do any work" (Ex 20:8-10; Dt 5:12-15).

"The Sabbath was made for man, and not man for the Sabbath; so the Son of Man is Lord even of the Sabbath" (Mk 2:27-28).

949. *What was the Old Testament understanding of the Sabbath?*

The Old Testament understood the Sabbath to commemorate God's creating the world and resting on the seventh day. Moreover:

- It was a memorial of Israel's liberation from Egypt.
- It was a sign of the unbreakable covenant between God and His people.
- It presented God as a model for human action. We are to rest periodically from our labors and not become slaves of labor and the worship of money. (2168-2172)

950. *How did Christ interpret the Sabbath?*

He did so by respecting the holiness of the Sabbath while authorizing the practice of compassion and charity on this day. (2173)

951. *How does Sunday commemorate the new creation?*

The Jewish Sabbath recalled the first creation of the world. Sunday commemorates the new creation that opened with Christ's Resurrection on Easter Sunday. It is the first of feasts, the Day of the Lord. (2174)

952. *How is Sunday the fulfillment of the Sabbath?*

Where the Sabbath prepared the people for Christ's coming, Sunday is a weekly preparation for man's eternal rest in God. (2175)

953. *What does the celebration of Sunday fulfill?*

It fulfills the moral commandment, inscribed in man's heart, "to render to God an outward, visible, public, and regular worship in recognition of His universal benefit to men" (St. Thomas Aquinas, *Summa Theologica*, II, II, 122. 4). (2176)

954. *What celebration is at the heart of the Church's life?*

It is the Sunday celebration of the Lord's Day and the Eucharist of the Lord. (2177)

955. *What feast days are likewise celebrated as holy days in the universal Church?*

They are the Nativity of Our Lord, Epiphany, the Ascension, and the feast of the Body and Blood of Christ; the feast of Mary the Mother of God, her Immaculate Conception, and Assumption; and the feasts of St. Joseph, the holy Apostles Peter and Paul, and All Saints. (2177)

956. *What is a parish?*

A parish is a particular community of the faithful established on a stable basis in a particular church, whose pastoral care is entrusted to a parish priest as its own pastor, under the authority of the diocesan bishop. (2179)

957. *Are Catholics obliged to assist at Mass on Sundays and holy days of obligation?*

Yes, it is binding under grave sin unless excused for a grave reason or dispensed by their own pastor. (2180)

958. *Why must Catholics assist at Mass on Sundays?*

Because the Sunday Eucharist is the basis and crown of all Christian practice. Moreover, the faithful thus give witness to their loyalty to Christ and His Church, testify to God's holiness and hope of salvation, and strengthen one another under the guidance of the Holy Spirit. (2182)

959. *Why are Sundays and holy days called "days of grace and rest from work"?*

Because they are days of special grace from God and because we are to abstain from work, which would be an obstacle to the worship due to God, the joy proper to the Lord's Day, works of mercy, and the necessary relaxation of spirit and body. (2184-2185)

960. *Should Christians seek to have Sundays and holy days recognized as legal holidays?*

Yes, out of respect for religious freedom and for the common good. (2188)

CHAPTER TWO
YOU SHALL LOVE YOUR NEIGHBOR
AS YOURSELF

The second part of the Decalogue covers the fourth through the tenth commandments. It is also an expression of the love we are to show to others.

To be kept in mind is that Christ elevated both commandments of love, of God and our neighbor, far beyond what they were in the Old Law.

Thus, where the Mosaic Law prescribed, "You shall love your neighbor as yourself," Christ told his followers, "Love one another as I have loved you."

ARTICLE 4: THE FOURTH COMMANDMENT

"Honor your father and your mother, so that your days may be long in the land that the Lord your God is giving you" (Ex 20:12; Dt 5:16).

"Then he went down with them... to Nazareth and was obedient to them" (Lk 2:51).

961. *How does the Fourth Commandment express the order of charity?*

After God, we should honor our parents, from whom we have received life and the knowledge of God. (2197)

962. *What is the scope of this commandment?*
* It concerns all our family relationships.
* It tells us to honor and love the elderly and our ancestors.
* It expresses the duties of pupils to their teachers, employees to their employers, subordinates to their leaders, and citizens to their country and to those in government. (2199)

963. *What are the benefits of observing the Fourth Commandment?*

The spiritual benefits are God's grace; the temporal benefits are peace and prosperity. Disobedience of this commandment causes great harm to persons and communities. (2200)

964. *What is a family?*

A man and a woman who are united with their children form a family. (2201-2202)

965. *Who instituted the family?*

God created the human family and endowed it with its fundamental constitution. (2203)

966. *What is the role of the state or public authority in the family?*

The state must recognize the family as instituted by God and respect its rights accordingly. (2202-2203)

967. *What is the Christian family?*

The Christian family is revealed by Christ as a communion of persons who reflect the communion of the Father, Son, and the Holy Spirit in the society of the Holy Trinity. (2205)

968. *What are some of the functions of the Christian family?*

The Christian family is to reflect the procreative and educational work of the Father. Moreover, it is called to share in the prayer and sacrifice of Christ. (2205)

969. *What is the mission of the Christian family?*

It is to proclaim the Gospel. (2205)

970. *How is the family a privileged community?*

It is a privileged community because it is called by God to achieve a union of thought between the spouses as well as a zealous cooperation of the parents in the education of their children. (2206)

971. *How is the family related to society?*

The family is the original cell of social life. It is the natural society in which man and woman are called to give themselves to each other in love and in the gift of life to their children. The authority, stability, and life relationships within the family lay the foundations of freedom, security, and fraternity in society. (2207)

972. *Whose responsibility is it to care for the young and old, the sick and handicapped, and the poor?*

It is first of all the responsibility of the family, with the help of other persons and families and, in a subordinate way, the help of society. (2208)

973. *What are the basic rights that the state is to assure the family?*
The state is to assure the family of the following:

- the right to found a family, have children, and raise them according to the parents' moral and religious convictions;
- the right to protect the stability of the marriage bond and the institution of the family;
- the right of parents to profess their faith and hand it on to their children with the necessary means and institutions;
- the right to private property and freedom of enterprise, to obtain work and lodging, and to emigrate;
- the right to medical care, assistance for the aged, and family benefits;
- the right to protection in security, public health, and especially against dangerous drugs, pornography, and alcoholism;
- the right to form associations with other families and so be represented before civil authority. (2210-2211)

974. *How does the Fourth Commandment affect our view of society?*

It enables us to see in everyone a person who is somehow related to us by origin or descent. (2212)

975. *Are contracts sufficient for the good government of human communities?*

No, their good government presupposes a natural good will, elevated by grace, that respects the dignity of human persons. (2213)

976. *What is filial piety?*

It is the children's respect for their parents out of gratitude to those who have brought them into the world and enabled them to grow in stature, wisdom, and grace before God and man. (2215)

977. *How is filial respect to be shown to parents?*

By loving sincerity and true obedience. (2216)

978. *What is the obedience that children owe their parents?*

Children are to obey their parents in everything that concerns the children's or the family's physical and spiritual well-being. The same holds for the obedience due to those chosen by the parents to teach or otherwise train the children. When children reach majority, the children are still to respect their parents, ask for their advice, accept their justified reprimands, and anticipate their parents' desires. (2217)

979. *What are the duties of adult children toward their parents?*

As far as they can, they should provide for material and moral needs, and assist their parents in loneliness, sickness, or old age. (2218)

980. *How does filial piety affect other family relationships?*

Filial piety fosters harmony among all blood relations, especially brothers and sisters, grandchildren and grandparents. (2219)

981. *Who deserves special gratitude from children?*

Those from whom the children received their gifts of faith, Baptism, and membership in the Catholic Church. (2220)

982. *What is the most fundamental and inalienable right and duty of parents?*

It is to provide for their children's moral education and spiritual formation. (2221)

983. *How do parents basically train their children to obey the laws of God?*

They do so by being themselves obedient to the will of the Father in heaven. (2222)

984. *How do parents first fulfill their responsibility to educate their children?*

They do so by creating a home for their children. The home should be ruled by loving-kindness, forgiveness, mutual respect, fidelity, and selfless generosity. (2223)

985. *How are these family virtues to be developed?*

By training the children to subordinate their natural desires for self-satisfaction to interior and spiritual values. (2223)

986. *How should parents teach their children to be on their guard?*

They should warn their children to guard against influences that would compromise the children's principles or degrade their moral and spiritual integrity. (2224)

987. *When should parents begin to catechize their children?*

Parents should initiate their children from infancy into the mysteries of the faith and the life of the Church. (2225)

988. *What is the role of family catechetics?*

Family catechetics is home religious education. It establishes, accompanies, and enriches all other forms of teaching the faith. (2226)

989. *What is the role of the parish in catechesis?*

As the Eucharistic community, the parish is a privileged place for the religious instruction of both parents and children. (2226)

990. *What especially contributes to the holiness of the parents and the family?*

It is mutual forgiveness among members of the family. Their readiness to forgive each other is essential for the well-being and even survival of the family. (2227)

991. *What do children most need in infancy and as they grow up?*

In infancy, parents are especially to care for their children's physical and spiritual needs. As they grow up, parents are to train the children in the right use of their reason and free will. (2228)

992. *How are parents primarily responsible in choosing schools for their children?*

Parents have the primary duty to choose schools according to their own convictions. As far as possible, parents are obliged to choose schools that support their Christian faith. Public authorities have the duty to ensure parents that these kinds of schools are available. (2229)

993. *How are parents to assist their children in choosing a state of life or a profession?*

Parents are not to coerce their children. But they are to give good advice, especially when their children plan to found families of their own. (2230)

994. *Is it ever advisable to sacrifice marriage?*

Yes, especially when such a sacrifice is made to care for one's parents, brothers, or sisters, or for other praiseworthy motives. From a Christian perspective this can be of great service to the human family. (2231)

995. *What is the Christian's first vocation?*

It is to follow Jesus Christ. Loving Him takes precedence over the bonds of family life. (2232)

996. *How are parents to view their children's call to a consecrated life or priestly celibacy?*

They should rejoice at this fact. It is a response to the special vocation that Christ promised to give some of His followers to sacrifice marriage for the sake of the Kingdom of Heaven. (2233)

997. *What are the basic duties of civil authorities?*
- They are to exercise their authority as a service—in Our Lord's words, "as a servant"—to those under authority.
- Their authority must be measured by the divine law.
- They should respect each person's freedom and responsibility; practice distributive justice; and resist the temptation to place their own interests ahead of those of the community. (2234-2236)

998. *Can the political rights of citizenship be suspended?*

Yes, but only for legitimate and proportionally grave reasons. (2237)

999. *What are the basic duties of citizens?*

They are to see their superiors as representatives of God. They are therefore to obey and cooperate with those in authority for the common good. They are to pay their just taxes, exercise their right to vote, and share in the defense of their country. (2238-2240)

1000. *Are more prosperous nations obliged to welcome immigrants in search of security and livelihood?*

Yes, as far as possible. Moreover, civil authorities are to respect the natural law that gives moral protection to the immigrant guests. (2241)

1001. *May citizens engage in lawful protests?*

Yes, they may even have the duty to protest against what they consider harmful to personal dignity and the good of the community. (2242)

1002. *Are citizens ever obliged to refuse obedience to civil authority?*

Yes, whenever the demands of civil authority contradict the demands of the moral laws of God, the fundamental rights of persons, and the teachings of the Gospel. (2242)

1003. *When may citizens resort to force in resisting political power?*

Whenever the political power becomes oppressive and the following conditions are fulfilled:

- The violated rights are fundamental, and the violations serious and prolonged.
- All other means of redress are exhausted.
- Worse disorders are not provoked.
- There is a well-founded hope of success.
- It is reasonably impossible to foresee better solutions.   (2243)

1004. *What is the Church's relation to the political community?*

The Church has been divinely endowed with revealed truths. She invites political authorities to measure their judgments against those inspired by Christ and His Church.   (2244)

1005. *Is the Church identified with any political society?*

No, because her commission and competence are with man's supernatural life and heavenly destiny.   (2245)

1006. *Does the Church ever pass judgment on political matters?*

Yes, she is divinely authorized to pass moral judgment on political matters whenever required by the fundamental rights of human persons or the salvation of souls.   (2246)

ARTICLE 5: THE FIFTH COMMANDMENT

"You shall not kill" (Ex 20:13).

"You have heard it was said to the ancients, 'You shall not kill,' and that 'whoever shall kill shall be liable to judgment.' But I say to you that everyone who is angry with his brother shall be liable to judgment" (Mt 5:21-22).

This prohibition to kill is the prohibition to murder, which means the killing of an innocent human person.

1007. *Why is murder forbidden by the divine law?*

Murder is forbidden because human life is sacred, which means it belongs to God. It comes into being through the creative action of God. It remains always in a special relationship with the Creator and is destined to be with

God as the end or purpose of its existence. Therefore, no one has the right directly to destroy any human being. (2258)

1008. *What does the Bible teach about the sinfulness of murder?*

From the Book of Genesis through the New Testament, the Scriptures forbid the killing of an innocent person. This prohibition is universally binding on everyone always and everywhere. (2259-2261)

1009. *How did Christ elevate the Fifth Commandment?*

He did so in two ways:

- by forbidding the interior sins of anger and envy, which lead to murder;
- by commanding His followers to love their enemies in imitation of His own love for those who unjustly condemned Him to death.

(2262)

1010. *What is legitimate defense?*

It is the use of violent means to defend one's own life or the life of others. In the words of St. Thomas, "Defense can encompass two actions: the preservation of one's own life and the aggressor's death...the first is intended, the second is not" (*Summa Theologica*, II, II, 64.7). (2263)

1011. *Why are we permitted to defend our own lives?*

The basic reason is that authentic self-love is a fundamental principle of morality. In fact, self-defense even to the point of allowing the aggressor to die can be a serious duty for those responsible for the lives of others and for the common good of the family or the state. (2264-2265)

1012. *May unjust aggressors against the state be resisted by force?*

Yes, in extremely grave situations the state may even resort to the death penalty. (2266)

1013. *Is capital punishment ever justified?*

Yes, as just explained, since justly condemned criminals are unjust aggressors of society. Moreover, civil authority has the duty to preserve public order, provide for the safety of its citizens, and inflict punishment as a compensation for the disorder caused by a crime. (2266)

1014. *Can we say that capital punishment is a last resource?*

Yes, if human lives can be protected against criminals and the public peace safeguarded without bloodshed, the state is obliged to do so.   (2267)

1015. *What is willful homicide?*

Willful homicide is the deliberate killing of an innocent human being. It is murder that nothing can justify, even if ordered by civil authority.   (2268)

1016. *What is the indirect provoking of a person's death?*

This is exposing anyone to mortal risk without serious reason, or refusing to help anyone in mortal danger. Examples of such would be tolerating deadly famines or drug trafficking.   (2269)

1017. *What is involuntary homicide?*

Involuntary homicide is allowing a person to die without directly intending his death. This is morally justified, provided there are very grave reasons for permitting the person to die.   (2269)

1018. *What is abortion?*

Abortion is the killing of an unborn human being in the mother's womb. A human being exists from the moment of conception—that is, when the ovum is fertilized by the male sperm.   (2270)

1019. *What is the Church's teaching on the morality of abortion?*

From the first century of the Christian era, the Church has condemned direct abortion as a grave sin. Direct abortion is the killing of the unborn child, whether willed as an end or as a means for some other purpose, no matter how noble that purpose may be. This teaching has never changed and is unchangeable. As stated in *The Teaching of the Twelve Apostles:* "You shall not murder the child by abortion and shall not kill the newborn" (*Didache*, 2, 2).   (2271)

1020. *What is the penalty for abortion?*

Besides the grave sin against God, everyone who has an abortion or cooperates in the abortion incurs automatic excommunication.   (2272)

1021. *Do unborn children have an inalienable right to life?*

Yes, this right is not dependent on any human authority. It belongs to a person by virtue of a creative act of God.   (2273)

1022. *What should be said of a state law that denies this right to life?*

Such a law is inherently unjust. It undermines the very foundations of the state.   (2273)

1023. *How is the human embryo to be treated?*

It must be treated as a person from the moment of conception. Therefore, prenatal diagnosis is morally licit only if it respects the embryo as a human being and is directed to either safeguarding or healing this unborn individual. So, too, medical intervention is permissible only if it respects the life and integrity of the embryo, does not involve disproportionate risks, and does not threaten the survival or recovery of the health of the embryo.   (2274-2275)

1024. *What is to be said about producing embryos?*

It is morally sinful to produce human embryos as disposable biological material. Also immoral is every attempt to produce human beings selected according to sex or other predetermined qualities.   (2275)

1025. *What is euthanasia?*

Euthanasia is the deliberate ending of the life of a handicapped, sick, or dying person.   (2277)

1026. *What is the morality of euthanasia?*

It is morally unjustified. Therefore, any action or omission which of itself or by intention causes death to end a person's suffering is murder.   (2277)

1027. *What means are to be used to sustain a person's life?*

Such means are to be used as are not dangerous, extraordinary, or dispro-portionate to the hoped-for results. Death is not intended; it is merely ac-cepted. However, ordinary care, like food and drink, may not be interrupted.
(2278-2279)

1028. *What is suicide?*

Suicide is the direct killing of oneself on one's own authority.

1029. *What is the morality of suicide?*

Suicide is gravely sinful for the following reasons:

- It contradicts the natural human inclination to remain alive out of an authentic love of self.

- It unjustly severs the bonds of solidarity with one's family and with human society.
- It is contrary to the love we owe to the living God.   (2280-2282)

1030. *What factors can diminish the guilt of suicide?*

Psychological disorders, anguish, or a deep fear of hardship, suffering, or torture can lessen the responsibility for committing suicide.   (2282)

1031. *What is the Church's attitude toward suicides?*

The Church does not despair of the eternal salvation of suicides. She prays for persons who take their own lives.   (2283)

1032. *What is scandal?*

Scandal is any action or omission, not necessarily sinful in itself, that leads another person to do something morally wrong.   (2284)

1033. *What is the morality of scandal?*

Scandal is a serious sin if by action or omission it deliberately induces others to do something gravely wrong.   (2284)

1034. *How can scandal be provoked?*

It can be provoked by the law, by institutions, fashion, or public opinion. Those in power who use their influence to produce evil are guilty of scandal.
    (2285-2287)

1035. *Are we obliged to respect our life and health?*

We are obliged to take reasonable care of our physical life and health as precious gifts of God. Two important norms are the needs of others and the common good.   (2288)

1036. *What is the worship of the body?*

It is the neopaganism that sacrifices all else for the welfare of the body. It idolizes physical perfection and success in sports.   (2289)

1037. *What is the virtue of bodily temperance?*

It disposes us to avoid overindulgence in food, alcohol, tobacco, and medicines. Those who by drunkenness or passion for speed endanger their own or other people's safety are guilty of grave sin. So, too, is the use of drugs except for strictly therapeutic reasons.   (2290-2291)

1038. *Is scientific experiment on human persons morally neutral?*

No. Such experiments must be at the service of human persons. It must respect their inalienable rights in keeping with the plan and will of God.

(2292-2294)

1039. *Is research on human beings permissible?*

Yes, but only if such research does not expose a person's life or physical and psychological integrity to disproportionate or avoidable risks. Moreover, such research demands prior informed consent. (2295)

1040. *Are organ transplants permissible?*

Yes, but only on certain conditions, namely:

- that the donor or those representing the donor give their informed consent;
- that the benefits for the recipient are proportionate to the risks incurred by the donor;
- that the organ transplant not cause the death or even disablement of a human being. (2296)

1041. *What are the basic norms for respecting bodily integrity?*

Kidnapping, taking hostages, terrorism, and torture are contrary to the respect for human dignity. Except for strictly therapeutic reasons, mutilation, amputation, and sterilization of innocent persons are also contrary to the moral law. (2297-2298)

1042. *What is the Church's teaching on care for the dying and the deceased?*

Dying persons should be prepared for eternity by prayer and the sacraments. The bodies of the deceased should be treated with respect and charity, based on faith and hope in the resurrection. Burying the dead is a corporal work of mercy that honors the deceased as children of God and temples of the Holy Spirit. Autopsies can be morally allowed for legal inquests or scientific research. The Church permits cremation, provided there is no questioning of faith in the resurrection of the body. (2299-2301)

1043. *What are the two main causes of murder?*

They are anger, which is a desire for revenge, and hatred, which deliberately wishes evil to another person. Both are condemned by Christ as contrary to charity. (2302-2303)

1044. What is peace?

Peace is the tranquility of order. Peace is the fruit of justice and the effect of charity. Peace on earth is the image and result of the peace of Christ. By the blood of His Cross, He merited our reconciliation with God, which is the foundation of peace among men. (2304-2305)

1045. Is it legitimate to renounce violence in order to safeguard human rights?

Yes, provided this can be done without injuring the rights and duties of other persons and societies. (2306)

1046. Is war ever justified?

Every citizen and government must strive to avoid war. Yet, legitimate self-defense by military force is justified under certain strict conditions, namely, if:

- the damage inflicted by the aggressor would be lasting, serious, and certain;
- all other means are impractical or ineffective;
- there is every serious prospect of success;
- the arms used may not cause worse damage than the evils to be eliminated. (2307-2309)

1047. Are citizens obliged to perform military service?

Yes, provided they are promoting the nation's common good and safeguarding peace. (2310)

1048. Is the moral law to be observed during war?

Yes, as taught by the Church and human reason. (2312)

1049. Are conscientious objectors to be recognized?

Yes, those who for reasons of conscience object to war should be excused from bearing arms. However, they must serve the community in some other way. (2311)

1050. What are some moral norms to be observed during military conflict?

The Second Vatican Council has provided many such norms:

- Noncombatants, wounded military people, and prisoners should be treated with respect and humanity.
- The indiscriminate destruction of whole cities or vast areas is a crime against God and humanity. (2312-2314)

1051. *Does the arms race ensure peace?*

No, rather than eliminating the causes of war, it aggravates them.
(2315-2316)

1052. *What are the main causes of war?*

The most common enemies of peace and causes of war are injustices, excessive economic and social inequalities, envy, distrust, and pride among people and nations. (2317)

ARTICLE 6: THE SIXTH COMMANDMENT

"You shall not commit adultery" (Ex 20:14).
"You have heard that it was said to the ancients, 'You shall not commit adultery.' But I say to you that anyone who so much as looks with lust at a woman has already committed adultery with her in his heart" (Mt 5:27-28).
The foundations for the Sixth Commandment were laid in the opening pages of the Book of Genesis. Thus, we read that God created the human race "male and female" and told our first parents to "be fruitful and multiply" (Gn 5:1-2). (2331)

1053. *How does sexuality affect our whole life?*

Sexuality affects our lives because it especially concerns our capacity to love and procreate. (2332)

1054. *What is God's plan for the two sexes?*

In God's plan they are to complement and cooperate with each other. The welfare of society greatly depends on this cooperation. Each of the two sexes is a reflection of the power and love of God, but in different ways. The union of man and woman in matrimony is an eloquent reflection, in the flesh, of the generosity and fruitfulness of the Creator. (2333-2335)

1055. *How does the Sixth Commandment include all of human sexuality?*

It does so because this has been the teaching of the Church's Magisterium since the time of Christ. (2336)

1056. *What is chastity?*

Chastity is the moral virtue of temperance that moderates the desire for sexual pleasure according to the principles of right reason and the Christian faith. Thus, the virtue of chastity integrates a person's sexuality with his whole being, producing an interior unity of his body and soul. (2337, 2341)

1057. *Is chastity possible without the grace of God?*

No, chastity is both a moral virtue and a gift from God. It is a supernatural fruit of the Holy Spirit, who enables the baptized to imitate the purity of Christ. (2345)

1058. *What are some of the blessings of chastity?*

The most fundamental blessing of chastity is to unify the powers of our body with those of the soul. Moreover, chastity provides internal freedom by enabling us to control our sex passions and enjoying the peace that only chaste people can experience. (2339)

1059. *How is the virtue of chastity to be maintained?*

To remain chaste requires self-knowledge, asceticism according to one's state of life, obedience to all of God's commandments, the practice of the other moral virtues, and prayer. (2340)

1060. *Are we to grow in the virtue of chastity?*

Yes, chastity is a long-term moral process and follows the laws of spiritual growth. This growth is achieved "day by day through many free decisions, knowing, loving, and doing the moral good according to the stages of growth" (*Familiaris Consortio*, 34). (2343)

1061. *Is growth in chastity only personal?*

No, it also requires cultural effort on the part of society. This means respect for the rights of others, especially the right to receive an education that recognizes the moral and spiritual dimensions of human life. (2344)

1062. *How is chastity related to charity?*

Chastity is directed not only to self-control, but to self-giving. Chaste people are witnesses to God's faithfulness and loving tenderness. Chastity fosters friendship between people of the same or of opposite gender. Chaste friendship leads to spiritual communion. (2345-2347)

1063. *What are the forms of chastity?*

The forms of chastity correspond to the different states of life. All the baptized are called to chastity. Married people have a vocation to conjugal chastity, others to the chastity of continence, which includes continence for those engaged to be married. (2348-2350)

1064. *What are the principal sins against chastity?*

They are sins of lust, which is the desire for or indulgence in sexual pleasure apart from procreation or conjugal love. Lust takes on a variety of forms:

- masturbation, which is voluntary stimulation of the sex organs outside of sexual intercourse;
- fornication, which is the carnal union between unmarried men and women;
- pornography, which is the display of sexual acts apart from the intimacy of married partners. Its purpose is to stimulate sinful sexual feelings;
- prostitution, which is the sale of sexual activity, usually by women but sometimes also involving men, children, and adolescents;
- rape, which is sexual intimacy under coercion.

All of these sins are gravely offensive and forbidden by the divine law.

(2351-2356)

1065. *What is the Church's teaching on homosexuality?*

Homosexuality is sexual experience between two men or two women. The Church's tradition has always taught that homosexual actions are intrinsically disordered. They are contrary to the natural law. They exclude the gift of life from the sexual act. In no case can they be morally approved. (2357)

1066. *Do some people have homosexual tendencies?*

Yes, but these tendencies are not chosen; they are for most persons a trial. Such people should not be discriminated against. They are called to chastity. As Christians, they are to unite themselves with the Cross of the Savior and, with God's grace, strive to attain Christian perfection. (2358-2359)

1067. *Is sexual pleasure in marriage pleasing to God?*

Yes. While practicing due moderation, the sexual pleasure enjoyed in the marital act is a gift from God. Its purpose is to foster the twofold end of marriage, namely the good of the spouses themselves and the transmission of human life. (2360-2363)

1068. *What is marital fidelity?*

It is the mutual lifelong commitment of husband and wife, who enter into a covenant with God to remain faithful to each other, irrevocably, until death. In the Sacrament of Matrimony, they become part of the mystery of Christ's fidelity to His Church. (2364-2365)

1069. *Must every marriage be open to the transmission of life?*

Yes, this is the unchangeable teaching of the Church's Magisterium. It reflects the humanly unbreakable connection between the unitive and the procreative purpose of marital intercourse.   (2366-2377)

1070. *Is birth regulation permissible?*

For unselfish reasons, a married couple may regulate the number of their children. But this regulation may not separate the twofold purpose of the marital act, namely the fostering of mutual love between the spouses and the procreation of children.   (2368-2369)

1071. *What is periodic continence?*

This is the control of human conception by restricting the marital act to the infertile periods of the wife. From the moral standpoint, natural family planning is permissible. As stated by Pope Paul VI, "If there are serious motives to space out births, which derive from physical or psychological conditions of husband or wife, or from external conditions, it is licit to take account of the natural rhythm inherent in the generative functions" (*Humanae Vitae*, II, 16).   (2370)

1072. *What is contraception?*

Contraception is the deliberate interference with marital intercourse in order to prevent conception.   (2370)

1073. *Is contraception forbidden by divine law?*

Yes, contraception has been forbidden from the earliest days of Christianity. The most significant document on the subject was issued by Pope Paul VI in *Humanae Vitae*. Its central teaching declares as intrinsically evil "every action which, whether in anticipation of the conjugal act, or in its accomplishment, or in the development of its natural consequences, proposes, whether as an end or as a means, to render procreation impossible" (II, 14).

As further explained by Pope John Paul II: "By means of contraception, the spouses separate the two meanings that God has inscribed into the being of man and woman [namely, unitive and procreative love]. They act as 'arbiters' of the divine plan and they 'manipulate' and degrade human sexuality, and with it themselves and their married partner, by changing its value of 'total self-giving'" (*Familiaris Consortio*, II, 32).   (2370)

1074. *What is the responsibility of the state in population growth?*

The state may provide its citizens with sound information. But it may not substitute itself for the initiative of the spouses, nor may it encourage immoral means of regulating population growth. (2371-2372)

1075. *Are large families encouraged?*

Yes. Sacred Scripture and the Church's traditional teaching view large families as a sign of God's blessing and the generosity of the parents. (2373)

1076. *Are artificial insemination and fertilization morally permissible?*

No, in both forms of artificial parenting.

- *Heterologous* artificial insemination and fertilization intrudes a third person between father and mother by the gift of sperm, ovum, or the loan of a uterus. This is wrong because it violates the child's right to be born of a father and mother, and the spouses' right to become parents only through each other.

- *Homologous* artificial insemination and fertilization entrusts the life and identity of the embryo into the power of doctors and biologists. It is morally wrong because it separates the sexual act from the procreative act. The conception and birth of a child are no longer the fruit of the married spouses but of other persons. This is contrary to the dignity and equality of that which must be shared by parents and children. (2374-2377)

1077. *When does a child have all the rights of a human being?*

From the moment of conception. (2378)

1078. *What is the Church's teaching on sterility?*

A married couple who cannot have children of their own should unite themselves with Christ on the Cross, who is the source of spiritual fruitfulness. They may adopt abandoned children or undertake some work of service for others. (2379)

1079. *Why is adultery a grave sin?*

Adultery is a grave sin because it is a great injustice to the married partner and violates the sanctity of the marital bond. It discredits the institution of marriage, and it compromises the good of human generation and the welfare of the children, who need the stable union of their parents. (2380-2381)

1080. *What are some of the Church's basic principles regarding divorce?*

- Christ restored the indissolubility of marriage. Therefore, divorce was abolished by the Savior.

- A valid sacramental and consummated marriage cannot be dissolved by any human power on earth.
- Separation from "bed and board" may be justified as explained in canon law.
- Civil divorce may be tolerated in certain grave situations.
- Divorce introduces disorder into families and a plague of instability into societies.
- If divorced people remarry according to civil law, they are living in a state of public adultery.
- Innocent victims of a civil divorce do not violate the moral law.

(2382-2386)

1081. *What are some other offenses against the dignity of matrimony?*

- The most notorious is polygamy, or a plurality of "wives." Polygamy contradicts the divinely established communion of marriage and is contrary to the equal personal dignity of men and women.
- Incest, or sexual relations between persons of the same family. It not only corrupts family life but shows a regression to animality.
- Sexual abuse of children, which may scar them for life.
- So-called free union, where a man and woman live together but without marriage. This is a reversion to pre-Christian paganism and destroys the very idea of a family.
- Trial marriages, which are a claim that matrimony is experimental and that true love demands a total and definitive self-giving.

(2387-2391)

ARTICLE 7: THE SEVENTH COMMANDMENT

The Seventh Commandment in both the Old and New Testaments is a simple prohibition, "You shall not steal" (Ex 20:15; Mt 19:18).

As Christianity understands this precept, it forbids either taking or keeping unjustly what belongs to someone else. It commands not only justice but also charity in the use of earthly possessions and the fruits of human labor.

Most importantly, this commandment teaches that the right to private property is not absolute. It must be consistent with the common good, and governed by the will of God and fraternal charity. (2401)

1082. *To whom do the goods of creation belong?*

They belong to the whole human race. (2402)

1083. *Why then are these goods divided among people?*

They are divided among people to bring everyone security in their lives, which are exposed to destitution and threatened by violence. (2402)

1084. *How is the right to private property related to promoting the common good?*

Promoting the common good is primary, even though it requires respect for private property. (2403)

1085. *How are owners the stewards of providence?*

They are stewards of providence because they have the duty to share the benefits of their possessions with as many other people as possible. Indeed, they are to reserve the better part for the guest, the sick person, and the poor. (2404-2405)

1086. *What is the right and duty of political authority?*

It is to regulate the lawful exercise of property rights for the common good. (2406)

1087. *What virtues are required to respect human dignity in economic matters?*

They are temperance to moderate attachment to the goods of this world; justice to respect our neighbor's rights; and solidarity to follow the Golden Rule and the example of Jesus Christ, who became poor that we might become rich (2 Cor 8:9). (2407)

1088. *What is theft?*

Theft is appropriating another person's goods against the reasonable will of the owner. It is therefore not theft to appropriate in some urgent or grave need. (2408)

1089. *What are examples of theft?*

It is theft to deliberately retain goods lent or objects lost; to defraud in business; to pay unjust wages; to speculate on the ignorance or hardship of others; to speculate at the grave disadvantage of others; to do bad work, to counterfeit checks or invoices, or to cause excessive waste and expense. In all these cases, restitution is necessary, according to one's participation in the theft. (2409, 2412)

1090. *Are contracts binding in conscience?*

Yes, contracts between persons are forms of commutative justice. Commutative justice is the foundation of human society and requires the protection of property rights, the payment of debts, and the fulfillment of whatever obligations were freely contracted. (2410-2411)

1091. *What is distributive justice?*

This is what the community owes its citizens according to their contributions and their needs. (2411)

1092. *What is the morality of gambling?*

Gambling as such is not sinful. It becomes sinful when it deprives people of what they need to provide for themselves and their dependents. As a passion, gambling can become an addiction. Cheating in gambling can be serious. (2413)

1093. *Is slavery sinful?*

Yes, to buy, sell, or exchange human beings like merchandise is a sin against the dignity and basic rights of human persons. (2414)

1094. *Does the Seventh Commandment oblige respect for the integrity of creation?*

We are obliged to respect animals, plants, and inanimate creatures, which are intended for the good of humanity in the past, present, and future. This means several things:

- Like God, we should treat animals kindly.
- We may use animals for food and clothing, also to assist us in our work and recreation.
- Reasonable experiments on animals are permissible; however we may not cause animals to suffer needlessly or waste their lives.
- We must not spend on animals sums of money that should be devoted to needy persons, or love animals with an affection that only people deserve. (2415-2418)

1095. *What are the principal norms of the Church's social doctrine?*

The Church's social teaching is based not only on human reason and experience but on divine revelation. It is ordered not only to peace and well-being here on earth but to eternal life. This doctrine holds the following:

- Any social system governed by economic factors alone is morally wrong.
- Any theory in which profit is the exclusive standard in business is likewise morally unjustified.
- Any system that subordinates individuals to collective production or reduces persons to making financial profit enslaves man and leads to idolatry of money and the spread of atheism.
- Communism and socialism—as well as individualism and the primacy of the market in capitalism—are all rejected by the Church.

(2419-2425)

1096. *What are the basic norms of social justice in economic activity?*

Economic activity must be subordinated to the Church's teaching on morality and social justice. Consequently:

- Work is a sacred duty that is also redemptive by our imitating the earthly labors of Christ at Nazareth.
- Work is to sanctify the person; the worker is not a mere robot who is put to work.
- Everyone has a right to economic initiative. People should use their talents for the common good.
- The conflicts arising between opposed interests should be reduced by negotiation.
- While the state is to be involved, the primary responsibility for economic activity belongs not to the state but to individuals and voluntary associations in society.
- As important as profits are to business leaders, these leaders are also to consider the well-being of the persons who are affected by their business.
- Employment should be available without discrimination for men and women, the healthy and the disabled, natives and immigrants.
- A just wage should provide for the material, social, cultural, and spiritual life of both the laborers and their dependents.
- While it is permissible to strike, it becomes wrong when the strike involves violence, or is called for a purpose not directly connected with working conditions, or is contrary to the common good.
- Contributions authorized for social security and welfare should be paid, because unemployment can be very harmful to both individuals and their families. (2426-2436)

1097. *Is there economic inequality among nations?*

Yes, it is notorious. Its causes are abusive and even usurious financial systems, iniquitous commercial relations among nations, and the arms race.

(2437-2438)

1098. *Do rich countries have an obligation to assist poorer nations?*

Yes. The obligation stems from human solidarity and charity, and, where the prosperity of rich nations is the result of injustice in paying for their resources, out of justice. (2439)

1099. *What is the value of direct international aid?*

It is laudable but inadequate to meet the serious evils resulting from destitution or to provide permanently for alleviating needs. A total reassessment should be made, especially of agricultural labor, which involves the majority of the people in the Third World. (2440)

1100. *What is the vocation of the laity?*

The laity are to "animate the temporal realities with Christian commitment, by which they show that they are witnesses and agents of peace and justice" (John Paul II, *Sollicitudo rei socialis*, 47). (2441-2442)

1101. *What is the Church's doctrine on our love for the poor?*

This doctrine is founded on the teaching of Christ. Thus we are told:

- Jesus Christ will recognize His own elect by what they have done for the poor.
- The Church's love for the poor is part of her revealed tradition. It stems from the Beatitudes, from Christ's poverty, and from His attention to the poor.
- Love for the poor is irreconcilable with the immoderate love of wealth or its egotistical use.
- St. John Chrysostom tells us, "Not to share our goods with the poor is to steal from them" (*Homily on Lazarus*, 2, 5).
- The works of mercy are to relieve both the material and the spiritual needs of others. Their spiritual needs include instruction in the faith, counseling and advising, and consoling and forgiving those who have offended us.
- People oppressed by poverty, whether physical or otherwise, draw the special compassion of Christ. We are to demonstrate the same compassion. (2443-2449)

ARTICLE 8: THE EIGHTH COMMANDMENT

"You shall not bear false witness against your neighbor" (Ex 20:16).

"Again, you have heard it was said to the ancients, 'You shall not swear falsely, but fulfill your oaths to the Lord'" (Mt 5:33).

The Eighth Commandment forbids falsifying the truth in relations with others. But more fundamentally, it prescribes the duty of our vocation as God's holy people to witness to Him who is and who wants the truth.   (2464)

1102. *What does it mean to live in truth?*

To live in truth first means to believe in Jesus Christ, who is Truth Incarnate. It further means to live according to Christ's teachings. It especially means living in conformity with Christ's example, and thus remaining in His truth. St. John reminds us, "If we say that we have fellowship with Him, while we are walking in darkness, we lie, and do not do what is true" (1 Jn 1:6).   (2465-2470)

1103. *How are believers in Christ to witness to the truth?*

They are to witness to Christ, who is the Truth, by their words and deeds. In this way, the true faith is transmitted to others. They are inspired to give this witness by the example of the martyrs over the centuries. The record of these martyrs is available in a library of literature, beginning with the letters of St. Ignatius of Antioch (107 A.D.).   (2471-2474)

1104. *How can we offend against the truth?*

- We can sin against the truth by making a false testimony in court, and compounding the evil by perjury in taking an oath to confirm what is a lie.
- We can further offend against the Eighth Commandment by rash judgment when we assume, without sufficient grounds, that someone has committed a sin.
- We sin by detraction when we disclose to others, without sufficient reason, the moral failures of people that we know.
- We commit calumny when we damage a person's reputation by telling lies about an individual.

The remedy for all these failures of the Eighth Commandment is to be more ready to give a favorable interpretation to people's conduct than to condemn it.   (2475-2479)

1105. *Why are flattery and servility sinful?*

They are sinful because they encourage others in their perverse conduct.

(2480)

1106. *Why are bragging and mockery sinful?*

Bragging and boasting are sinful either because they go beyond the truth or because the braggart is deceitfully taking personal credit for something that should be credited to God. Mockery is sinful because it maliciously caricatures some aspect of a person's behavior. (2481)

1107. *What is a lie?*

A lie is speaking a falsehood with the intention to deceive. It is speech contrary to the mind. It is withholding the truth from someone who has a right to it. (2482-2483)

1108. *Why is lying sinful?*

Lying is sinful because it is a profanation of language, a failure in justice and love, an act of violence against others. It sows the seeds of division of opinion, undermines trust among people, tears apart the fabric of social relations, and is disastrous to human society. (2484-2486)

1109. *Do sins against the Eighth Commandment require restitution?*

Yes, because every offense against justice and truth demands reparation. This holds even if the guilty person has been pardoned. If the injury cannot be repaired directly, then moral reparation should be made in the name of charity. (2487)

1110. *What are some basic principles for respecting the truth?*

The fundamental norm is that the right to communicate the truth is not conditional. We must conform our lives to the Gospel precept of fraternal charity. Among other reasons for not revealing what we know are the good and security of others, the duty to avoid scandal, and realizing that not everyone has a right to know the truth.

The seal of confession is absolute so that a confessor may not betray the penitent in any way, for any reason, whether by word or by any means of communication.

What are called professional secrets, confided to doctors or lawyers or in confidence, may not be divulged unless grave harm would otherwise result.

In general, we should practice reserve about the private lives of other people. (2488-2492)

1111. *What is the Church's teaching on the use of mass media?*

Society has a right to information based on truth, freedom, justice, and solidarity.

Viewers, listeners, and readers should exercise great discretion, moderation, and discipline in the use of the media. Otherwise, they can become passive victims of the untruth.

Journalists, like other public informants, must observe the truth and not offend against charity.

Civil authority has the duty to punish any violation of a person's right to privacy and a good reputation. Civil authority has the corresponding duty not to violate the freedom of any individuals or groups in a society.

It is a scourge in any country where the state systematically falsifies the truth, exercises political control over the media, manipulates people in public trials, and represses every view that is contrary to that of the state.

(2493-2499)

1112. *What is the relationship between truth and beauty?*

As the Book of Wisdom makes clear, truth is beautiful and attracts on being seen. The fine arts are inspired by the desire to portray truth beautifully. When authentic, the arts express the truth of a reality in language accessible to sight and sound.

Sacred art is true and beautiful when it corresponds in its form to the purpose of sacred art, which is to evoke and glorify the inexpressible mystery of God in faith and adoration. This divine beauty is fully revealed in Christ and reflected in the most blessed Virgin Mary, the angels, and the saints. That is why bishops should promote sacred art and remove from the liturgy and church buildings whatever is alien to the truth of the faith or to authentic beauty of sacred art. (2500-2503)

ARTICLE 9: THE NINTH COMMANDMENT

"You shall not covet your neighbor's wife" (Dt 5:21).

"Anyone who so much as looks with lust at a woman has already committed adultery with her in his heart" (Mt 5:28).

At the root of all sins of the flesh is concupiscence, or the desire for carnal pleasure. It began with the disobedience of our first parents, and it unsettles our moral equilibrium and inclines us to sins of the flesh. (2514-2515)

1113. *What does the Ninth Commandment forbid?*

It forbids all internal sins of thought and desire against chastity. It forbids our flesh to dominate our spirit. (2516)

1114. *What does the Ninth Commandment prescribe?*

It prescribes purity of heart. As expressed in the sixth Beatitude, "Blessed are the pure of heart, for they shall see God." We are told to purify our hearts in these ways: in love (or charity), in chastity (or sexual integrity), and in love of the truth (or orthodoxy). These three are closely interrelated. True charity is chaste; true chastity is based on the true faith. (2517-2519)

1115. *What is the struggle for purity?*

This is the lifelong struggle that we Christians must expect in conflict with concupiscence and disorderly appetites. Four conditions must be fulfilled to remain chaste:

- We must rely on our infused virtue and gift of chastity.
- We must sincerely strive to do God's will in everything.
- We must discipline our emotions, imagination, and thoughts.
- We must pray for the grace of chastity. (2520)

1116. *How is modesty related to chastity?*

Modesty is the virtue that moderates the internal and external movements of a person according to one's endowments, possessions, and station in life. Thus understood, modesty is necessary to preserve our own chastity and that of others. Why? Because we have a fallen human nature. Modesty avoids unnecessary stimulation of the sex appetite, protects us from sexual seduction, preserves the mystery of persons and their love, guards a person's privacy, inspires the choice of clothing, and maintains silence or reserve in the presence of vain curiosity. Modesty is decency, and should be taught children from their tenderest years. (2521-2524)

1117. *How does Christian purity depend on the social climate?*

Christian purity calls for a purification of the social climate, especially the media. The widespread eroticism that characterizes the modern world rests on a false idea of human freedom. Only the moral teaching of Jesus Christ provides the principles and supernatural resources necessary to preserve and grow in Christian chastity. (2525-2527)

ARTICLE 10: THE TENTH COMMANDMENT

"Neither shall you desire your neighbor's house, or field, or male or female slave, or ox, or donkey or anything that belongs to your neighbor" (Dt 5:21).

"For where your treasure is, there your heart will be also" (Mt 6:21).

The Tenth Commandment completes the divine precepts of the Decalogue. As the Ninth Commandment prescribes our control of the concupiscence of the flesh, the Tenth Commandment prescribes our mastery of the natural desire to possess. (2534)

1118. *What is the disorder of covetousness?*

It is one of the seven capital disorders of our fallen human nature. It is therefore the natural tendency to unlimited acquisition of earthly goods, unbridled greed for riches and power, and the desire to deprive our neighbor unjustly of his temporal possessions. (2535-2536)

1119. *Who must struggle most to keep the Tenth Commandment?*

Those whose position, profession, or livelihood depends upon people who are in need, or those who are suffering or in trial. Examples include merchants, physicians, and lawyers. (2537)

1120. *How is envy a sin against the Tenth Commandment?*

Envy is sorrow at another person's possessions or achievement. It includes the sinful desire to appropriate what someone else has. According to St. Augustine, envy is *the* diabolical sin, since it was out of envy that the devil seduced our first parents from Paradise. Even as envy comes from pride, Christians train themselves to live in humility. (2538-2540)

1121. *What is poverty of spirit?*

Poverty of spirit is putting the first Beatitude into practice. It means having one's heart set on the Kingdom of Heaven instead of any earthly kingdom. It is surrender to the providence of God, which frees us from anxiety about tomorrow. (2544-2547)

1122. *How are we liberated by our desire for true happiness?*

We are liberated by our deliverance from inordinate attachment to anything in this world. Our thirst for God is quenched only by eternal life. (2548)

1123. *What is the price we must pay to gain eternal life?*

The price is high. It is nothing less than mortifying our natural cravings. With God's grace, it means that we overcome the seduction of pleasure and power. (2549)

1124. *Is there a one-paragraph description of our heavenly destiny?*

It is expressed in St. Augustine's classic *City of God*, in which he says, "God Himself will be the goal of our desires; we shall contemplate Him without end, love Him without surfeit, praise Him without weariness. This gift, this state, this act, like eternal life itself, will assuredly be common to all" (22:30). (2550)

PART FOUR
CHRISTIAN PRAYER

SECTION I:
PRAYER IN THE CHRISTIAN LIFE: WHAT IS PRAYER?

Our faith is a great mystery. The Church professes and celebrates this faith in the Apostles' Creed. She celebrates this faith in the sacraments and the liturgy. The faithful live out this faith in their following of Christ. These were the first three parts of *The Catechism of the Catholic Church*.

Now we are to see how the following of Christ is to be a vital and personal relationship with the living and true God. This relationship is prayer.   (2558)

"For me, prayer is an outreach of the heart. It is a simple looking up to heaven. It is a cry of recognition and of love, whether in the depths of trial or in the peak of joy," wrote St. Thérèse of Lisieux (*Autobiography*, 25).

1125. *What is the foundation of prayer?*

Humility is the foundation of prayer. The one who humbles himself will be exalted by being given the grace to pray. In the words of St. Augustine, "Man is a beggar before God."   (2559)

1126. *How is prayer a response to God's thirst for our love?*

As shown in Christ's dialogue with the Samaritan woman at the well, God wants us to love Him. We may say He thirsts for the response of our hearts to His, which is the essence of prayer.   (2560-2561)

1127. *Where does prayer come from?*

It comes from the heart. When the heart is separated from God, there cannot be prayer.   (2562)

1128. *What is the heart?*

It is the center of our being, where we choose life or death. It is also the place of our covenant with God.   (2563-2564)

1129. *How is prayer a communion?*

It is the ongoing relationship between God and ourselves. It means the habit of living in the presence of the thrice holy God.   (2565)

CHAPTER ONE

THE REVELATION OF PRAYER

Human beings have always sought God. It is therefore not surprising that God revealed Himself to mankind from the dawn of salvation history. He wants us to respond to His revelation in the covenant drama that engages our heart, which is at the root of prayer.   (2566-2567)

ARTICLE 1: IN THE OLD TESTAMENT

The revelation of prayer in the Old Testament spans the long centuries between the fall of our first parents and the redemption of the human race by the Son of God, who told His heavenly Father, "I have come to do your will, O God" (Heb 10:7).   (2568)

1130. *What is the basic source of prayer?*

As revealed in the first nine chapters of Genesis, the basic source of prayer is the fact of creation. God is our Creator; we are His creatures. Therefore, we *must* pray.   (2569)

1131. *How is Abraham our model of prayer?*

By the complete submission of his heart to the will of God. Abraham was ready to sacrifice even his son, Isaac. Our willingness to sacrifice enables us to share in the power of God's love.   (2570-2572)

1132. *How is prayer a struggle and a triumph?*

Prayer is a struggle because we pray in faith, believing that our prayers will be heard. It is a triumph because we are sure of our destiny, provided that we persevere in prayer.   (2573)

1133. *How is Moses a model of the prayer of mediation?*

Moses, as a friend of God, more than once mediated between God and the people of Israel. Because of this prayerful mediation, the Israelites were spared the punishment they deserved for their unfaithfulness, and were finally led to the Promised Land.   (2574-2577)

1134. *How was King David the first prophet of Jewish and Christian prayer?*

He was a king "according to God's heart." His many prayers, especially the Psalms, became the norm for Jewish prayer and are an integral part of Christian worship. The prayer of Christ was the fulfillment of the prayerful prophecies of King David. (2578-2580)

1135. *What are the main features of Elijah's prayer?*

- Elijah's prayer was joined to a life of righteousness.
- His prayer was full of confidence in God's power, as seen in the sacrifice on Mount Carmel.
- Like Moses, Elijah humbled himself before God.

His prayer set the pattern for the prophets who followed him. It was a prayer of intercession for his people, preparing them for the intervention of God the Savior, the Lord of history. (2581-2584)

1136. *What are the main features of the Psalms?*

- They were the leading prayer of the Chosen People in the Temple and the synagogues.
- They were both the common prayer of the Jewish assembly and the personal prayer of each believer.
- They both commemorate past events and anticipate the future, even to the end of time.
- They are an essential part of the Church at prayer.
- They reflect both the simplicity and spontaneity of prayer.
- They express God's special love for those who believe in Him, even when He tries their loyalty to His name. (2585-2589)

ARTICLE 2: IN THE FULLNESS OF TIME

The full revelation of prayer did not come until the coming of Christ. Accordingly, there are three aspects of prayer as revealed in the New Testament that should be considered: *contemplate* our Lord in prayer, *see* what He teaches us about prayer, in order that He might *hear* our prayers. (2598)

1137. *What is most distinctive about the prayer of Jesus?*

It is the prayer of the eternal Son of God to His heavenly Father, praying in His humanity for us human beings. (2599)

1138. *What aspects of Christ's prayer are emphasized by St. Luke?*

- Jesus prayed before decisive moments of His mission.
- He also prayed before decisive moments in missions of the Apostles.
- His prayer inspired the disciples to learn how to pray.
- He often withdrew to pray alone, spending even a whole night in solitude. (2600-2602)

1139. *What is the significance of Christ's words, "Your will be done"?*

These words synthesize the whole prayer of Jesus, namely the loving commitment of His human heart to the mystery of the Father's will. (2603)

1140. *How are we to follow Christ's example in prayer?*

Like Him, we should first give ourselves to God, since He is our Treasure. Praying in this way, we also obtain what we ask for. (2604)

1141. *What prayer of Jesus sums up all the prayers of human history?*

It was the prayer of Jesus on the Cross, when He said, "Father, into your hands I commend my spirit." In the last analysis, this is what we are always to be saying to God: entrusting every trial into the loving hands of God.
(2605-2606)

1142. *What are the main lessons Jesus taught us about prayer?*

The primary lesson He gave us was His own example in prayer. However, He also gave us detailed directives on how to pray. Among these, the most important are:
- conversion of heart as the precondition for prayer;
- reconciling with those from whom we may be estranged;
- praying for those who dislike us or even openly persecute us;
- no ostentation in prayer;
- avoiding empty phrases in prayer;
- forgiving injuries in heartfelt prayer;
- sinlessness and chastity of heart;
- seeking first the Kingdom of God before everything else;
- childlike faith in prayer, beyond what we naturally feel or understand;
- filial boldness by thanking God even before we receive the gifts we are praying for;
- conformity of our wills with the divine will;
- avoiding unnecessary exposure to temptation and looking forward to union with Christ in glory. (2607-2612)

1143. *What are the three principal parables of Jesus on prayer?*

- The importunate friend. Christ's lesson to us is to keep knocking and the door will be opened to us.
- The importunate widow. Christ's lesson here is to pray always without ceasing, yet with the patience of faith.
- The Pharisee and the tax collector. Christ tells us to pray with humility. Hence the Church's constant prayer, "Kyrie eleison! Lord, have mercy."

(2613)

1144. *What are the new elements that Christ introduced into prayer?*

He told us to pray to the Father in His name. Jesus is the Son of God who became man, our divine Intercessor with the Father. He promised to send us "another Advocate," the Holy Spirit, who will ensure that our joy is complete.

(2614-2615)

1145. *How does Jesus hear our prayers?*

He hears them even as He heard them in Palestine. He works miracles in favor of those who pray to Him in faith. As St. Augustine says, "Jesus prays *for* us as our priest. He prays *in* us as our Head. He is prayed to *by* us as our God. Therefore, let us acknowledge *our* voice in Him and *His* voice in us" (*Enarrationes in Psalmos* 85, 1). (2616)

1146. *What are the two beginnings when the prayer of Mary is revealed to us?*

Mary prayed at the dawn of the Incarnation; her *Fiat* brought the Son of God to become her son in the flesh. Mary also prayed at the dawn of the outpouring of the Holy Spirit on Pentecost Sunday. (2617)

1147. *How is the power of Mary's intercession demonstrated with her divine Son?*

At Cana, her intercession wrought the miracle that prefigured the miracle of the Eucharist. Christ gives His Body and Blood at the request of the Church, His bride. On Calvary, Mary's silent prayer under the Cross entitled her to become the Mother of all the living. (2618)

1148. *How is Mary's* Magnificat *the song of both the Mother of God and of the new People of God?*

On both levels, the *Magnificat* is a song of thanksgiving both for the graces bestowed on Mary and the communication of graces to the world through the Church. But the *Magnificat* is also the song of the poor. Their hope is fulfilled in God's keeping the promises He made to Abraham and his descendants forever. (2619)

ARTICLE 3: IN THE AGE OF THE CHURCH

Not surprisingly, as the disciples and Mary awaited the coming of the Holy Spirit, they were gathered together in prayer. Once the Holy Spirit came, He taught the infant Church what Christians should know about prayer, even to the end of time. These forms of prayer, revealed in the apostolic Church, have become normative for all the followers of Christ.   (2623-2625)

1149. *How does blessing express the fundamental movement of prayer?*

It does so in two ways:
- We bless God for His goodness to us, and beg Him for the graces we need.
- He blesses us by giving us what we ask for.   (2626-2627)

1150. *What is the prayer of adoration?*

It is the acknowledgment of ourselves as creatures before our Creator. It is the homage of our spirit before the King of Glory and the respectful silence we owe to the "ever greater God."   (2628)

1151. *What is the prayer of petition?*

In New Testament terms, it is variously described as: asking, insistently calling, beseeching, invoking, entreating, crying out, and even wrestling in prayer. But the most common term is "petition."   (2629)

1152. *Are there any lamentations in the New Testament?*

Scarcely any, in contrast with their frequency in the Old Testament. Such lamentations as occur in St. Paul are really expressions of his deep desire to be delivered from the sorrows of this life and to be united with Christ. (2630)

1153. *What is the basic object of the prayer of petition?*

It is to beg forgiveness for our sins. This plea for mercy is the prelude to both the Eucharistic liturgy and personal prayer.   (2631)

1154. *Is there a hierarchy in our prayers of petition?*

Yes. We should first pray for the coming of the kingdom. Then we ask for what is necessary to accept it, and finally for grace to cooperate in its attainment.   (2632)

1155. *Can every need be the object of petition?*

Yes, we should see in every need in our lives the occasion for asking God for the grace to meet this need. (2633)

1156. *What is the prayer of intercession?*

This is the prayer of petition for the needs of others. Our prayers of intercession should know no boundaries. We should intercede for the needs of our fellow Christians and extend our prayer even for the salvation of those who reject the Gospel. (2634-2636)

1157. *How does the prayer of thanksgiving characterize the Church?*

The Holy Eucharist is *the* great prayer of thanksgiving; as believers we participate in Christ's thanksgiving to His heavenly Father. As with petition, we should express our gratitude to God in every event and need of our life.

(2637-2638)

1158. *What is the prayer of praise?*

In the prayer of praise, we sing the glory of God not for what He has done but because of who He *is*. Praise integrates the other forms of prayer and raises them to Him who is the Source and Goal of all creation. (2639)

1159. *How does St. Luke emphasize the prayer of praise?*

He does so by his praise of the wonders of Christ and the marvels of Christ's Spirit in the Church. (2640)

1160. *How did St. Paul instruct the early Christians on the prayer of praise?*

He told them: "Sing psalms, and hymns, and spiritual songs among yourselves; singing and making melody to the Lord in your hearts" (Eph 5:19).

(2641)

1161. *What does the Apocalypse tell us about the prayer of praise in heaven?*

It is filled with revelation of the canticles of the heavenly liturgy. The martyrs and saints continue praising God for their victory over suffering and persecution. The Church on earth unites herself with the Church Triumphant, since faith is pure praise. (2642)

1162. *What is* the *sacrifice of praise?*

It is the Holy Eucharist, in which the whole body of Christ is offered to the glory of God's name. (2643)

CHAPTER TWO
THE TRADITION OF PRAYER

Building on the revelation of prayer in the Old and New Testaments, the Church has preserved this revelation over the centuries. Under the guidance of the Holy Spirit, she has shaped the Christian tradition of prayer. In this way, the faith of believers has been safeguarded and developed through penetration into the spiritual realities they have experienced.   (2650-2651)

ARTICLE 1: SOURCES OF PRAYER

1163. *What are the principal sources of prayer?*

They are Sacred Scripture; the Church's liturgy; the practice of the virtues of faith, hope, and charity; and the daily encounter of God's providence in our lives.

- The Scriptures provide us with the food for prayer.
- Prayer interiorizes and assimilates the liturgy during and after its celebration.
- Faith provides us with the content of our prayer, hope gives us the promise of reaching the goal of our prayer, and love enables us to respond to Christ's love for us by our prayer.
- The awareness of God's providence in every event of our lives is one of the secrets of the kingdom revealed to little children.   (2652-2660)

ARTICLE 2: HOW TO PRAY

1164. *What is our pathway in the practice of prayer?*

It is the authority of the Church, based on apostolic tradition and always directing our prayer in relation to Jesus Christ. His humanity is the road by which the Holy Spirit teaches us to pray to God our Father.   (2663-2664)

1165. *How is Jesus the primary focus of our prayer?*

By the fact that He is our God who became man precisely to become the object of our worship and the inspiration of our love. The name of Jesus contains everything: God, man, and the whole economy of creation and salvation.   (2665-2669)

1166. *What is the role of the Holy Spirit in Christian prayer?*

The Holy Spirit is the interior Teacher of Christian prayer. He is always present by His grace in our souls. We should be conscious of His presence and, as Jesus told us, invoke the help of His enlightenment and strength.

(2670-2672)

1167. *How should our prayer be in communion with the Mother of God?*

Since Christ assumed His humanity from Mary, she is to be an integral part of our life of prayer. (2673-2674)

1168. *What has been the pattern of the Church's Marian prayer over the centuries?*

It has had two prominent features:
- centering on Christ and magnifying the Lord for the great things He has done for Mary and for all humanity;
- entrusting God's praises and supplications of His children to the Mother of Jesus. (2675)

1169. *How are these two features fulfilled in the* Ave Maria?

- "Hail Mary" reflects the high regard of the Lord for His lowly servant.
- "Full of grace, the Lord is with thee." She is full of grace because the Lord is with her.
- "Blessed art thou among women and blessed is the fruit of thy womb, Jesus." Because of her faith, Mary became the Mother of believers in Him who is the source of blessing to all nations.
- "Holy Mary, Mother of God." With Elizabeth, we address Mary as the Mother of God and our mother, entrusting ourselves to her prayer.
- "Pray for us sinners, now and at the hour of our death." We recognize our sinfulness. We ask Mary to be with us at the hour of our death, as she was on Calvary at the death of her Son. We pray she may lead us to Him in paradise. (2676-2677)

1170. *What are some of the most popular devotions to Our Lady?*

In the West, the rosary became a medieval substitute for the Liturgy of the Hours. In the East, there is a Marian litany similar to the choral office, as well as a variety of popular hymns and songs addressed to Our Lady. (2678)

1171. *How are we, like the beloved disciple, to welcome Mary into our homes?*

We do so by praying with Mary, the Mother of all the living; and to Mary, who is the Mother of God. (2679)

ARTICLE 3: GUIDES FOR PRAYER

Our special guides for prayer are also our great intercessors before God. They are the countless persons who have preceded us to heavenly glory. They have left us the inspiring example of their holy lives and a treasury of writings.

The variety of their approaches to God has given the Church what we may call different spiritualities. Yet, all are at one in the Spirit, who guided them during their stay on earth. In the words of St. Basil, "The Spirit is truly the dwelling place of the saints and the saint is for the Spirit his proper dwelling place, since the saint offers to dwell with God and is called His Temple" (*De Spiritu Sancto,* 26, 62: *Patrologia Graeca* 32, 184).   (2683-2684)

1172. *What is the first place for education in prayer?*

It is the Christian family. For young children especially, daily family prayer is their first experience of the Church being brought up by the Holy Spirit.

(2685)

1173. *What is the responsibility of ordained ministers?*

They are ordained precisely to guide the People of God to the living sources of prayer. (2686)

1174. *What is the responsibility of religious?*

Their consecrated life cannot be maintained or propagated without prayer. It is one of the living sources of contemplation and the spiritual life in the Church. (2687)

1175. *What is catechesis in prayer?*

It is an essential part of catechetical instruction of children, young people, and adults. They should be trained in personal prayer and the liturgy. Basic prayers are to be memorized and their meaning explained. (2688)

1176. *What is the significance of prayer groups?*

They are a sign of the renewal of prayer in the Church and evidence of the need for communion in prayer. However, these groups must be nourished on the authentic sources of Christian prayer. (2689)

1177. *What is the role of spiritual direction in prayer?*

Spiritual directors are to be persons gifted in faith, wisdom, and discernment of spirits for the common good. They should be experienced in the spiritual life. (2690)

1178. *What are the places suitable for prayer?*

A Catholic church is the first suitable place for liturgical prayer and for prayer before Our Lord in the Blessed Sacrament.

- For personal prayer, there can be a prayer corner with the Sacred Scriptures and sacred images for members of the family to pray together or "in secret" before our Father.
- Monasteries should encourage the faithful to participate in the Liturgy of the Hours and spend some time in more intense solitary prayer.
- Pilgrimages are a reminder of our journey to heaven. Shrines are special places for pilgrims to nourish their Christian prayer "in church." (2691)

CHAPTER THREE
THE LIFE OF PRAYER

Prayer should animate every moment of our lives. Otherwise, we are liable to forget Him who is our Life and our All. In the words of St. Gregory Nazianzen, "We should remember God more often than we breathe."

The Church provides us with rhythms of prayer: morning and evening prayers, grace before and after meals, the Liturgy of the Hours, Sunday and weekly celebration of the Eucharist. There are feast days and the whole cycle of the ecclesiastical year. (2697-2698)

ARTICLE 1: EXPRESSIONS OF PRAYER

Christian tradition gives us three principal expressions of prayer that deserve to be carefully explained. They are vocal prayer, meditation, and mental prayer. (2699)

1179. *What is vocal prayer?*

Vocal prayer is bodily prayer. It is prayer in which our senses are involved. (2700-2702)

1180. *Why is vocal prayer necessary?*

Vocal prayer is basically necessary because we are not angels but human beings. We have a body and a soul. We are therefore to pray with our whole being. Moreover, God wants us to honor Him with all our faculties. Finally, vocal prayer enables us to pray as social beings, where we join with others, and they with us, in vocal and sensibly perceptible harmony.   (2701-2704)

1181. *What is meditation?*

Meditation is a search or a quest. In meditation, the mind seeks to know and understand. It is the universal plea of the blind man in the Gospel, "Lord, that I may see." It is the prayer that needs to see what God wants us to do, why He wants it, and how He wants it done. Meditation is reflective prayer.   (2705)

1182. *What are some useful aids to meditation?*

They are as varied as our needs. The Scriptures and writings of the saints, sacred images and works of art, the texts of the liturgy—all are useful for meditation.   (2705)

1183. *What is most important in meditation?*

Most important is to be practical. In meditation, we are to focus on our own personal needs, on the present circumstances of our life, and on the here and now of our relationship to God.   (2706)

1184. *What are the methods of meditation?*

They are numerous, but two things should be kept in mind. We must cultivate the habit of meditating regularly. And we must be convinced of the necessity for meditation, at the risk of becoming the first of the three fruitless soils in the parable of the sower. The evil spirit steals the word of God from the hearts of those who fail to understand it.   (2707)

1185. *What faculties should be engaged in meditation?*

Literally, all the faculties: thought, imagination, emotion, and desire. What is most important is that, through meditation, we deepen our convictions of faith, arouse the conversion of our heart, and strengthen our resolve to follow Christ.   (2708)

1186. *What is mental prayer?*

In the words of St. Teresa, "As I see it, mental prayer is simply an intimate exchange of friendship where one enters into frequent conversation with God who, as we know, loves us" (St. Teresa of Jesus, *The Life of St. Teresa of Avila by Herself,* 63).   (2709)

1187. *What are some practical guidelines for mental prayer?*

We should have a definite time and duration for mental prayer. We cannot always meditate, but we can always engage in mental prayer, which is simply opening our hearts to God, for Him to open His heart to us.   (2710-2712)

1188. *What are some synonyms for mental prayer?*

- Mental prayer is the most simple expression of the mystery of prayer.
- Mental prayer is the most powerful time of prayer.
- Mental prayer is contemplation in which our eyes of faith are fixed on Jesus. "I look at Him, and He looks at me," the Curé of Ars quoted a peasant's comment about his prayer before the tabernacle.
- Mental prayer listens to the word of God. It shares in the "yes" of Christ to His Father, and the *Fiat* of Our Lady to God's will.
- Mental prayer is silence and the symbol of the world to come. There are no speeches. There is only kindling that feeds the fire of love.
- Mental prayer is the prayer of union with Christ insofar as it enables us to share in His mystery.
- Mental prayer is a communion of love sustaining the life of the world. But only in the measure that we are willing to remain in the darkness of faith.   (2713-2719)

ARTICLE 2: THE STRUGGLE OF PRAYER

Prayer is certainly a gift of divine grace. But it is also the fruit of our own determined effort. As the great figures of prayer down the ages make plain, it is a struggle to pray:

- a struggle with the evil spirit who wants nothing more than to keep us from praying;
- a struggle with ourselves, to overcome our natural disinclination to prayer.

We pray as we live, because we live as we pray. The built-in conflict of the Christian life is inseparable from the conflict of prayer.   (2725)

1189. *What are the main objections to prayer?*

They arise from three different sources and must be overcome if we are to pray as we should. They are:

- erroneous ideas;
- the modern mentality;
- personal experience.

Erroneous ideas:

- There is the false claim that prayer is a simple psychological activity.
- Others, again, look upon prayer as a concentrated effort to reach an emptiness of mind.
- For many Christians, prayer is incompatible with all we have to do. "We do not have time to pray," they say.

Modern mentality:

- Truth is said to be attained only by reason and science, whereas prayer is a mystery surpassing our natural mind.
- Emphasis on money and material values makes prayer seem useless.
- Preoccupation with sensuality and comfort contradicts the beauty of prayer concerned with the glory of the living and true God.
- Activism reduces prayer to a flight from the world.

Personal experience. We are tempted:
- to discouragement through dryness in prayer;
- to sadness at not giving ourselves wholly to the Lord;
- to deception when we do not get what we ourselves want;
- to dwell on our wounded pride, which keeps us from seeing ourselves as sinners, and our unwillingness to see prayer as a free gift of grace.

There is only one remedy: humility, confidence, and perseverance in prayer. (2726-2728)

1190. *How is humble vigilance of heart necessary for prayer?*

Our distractions in prayer reveal preoccupation with created things. Our dominating possessiveness contrasts with Christ's warning to be always on guard. And our dryness in prayer tells us to remain faithful to Jesus, even when we do not experience consolations. It may also tell us we need a moral conversion. On all these counts, watchful humility is necessary.

(2729-2731)

1191. *What are the principal temptations in prayer?*

They are a lack of faith and laziness. On the side of faith, we need to be convinced of our Lord's warning, "Without me, you can do nothing" (Jn 15:5). On the side of laziness, we must humbly admit our sloth and practice self-discipline. (2732-2733)

1192. *What is the single greatest need in our prayers of petition?*

It is childlike confidence in God. This calls for the right answers to two basic questions: Why do we think that our petition has not been heard? How is our prayer heard, that is, effective?   (2734)

1193. *Why do we think our prayers are not heard?*

We are prone to ask for what *we* want and not for what God wants. We must learn not to pray with a divided heart, attached to our own selfish desires while praying as though we were open to the will of God.

(2735-2737)

1194. *How is our prayer efficacious?*

Our prayer is assured of being effective when it is grounded on the merits of Jesus Christ. Its efficacy is assured on two counts: Our Lord is praying in us and with us, and He is constantly praying for us. The secret is to have the trust and boldness of children who are sure of their father's love. (2738-2741)

1195. *What does it mean to "pray without ceasing"?*

This teaching of St. Paul tells us that we are to persevere in our love for God, which is at the heart of prayer. Behind this revealed injunction are three truths of our faith:

- *It is always possible to pray.* The grace is always available. In the words of St. John Chrysostom, "It is possible to offer frequent and fervent prayer even while walking in public or strolling alone or seated in your store, while begging or selling or even while working in the kitchen" (*De Anna* 4, 5: *Patrologia Graeca* 54).
- *Prayer is a vital necessity.* Again in the words of St. John Chrysostom, "Nothing is more valuable than prayer" (*De Anna* 4, 5: *Patrologia Graeca* 666). St. Alphonsus Liguori expresses the mind of the Church when he says, "Those who pray are certainly saved; the one who does not pray certainly damns himself" (*Del Gran Mezzo della Preghiera*).
- *Prayer and the Christian life are inseparable.* They are inseparable because both proceed from the same love of Jesus Christ, the same renunciation of self, the same filial and loving conformity to the Father's love.   (2742-2745)

ARTICLE 3: THE PRAYER OF JESUS IN HIS LAST HOUR

The priestly prayer of Jesus at the Last Supper is a perfect prelude to our reflection on the Lord's Prayer.

We are inspired to say everything that Jesus said in His prayer to the Father on Holy Thursday night when we recite the Our Father. Like the Savior, we are to be concerned for the honor of the Father's name. Like Jesus, we are to have a passionate zeal for the glory of God and the extension of His kingdom. Like the Redeemer, we are to fulfill the will of the Father, His plan of salvation, and His deliverance of the world from evil.

Finally, it is in this prayer on the night before He died that Jesus reveals to us and gives us the inseparable knowledge of the Father and the Son, which is the very mystery of the life of prayer.   (2746-2751)

SECTION II:
THE LORD'S PRAYER

The Lord's Prayer is exactly that. It was Our Lord Himself who gave us this prayer in answer to the request of His disciples: "Lord, teach us to pray, as John taught his disciples" (Lk 11:1). Jesus then said, "When you pray, say...," followed by the text of the Our Father.   (2759)

In the early Church, there was a liturgical addition to the Lord's Prayer, which is now restored in the Common Missal. It reads: "For thine is the kingdom, and the power, and the glory forever." This doxology, or song of praise, dates from the first to the fifth centuries of the Christian era.   (2760)

CHAPTER ONE
THE LORD'S PRAYER AS A
SUMMARY OF THE GOSPEL

1196. *How is the Lord's Prayer a summary of the whole Gospel?*

Because it contains, in the form of petitions, everything that Christ came into the world to teach the human race.   (2761)

1197. *How is the Lord's Prayer at the center of the Scriptures?*

Because the center of the Scriptures is Jesus Christ, and the Lord's Prayer is His own summary of our approach to the heavenly Father.   (2762)

1198. *Why is the Lord's Prayer the most perfect prayer we can say?*

It is the most perfect prayer because it not only expresses all the requests that we can justly make of God, but even gives us the order in which our petitions should be made. (2763)

1199. *How is the Our Father related to the Sermon on the Mount?*

In the Sermon on the Mount, Our Lord teaches us the new life that He brought to the world. In the Our Father, He shows us how to ask for this new life in prayer. (2764)

1200. *How is the Our Father the prayer of the Lord?*

It is the prayer of the Lord because:
- it was taught by the Lord;
- it was given to us by Our Lord Himself;
- it is the prayer which Our Lord received from the Father;
- it is the prayer which expresses what Our Lord, in His human heart, knows are the needs of His human brothers and sisters;
- it is the prayer of Our Lord, who is the model of our prayer. (2765)

1201. *What does Christ give us in the Lord's Prayer?*

He gives us more than just the words of this prayer. He infuses His Spirit into us. We are thus assumed into the mission of the Second and Third Persons of the Holy Trinity. (2766)

1202. *When did the Church begin to use the Lord's Prayer?*

Already in apostolic times. The Lord's Prayer was recited three times a day by the Christian communities in place of the eighteen benedictions of Judaism. (2767)

1203. *How is the Our Father essentially a liturgical prayer?*

As explained by St. John Chrysostom, "The Lord teaches us to make our prayers in common for all our brethren. He did not say, 'my Father' who art in heaven, but 'our' Father, so that our prayer would be as of one soul, for the whole Body of the Church" (*Hom. in Mt.* 19, 4: *Patrologia Graeca* 57, 278).

In all Catholic liturgical traditions, the Our Father is an integral part of the hours of the Divine Office. But especially prominent is its ecclesial character in the three sacraments of initiation.
- In Baptism and Confirmation, the "handing on" (tradition) of the Lord's Prayer signifies the new birth in the divine life. That is why

most of the patristic commentaries on the Our Father are addressed to catechumens and neophytes.

- In the Eucharistic Liturgy, the Lord's Prayer appears as the prayer of the whole Church and reveals its full meaning and efficacy. Placed between the Eucharistic Prayer and the Liturgy of Communion, it sums up all the intercessions following the Consecration and all the hopes of the heavenly kingdom that Holy Communion anticipates.

- In the Eucharist, the Lord's Prayer reveals its eschatological character. Unlike the prayers of the old covenant, its petitions assume that the Savior has already come, and is due to return on the last day.

- From this unshakable faith comes the hope that underlies each of the seven petitions. The Eucharist and the Our Father look forward to the coming of the Lord. (2768-2772)

CHAPTER TWO
"OUR FATHER WHO ART IN HEAVEN"

The opening of the Lord's Prayer is a filial address to God as our Father in heaven. The seven petitions that follow are founded and inspired by our confident profession of faith in the fatherhood of our God.

This is in stark contrast with the extreme deference toward God that characterized the old covenant. Moses was told by God, "Do not come closer. Take off your sandals."

Elevated by the Spirit of Christ, we address God as our Father. As expressed by St. Peter Chrysologus, "When would a weak mortal dare call God his Father, unless the deepest recesses of man were animated by the Power from on high?" (2777-2778)

1204. *What must we avoid in speaking of God as Father?*

We must avoid being misled by the false images of fatherhood taken from this world. Terms like "paternal" or "maternal" are loaded with cultural and personal implications that would falsify our understanding of God as Father. They can become idols that destroy our knowledge of the one true God.

(2779)

1205. *How then can we invoke God as Father?*

We can do so because we believe that Jesus Christ is the Son of God become man. He revealed our participation in that sonship, which is beyond the grasp of angels or men. (2780)

1206. *How do we become children of God?*

We become children of God through Baptism. This entitles us to address God as "Abba, Father!" because we have become His adopted children by grace, sharing in the natural filiation of His Son, Jesus Christ.   (2781-2782)

1207. *How does* our *relation to God differ from that of Christ?*

Unlike Christ, who is the natural Son of God, we are all God's creatures. The triune God is not our natural Father. He is our Creator. Only by grace do we become His adopted children.   (2783)

1208. *What are the consequences of this free gift of adoption?*

They are mainly two: the desire and will to become like Him; and a humble and trustful heart. In the words of St. Gregory of Nyssa, "We must constantly behold the beauty of the Father in order to shape our souls accordingly" (*De Orat. dom.* 2: *Patrologia Graeca* 44, 1148B). And in the words of St. Augustine, "Our Father... how could He refuse His children anything they ask for when He has already allowed them to be His children?" (*De Sum. Dom.* 2, 4: *Patrologia Graeca* 34, 1276).   (2784-2785)

1209. *What does the word "our" tell us about the fatherhood of God?*

It tells us many things, all arising from our new relation to God with the coming of Christ.
- With Christ, we have become His people of the new covenant.
- We respond to His grace and truth with love and fidelity.
- We look forward to joining God in the heavenly Jerusalem.
- We address God as the Father whom we adore and glorify with the Son and the Holy Spirit.
- We pray to God together as members of the Church founded by His divine Son.
- In spite of the divisions in Christendom, we share in the prayer of Christ for the unity of His followers.
- We pray for the grace to overcome our divisions. We honestly exclude no one from the last four petitions of the Lord's Prayer.
- Our prayer should be inspired by the love of God that knows no bounds. It should extend to all mankind.   (2786-2793)

1210. *What does the expression "heaven" mean in the Lord's Prayer?*

Heaven means state of being. It designates God's majesty. It means that God is in the heart of the just. It finally means the heavenly world where

God lives and moves in those who enjoy His celestial vision.

When the Church prays, "Our Father, who art in heaven," she professes that we are already the People of God, "hidden with Christ in God" (Col 3:3). Yet at the same time, we groan, looking forward to our heavenly dwelling place. In the words of a famous letter of the second century, "Christians are in the flesh but they do not live according to the flesh. They pass their life here on earth, but they are citizens of heaven."   (2794-2796)

CHAPTER THREE
THE SEVEN PETITIONS

The opening of the Lord's Prayer places us in God's presence. We therefore first adore Him, love, and bless Him. Then we are ready to open our hearts to ask Him for what we need.   (2803)

There are seven petitions. The first three are concerned for *His* kingdom, *His* will. The next four may be called eucharistic needs in this world: "Give *us*...forgive *us*...lead *us* not...deliver *us*." The fourth and fifth petitions concern our life as such, our need for nourishment, and healing from sin; the last two petitions concern our struggle for the victory of life, the same struggle that involves our prayer.   (2804-2805)

By the first three petitions, we are strengthened in faith, filled with hope, and inflamed by charity. But we are creatures and sinners. So we must beg for ourselves—representing history and the world—that we may offer God our boundless love.   (2806)

I. "Hallowed Be Thy Name"

1211. *What does the word "hallowed" mean?*

The word "hallowed" or "sanctified" here does not mean we are asking for God to be made holy. He *is* the all-holy One. Rather, we are asking that His holiness may be recognized and that His name may be treated in a holy manner.   (2807)

1212. *What obligation do we have to sanctify the name of God?*

God has revealed His name in the decisive periods of salvation history. But He also revealed that His salvific work is accomplished for us and in us only if we sanctify His name.   (2808)

1213. *Has there been progress in God's revelation of His holiness?*

Yes. The holiness of God is an inaccessible mystery. The manifestation of this holiness in creation and history is called "glory" in Scripture. But once the world had sinned, God went beyond creation and history to reveal His very name, in order to restore the world to the image of the Creator.   (2809)

1214. *What is the record of God revealing His name in the Old Testament?*

After the promise He made to Abraham, God gradually revealed His name through Moses and the prophets. By the covenant of Sinai, God formed His people to be holy and consecrated in His name. Yet, time and again the people turned away from the Holy One of Israel.   (2810-2811)

1215. *How is the name of God revealed in the flesh?*

In Jesus, the name of God is revealed and given to us in the flesh. At the end of His Passover, the Father gives Christ the name that is above every name, "Jesus Christ is Lord, to the glory of God the Father."   (2812)

1216. *How are we sanctified?*

In the water of Baptism, we have been sanctified in the name of the Lord Jesus Christ. But after Baptism, we have sinned; indeed we sin daily. That is why, in St. Cyprian's third-century commentary on the Lord's Prayer, "We need to be daily purified of our sins by a daily sanctification" (*De Dom. orat.* 12: *Patrologia Latina* 4, 527A; Lev 20:26).   (2813)

1217. *For whose sanctification do we pray?*

We pray not only for our own sanctification but also for that of the whole world, even for our enemies.   (2814)

1218. *How is the first petition related to the others?*

This first petition contains all the others. Moreover, like the others, it is fulfilled in Christ's own priestly prayer at the Last Supper when he says, "Holy Father, in your name, protect those whom you have given to me" (Jn 17:11).
(2815)

II. "Thy Kingdom Come"

1219. *What is the New Testament meaning of the kingdom?*

The New Testament word *basileia* can be translated "royalty," "kingdom," or "reign."   (2816)

1220. *How can we speak of the coming of God's kingdom?*

God's kingdom is brought near by the Word incarnate. It is announced throughout the Gospel. It is come in the death and Resurrection of Christ. It comes to us in the Eucharist. It will come when Christ hands the kingdom over to His Father. According to St. Cyprian, "We may even say that the Kingdom of God is Christ in person. We desire His coming daily" (*De Dom. orat.* 13: *Patrologia Latina* 4, 544C-545A).   (2816)

1221. *How is this petition the cry, "Come, Lord Jesus"?*

It is the cry of the martyrs asking the Lord to come to judge the world at the end of time. It is the cry of hope of those who had served God and suffered for His name.   (2817)

1222. *To what does this petition principally refer?*

It mainly refers to the final coming of God's kingdom with the return of Jesus Christ. The Church He established has her mission in the world. We pray that this mission will be accomplished by the Holy Spirit, who completes the work of the Savior on earth, which is our full sanctification. (2818)

1223. *Who alone can truly say, "Thy kingdom come"?*

Only those who have fought the decisive battle between the flesh and the spirit. "Only those who have purified themselves in their actions, thoughts, and words can say to God, 'Thy kingdom come!'" as we read in St. Cyril of Jerusalem's catechism of the third century.   (2819)

1224. *Are we to distinguish between the growth of the kingdom of God and the progress of the society in which we live?*

Indeed, there is no necessary connection between the growth of the two. Yet, only the Spirit of God enables us to make the distinction.   (2820)

1225. *Are the two societies to be separated?*

By no means. Our vocation to eternal life does not suppress but rather reenforces our duty to use the means given to us by the Creator for the promotion of justice and peace in this world.   (2820)

1226. *How is this petition offered and answered in the prayer of Jesus at the Last Supper?*

Jesus prayed to His Father for the advent of His kingdom by the sanctification of His followers here on earth, and their attainment of heavenly glory in the life to come. His prayer has been answered by the assurance of the grace we need. But we must cooperate with the graces received. (2821)

1227. *How is this petition present and effective in the Eucharist?*

Because the Eucharist is Jesus Christ, from whom we receive the light and strength we need to ensure the coming of the kingdom of God. (2821)

1228. *How does this petition bear fruit in the new life of the Beatitudes?*

As the followers of Christ live out the Beatitudes they are in effect bringing this petition to fruition. How so? Every practice of every Beatitude advances the advent of Christ's kingdom: here on earth by the Church's growth in sanctity, and in the life to come by the increase in the number and happiness of the elect, according to the mysterious designs of God. (2821)

III. "Thy Will Be Done on Earth As It Is in Heaven"

1229. *What is the basic will of God?*

The basic will of God is that "everyone should be saved and come to the knowledge of the truth" (1 Tim 2:4). This means that God wants everyone to reach heaven and attain to the beatific vision. (2822)

1230. *Does everyone do the will of God, so as to reach heaven?*

No. As St. Peter told the first-century Christians, God "is patient with you, not wanting anyone to perish" (2 Pet 3:9). The patience of God is demonstrated in His forbearance, in His tolerating our sins to allow us time to reform and do penance. (2822)

1231. *What is the most fundamental commandment of the will of God?*

It is the commandment He gave us at the Last Supper, "that you love one another, even as I have loved you, that you also should love one another" (Jn 13:34). We may say that this commandment is a synthesis of all the other divine commandments, and tells us the whole divine will. (2822)

1232. *Who has given us the perfect example of doing the will of God?*

Jesus Christ. His human will was always conformed to the divine will of His Father. Christ alone could say, "I always do what is pleasing to Him" (Jn 8:29). (2823-2824)

1233. *Did Christ always find it easy to do His Father's will?*

No, as we know from His agony in the Garden of Gethsemane, He prayed, if it were possible, "that this chalice should pass from Me. Yet, not My will but Thine be done" (Mt 26:39). So, we too must not expect doing God's will to be always easy. (2824)

1234. *Where do we get the strength to do God's will?*

From the merits of Christ. In the words of St. Paul, Jesus "gave Himself for our sins to set us free from the present evil age, according to the will of our God and Father" (Gal 1:4). Thus, through the merits of Christ, we are set free from the bondage of self-will and empowered to conform to the will of God. (2824)

1235. *What, then, is our prayer?*

Our prayer is to unite our will with the will of Christ so that, like Him, we might do the will of God. (2825)

1236. *Are we powerless of ourselves, powerless to do God's will?*

Yes. We do have a free will, but without the grace that comes from Christ, we cannot do anything, of ourselves, to reach our heavenly destiny. That is why we need to pray. Through prayer, we are united with Jesus and empowered by His Holy Spirit to surrender our will. Thus, we are able to choose what the Son of God always chose—namely, to please the Father. (2825)

1237. *What are we really asking for in this petition of the Lord's Prayer?*

We are asking to follow the teaching of Christ on many levels:
* to be humble so we can see that our virtue does not depend only on us but mainly on the grace of God;
* to pray not only for ourselves but for the whole world;
* to pray that error will be banished and the truth be established throughout the earth;
* to pray that vice be destroyed and virtue flourish, so that earth should become more and more like heaven. (2825)

1238. *How is the will of God done in heaven?*

The will of God is done in heaven *universally;* everyone does the will of God. The will of God is done *perfectly;* there is no resistance to the will of God. The will of God is done *distinctively;* everyone does the divine will according to each person's capacity and variability. The will of God is done *lovingly;* there is no envy among the angels and saints, although each of the blessed differs in their response to God's will. The will of God is done *cooperatively;* there is no competition in heaven but only generous and cooperative charity. The will of God is done *joyfully;* indeed this is the beatitude of heaven, that everyone wants to do the will of God and is supremely happy in doing so. (2825-2826)

1239. *What are the two essential graces for which we are praying in this petition?*

They are the graces we need in the mind and the will.

* In the mind, we are asking for the light we need to recognize the will of God: for supernatural discernment to know *what* God wants and *how* He wants us to do it.
* In the will, we are asking for strength not only to begin but the perseverance necessary to continue doing what God wants of us. (2826)

1240. *What is Christ's warning about reaching heaven?*

He tells us that no one enters the kingdom of Heaven by words but, as He says, "by doing the will of my Father who is in heaven" (Mt 7:21). Thus we are being told that, while prayer is indispensable to obtain the grace of God, *we must then cooperate with this grace* if we wish to reach our heavenly destiny. (2826)

1241. *Are we sure that God listens to our prayer for His grace?*

Yes, but on one condition. As recorded in St. John's Gospel, "If anyone does the will of God, God listens to him" (Jn 9:31). Our prayer for grace is listened to, provided we are sincerely doing the will of God. (2827)

1242. *What is the most powerful prayer of petition we can offer to God?*

It is the prayer in the Holy Eucharist, where the One to whom and with whom we are praying is the incarnate Son of God. (2827)

1243. *With whom should we join our prayer of petition to do the will of God?*

We should join our prayer with the intercession of Our Lady, the Mother of God. (2827)

1244. *Are we here asking to do God's will as Christ Himself is doing the will of His Father?*

Yes, Jesus Christ is now in heaven perfectly conformed to the will of the Father. In the words of St. Augustine, we are here asking, "Thy will be done in the Church as in our Lord Jesus Christ Himself," or "in the Bride to whom He is espoused as in the Bridegroom who has accomplished the will of the Father" (*De Serm. Dom.* 2, 6: *Patrologia Latina* 34, 1279). (2827)

IV. "Give Us This Day Our Daily Bread"

1245. *What do we acknowledge in this petition?*

We recognize the goodness of God, who makes His sun to rise on the good and the bad and sends rain on the just and the unjust. (2828)

1246. *What do we express by praying, "Give us this day our daily bread"?*

We express our solidarity with the whole human race. We pray to the Father of all people, uniting ourselves with their sufferings and needs. (2829)

1247. *What are we saying by asking for our bread?*

We show our trust in God, who gave us our life, that He will also provide for the material and spiritual nourishment we need to sustain this life. (2830)

1248. *How is this petition our confidence in the providence of God?*

It is not passivity but a childlike trust that cooperates with the providence of our Father. Its purpose is to relieve us of all anxious worry, as Jesus insisted in His Sermon on the Mount. (2830)

1249. *What is Christ's promise?*

He promised that those who seek the kingdom and justice of God will receive everything else besides. As expressed by St. Cyprian, "God owns everything. Nothing is wanting to the person who does not lack God" (*De Dom. Orat.* 21: *Patrologia Latina* 4, 551C). (2830)

1250. *What is our Christian responsibility toward those suffering from hunger?*

We who pray are to put into practice our responsibility toward people in need. This refers not only to people's personal needs but to the needs of the whole human family. This petition of the Lord's Prayer cannot be isolated from the parallel of the poor Lazarus and the Last Judgment. (2831)

1251. *What does this petition tell us about the practice of justice?*

It tells us that Christ's kingdom should reflect His Spirit. This means the institution of justice in personal, social, economic, and international relations.

Never to be forgotten is that there are no just structures without people who want to be just. (2832)

1252. How does this petition reflect the first Beatitude?

The Beatitude promises blessedness to the poor in spirit. This is the virtue of sharing. We are called to communicate and share our material and spiritual goods, not from constraint but out of love. Thus, the abundance of some becomes the remedy to meet the needs of others. (2833)

1253. How important is saying grace at meals?

Very important. Christian families say grace at table to both ask God for the gift He is giving us and thank Him for the gift just received. There is no contradiction in this. No doubt the nourishment is the fruit of our labor. But we are to both pray and work. In the words of St. Ignatius Loyola, "Pray as though everything depended on God, and work as though everything depended on you." (2834)

1254. What is the specially Christian understanding of this petition?

It refers to hunger of spirit on two levels: hunger for the truth of God's revealed Word and hunger for the Holy Eucharist. (2835)

1255. What, then, is the bread needed to satisfy the hunger for God's truth?

It is the Gospel of Jesus Christ. As Christians, we have the duty to mobilize our efforts to proclaim the Good News of salvation to the poor. There is a famine on earth, not a famine for bread or a thirst for water but a famine for hearing the Word of God. (2835)

1256. What is the bread needed to satisfy the hunger for the Eucharist?

It is the spiritual hunger for receiving the Body of Christ in Holy Communion. (2835)

1257. What do the words "this day" mean in our asking God to "give us this day our daily bread"?

"This day" is the "today" of God. The bread for which we pray is mainly the bread of God's truth and His Son's Body. We are therefore asking for the everlasting possession of divine truth and the communion with Jesus Christ in the eternal Eucharist of the heavenly kingdom. (2836)

1258. *What, then, is the heavenly meaning of this petition of the Our Father?*

It is a prayer for the coming of the Day of the Lord, anticipated in the Holy Eucharist. Thus, the daily Eucharist is a foretaste of the kingdom to come. (2837)

1259. *How is Christ Himself this bread of heaven?*

"He is the bread who, sown in the Virgin, raised up in the flesh, molded in the Passion, baked in the oven of the tomb, kept in reserve in the Church and brought to our altars, provides the faithful each day with their heavenly nourishment" (St. Peter Chrysologus, *Sermo 67*). (2837)

V. "Forgive Us Our Trespasses As We Forgive Those Who Trespass against Us"

1260. *What is unique about this petition of the Lord's Prayer?*

It is unique in having a condition attached to receiving the request from God. No doubt, what we ask for is in the future, but this will be granted only if we fulfill the divine demand. (2838)

1261. *What is the confession we make in this petition?*

It is the admission that we have sinned. Like the Prodigal Son and the Publican, we recognize that we are sinners before God. Yet, even as we confess our misery, we profess our faith in His mercy. (2839)

1262. *What are the grounds for our confidence of being forgiven?*

We find the effective and unquestionable sign of our forgiveness in the sacraments of the Church. (2839)

1263. *To what degree does God's mercy penetrate our heart?*

Only to the extent that we forgive those who offend us. Love, like the Body of Christ, is indivisible. We cannot love God, whom we do not see, unless we love our brother and sister whom we do see. If we refuse to pardon them, we close our hearts to the penetration of the Father's mercy. In the confession of our sin, we open our heart to His grace. But this confession must include our readiness to forgive our offenders. (2840)

1264. *How do we know this petition is specially important?*

Because it is the only one to which Our Lord returns in His Sermon on the Mount and goes on to explain in detail. (2841)

1265. *How difficult is it to live up to this petition?*

It is not only difficult but impossible for human beings alone. But "everything is possible to God" (Lk 18:27). (2841)

1266. *What is our model of this merciful forgiveness?*

It is God our Father, revealing His mercy through His Son, Jesus Christ. His mercy toward us sinners is the pattern of our mercy to others; even as our mercy to them is a condition for God's mercy to us. (2842)

1267. *What kind of mercy are we to practice?*

It must be deeply interior. Of ourselves, we cannot erase or forget the injury another causes us. But once we offer our heart to the Holy Spirit, He changes the injury into compassion and purifies our memory by transforming the offense into intercession. (2843)

1268. *How does Christian prayer transfigure Christ's disciples into reflections of their Master?*

When Christian prayer extends to the forgiveness of our enemies. Moreover, forgiveness bears witness to the world that love is stronger than sin. This, in fact, is the great witness to Jesus that all the martyrs of the past and present have given to the world. (2844)

1269. *What is the fundamental condition for reconciliation with God and among men?*

The fundamental condition for reconciliation is forgiveness.
- We cannot be reconciled with God unless He forgives us.
- We cannot be forgiven by God unless we forgive others.
- We cannot be reconciled with others unless we forgive them.
- Others cannot be reconciled with us unless they forgive us. (2844)

1270. *In what sense are we always debtors?*

We are always debtors because we owe everyone our love. (2845)

1271. *What is the most beautiful sacrifice we can offer to God?*

It is the sacrifice of our peaceful concord with one another. It is the community of all the faithful people united in the Father, Son, and Holy Spirit.

(2845)

VI. "Lead Us Not into Temptation"

1272. *How does this petition go to the root of the preceding one?*

It goes to the root because our sins are not coercive. We sin not because we are tempted but because we consent to the temptations. (2846)

1273. *What are we really praying for in this sixth petition of the Our Father?*

We are praying not to be allowed to enter into temptation that would lead us into sin. (2846)

1274. *Does God tempt anyone?*

No, God tempts no one to evil. On the contrary, He wants to free us from the evil of sin. (2846)

1275. *Do we have to struggle to avoid sin?*

Yes, there is within us the conflict between the flesh and the spirit. In this petition, we ask the Holy Spirit for discernment and strength. (2846)

1276. *What is the first discernment for which we are praying?*

We ask to distinguish between a trial that would help us grow in virtue and temptation that leads to sin and death. (2847)

1277. *What is the second discernment for which we are praying?*

We ask to further distinguish between being tempted and actually consenting to temptation. No matter how long, or strong, or pleasant a temptation, there is no sin unless the will freely gives in to the pleasure or satisfaction of the temptation. Moreover, the degree of guilt depends on the measure of voluntary consent to accepting or not resisting the temptation. (2847)

1278. *What else are we asking for in this petition?*

We ask for the light to recognize a temptation for what it is. Every temptation is attractive. Every temptation is alluring. What we need is the grace to unmask the lie of a temptation, to see it as attractive indeed, but seductive.

Temptations, as we learn already from the Fall of Eve, are pleasant to the eyes and desirable, but in reality their fruit is death. (2847)

1279. *Why does God allow us to be tempted?*

Because He does not want to impose virtue. He wants us to live freely as human beings. Moreover, temptations reveal us to ourselves. They open our eyes to our sinful inclinations and inspire us with gratitude for the mercy of God. (2847)

1280. *How does this petition imply a decision of the heart?*

As Christ tells us, where our treasure is, there our heart will also be. We must either resist or give in to a temptation, according to our predisposition of heart. If our heart is set on doing the will of God, we will resist the temptation. But if our heart is set on doing our own will, we shall consent to the temptation. (2848)

1281. *Will God allow us to be tested beyond our strength?*

No, He will never allow us to be tempted beyond our strength. He always provides the means not only for resisting a temptation but even for growing in virtue because of the temptation. (2848)

1282. *What do we mean in saying that God always provides the means for overcoming temptations?*

God always gives us the grace to pray for the light and strength needed to resist temptation. (2849)

1283. *How did Jesus show us the necessity for prayer to overcome temptations?*

He did so at the beginning and at the end of His public ministry.

- At the beginning, He allowed Himself to be tempted by the devil. But before the temptation, He prayed and fasted forty days in the desert.
- At the end of His public life, in the agony in the garden, He prayed earnestly to do the will of His Father.

Absolutely speaking, Christ did not have to pray, any more than, as God, He had to become man and die for our sins. But He prayed to teach us the absolute necessity of prayer in *our* struggle with temptation. (2849)

1284. *Is it only prayer that we need to overcome temptation?*

No, besides prayer we must be constantly on our guard. In the Garden of Olives, Jesus told His disciples to watch and pray. Both vigilance and prayer are necessary. (2849)

1285. *What is this vigilance that we need to gain victory over temptation?*

It is a multiple vigilance, as all the masters of the spiritual life teach us.

- We must expect to be tempted. Temptation is part of our probation here on earth. We are not yet in the Church Triumphant. We are still in the Church Militant. And the essence of our military service is to battle with temptations.
- We should expect to be tempted according to our weaknesses. We must know our own sinful tendencies and be specially on guard in those areas where experience tells us we are most likely to give in.
- We should anticipate temptations. There is such a thing as foreseeing where we will be, whom we will see, with whom we will speak. Thus, to be forewarned is to be forearmed.
- We need not be exposed to every temptation. We are to avoid those places, persons, and situations that we know or suspect would be proximate occasions of sin for us.
- We must be prudent in our use of the senses, especially our eyes and ears. No two people are alike. Knowing myself, I must not allow myself to be exposed to sense stimuli that I prudently foresee would be too much for me. (2849)

1286. *What is the one temptation we must specially pray to resist?*

It is the last temptation of our life, the temptation to discouragement or even despair as we face eternity. (2849)

1287. *Can this grace of final perseverance be merited by even a lifetime practice of virtue?*

The Church tells us no. The grace of final perseverance must be prayed for. It is the fruit of prayer. It is this grace especially that we pray for in the Our Father when we ask the Lord, "Lead us not into temptation." It is also this grace that we ask Our Lady to obtain for us when we say, at the close of the Hail Mary, "Pray for us sinners… at the hour of our death."

(2849)

VII. "Deliver Us from Evil"

1288. *What is the basic evil from which we ask to be delivered in the last petition of the Lord's Prayer?*

It is deliverance from the devil. Thus, the last petition of the Our Father is also part of Christ's prayer at the Last Supper. Jesus prayed to his Father, "I am not asking You to take them out of the world, but I ask You to protect them from the Evil One" (Jn 17:15). (2850)

1289. *For whom are we praying in this petition?*

We are praying as believing Christians, therefore in solidarity with the whole Church; we are also praying for the whole family of mankind. (2850)

1290. *Are we here asking to be delivered from an abstract evil?*

By no means. We pray to be liberated from a person. He is variously called Satan, the Evil One, or the devil, which literally means "the one who throws himself across" the plan of God and His work of salvation fulfilled in Christ. The devil is the angel opposed to God. (2851)

1291. *What are some of the names in Scripture by which the devil is identified?*

He is a "murderer from the beginning." He is "a liar" and "the father of lies." He is "the deceiver of the whole world." These names bring out the fundamental malice of the devil; he sows the seeds of error in people's minds and thus brings them to ruin. The devil's chief weapon, therefore, is deceit. Through deceit, he destroys divine life in human souls and thus murders their supernatural life. (2852)

1292. *Who first brought sin and death into the world?*

It was the devil who seduced Eve, who in turn persuaded Adam to join her in disobeying God. That is how sin first entered the human race. Through the Fall of Adam and Eve, all human beings are conceived estranged from God. Through original sin, they are also deprived of the bodily immortality they would have had if our first parents had remained faithful to the Lord. (2852)

1293. *What is one of the principal effects of Baptism?*

In the teaching of St. John, those who are born of God are specially protected from the Evil One. Sanctifying grace shields them in an extraordinary way from the malice of Satan. (2852)

1294. *Can we say that the whole world lies under the power of the devil?*

Yes, this again is the teaching of St. John, who writes, "We know that we are God's children, and that the whole world lies under the power of the Evil One" (1 Jn 5:19). So true is this, that one of the major heresies in early Christianity claimed that the devil is a god who created an evil world. (2852)

1295. *What should be our attitude toward the devil?*

We should implicitly trust in God. This is beautifully expressed by St. Ambrose, who lived in the period when the heresy just described was seducing so many people. "The Lord," wrote Ambrose, "who has taken away your sin and pardoned your faults is the same who protects you and guards you against the wiles of the devil who is attacking you. This is so that the enemy, who is used to seducing into sin, may not overcome you. The one who entrusts himself to God is not afraid of the demon. 'If God is for us, who can be against us?'" (*De Sacr.* 5, 4, 30: *Patrologia Latina* 16, 454). (2852)

1296. *When was the victory won over the ruler of this world?*

It took place when Jesus freely gave up His life for us on Calvary. (2853)

1297. *How did the devil react?*

As described by St. John in the Apocalypse, the devil saw that he had been cast out. So "he pursued the woman who had given birth to the male child." But he had no hold on her. "Then the dragon was angry with the woman and went off to make war on the rest of her children" (Rev 12:11-17).

The Church interprets this symbolic language as referring to the devil's opposition to Mary, who was protected from sin by her immaculate conception and spared bodily corruption by her assumption. The devil never ceases opposing Mary's children, who are believers in her divine Son, but Christ's coming at the end of time will finally deliver them from all molestation by the Evil One. (2853)

1298. *Is it only deliverance from the devil for which we are praying?*

No, we ask God to deliver us from all evils, present, past, and future, whose author or instigator is the devil. In this petition, the Church brings before the Father all the distress of the world. (2854)

1299. *Do we ask for deliverance from the absolute evil of eternal death?*

Yes, the Church prays with emphasis for the precious gift of peaceful expectation of Christ's return and of perseverance in His grace until He comes. (2854)

CHAPTER FOUR
THE FINAL DOXOLOGY

Since the first century of the Christian era, the Church's liturgy has included an addition to the Lord's Prayer that we call the Final Doxology. Literally, this means the "closing prayer of praise."

1300. *What is the text of this Final Doxology?*

Addressing God, it says, "For Yours is the kingdom, the power, and the glory." (2855)

1301. *What do these three praises express?*

They express the first three precepts of the Lord's Prayer, namely:

- the glorification of His name;
- the coming of His kingdom;
- the power of His saving will. (2855)

1302. *How do these three praises differ from the three petitions?*

They differ as heaven differs from earth. In the Lord's Prayer, we are asking that God's name be glorified, that His kingdom come, and the power of His saving will be accomplished. But in the Doxology, we assume that all these prayers will have been fulfilled with Christ's final triumph in a heavenly eternity. Consequently, what are petitions in the Our Father become acts of praise and thanksgiving in the Final Doxology. (2855)

1303. *How does the Final Doxology glorify Christ over the prince of this world?*

The devil, as ruler of this world, falsely attributes to himself the three titles to kingship, power, and glory. These titles, by divine right, belong to God. At the end of time, Christ will have overcome the demonic usurper and restore these titles to His Father and our Father. Then the mystery of salvation will be completed and God will be all in all. (2855)

1304. *How does the devil exercise these three attributes in the world?*

He does so by usurping political control in civil societies. Over the centuries he has penetrated the State, where those in civil authority arrogate to themselves rights that are in conflict with the rights of God.

- They claim to be rulers or kings making laws and regulations that openly contradict the laws of God. Thus, the abortion laws are an arrogation of rights in open contradiction to the mind and will of God.

- They claim to have power over their citizens that deprives the people of even the most elementary rights of the natural law. The powers of dissolving valid, sacramental, consummated marriages and of regulating births by contraception are contrary to the basic teachings of Christianity.

- They demand recognition by arrogating honor and glory to themselves, to which, under God, they have no right.

(2855)

1305. *What is the meaning of "Amen," at the close of the Lord's Prayer?*

It literally means, "So be it." (2856)

1306. *Why do we say "Amen"?*

The "Amen" is our "countersignature," so to speak, to everything that God has taught us in the Lord's Prayer. It is our acceptance by faith, testifying that we believe with our minds. It is also our agreement in love to conform our wills to what Christ in the Our Father tells us to pray. (2856)

INDEX